Contents

Introduction   1

Section 1
Something Good and Fun   3
Children's and parents' views on play and out-of-school provision

Section 2
The Value of Children's Play and Play Provision   35
A systematic research review

Section 3
The Planning and Location of Play Provision in England   105
A mapping exercise

Section 4
The State of Play   183
A survey of play professionals in England

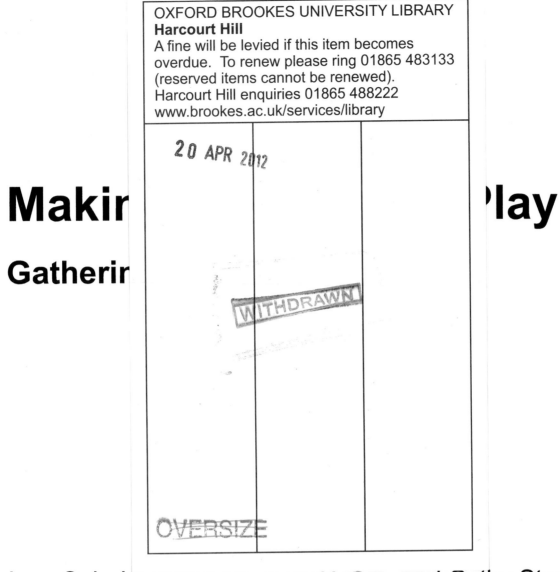

Makir   'lay

Gatherin

Issy Cole-Hamilton, Andrew Harrop and Cathy Street

NATIONAL
CHILDREN'S
BUREAU
Enterprises Ltd

00 888967 0X

The **Children's Play Council** aims to raise awareness of the importance of play in children's lives and the need for all children to have access to better play opportunities and play services.

Set up in 1988, CPC is an alliance of national and regional organisations and local authorities. Its work reaches wherever children play: at home, in play areas, parks, school playgrounds and streets, in play and childcare centres, in hospitals and community health settings, in cities and in the countryside.

The **New Policy Institute** is a progressive think tank, founded in 1996. Its mission is to advance social justice in a market economy. Wholly independent, its funding is project-based, from charitable foundations, companies, trade unions, voluntary organisations and public bodies. Its work focuses on: poverty, social exclusion and inequality; the tax and benefits system; and the performance of 'essential' services – from utilities and finance to education. Projects include policy formulation, policy evaluation, the identification of good practice, analytical modelling, design and interpretation of statistical indicators, and the assessment of needs.

Published by National Children's Bureau Enterprises Ltd, the trading company for the National Children's Bureau, Registered Charity number 258825. 8 Wakley Street, London EC1V 7QE. Tel: 020 7843 6000

© National Children's Bureau, 2002
Published 2002

ISBN 1 900990 34 2

British Library Cataloguing in Publication Data
A catalogue record for this book is available from the British Library

Printed and bound by CopyTech

Introduction

Between August 2000 and December 2001 the Children's Play Council (CPC) undertook a programme of research and policy development funded by the Department of Culture Media and Sport.

The programme had three strategic objectives:
- To identify the potential for play initiatives to inform and support key government policies, in order to find out what could work and why, in relation to play.
- To identify the key building blocks (both service models and processes) of an efficient and effective 'play development strategy' (that is, a coordinated approach to enhancing children's play opportunities, at local, regional or national level).
- To build consensus and understanding of policy issues, research findings and good practice within the play sector and in related fields.

To inform this work CPC developed a programme of research which:
- Reviewed the evidence base for the value of play in children's lives and healthy development.
- Investigated the benefits of play provision to families and communities, as well as children.
- Measured the extent to which an adequate range of play opportunities currently exists for all children.
- Identified the role that children's play provision currently plays in supporting national and local government policy agendas.
- Identified existing structures for developing and supporting play opportunities and provision.

The findings of this research have been summarised and used as the basis of the companion report to this *Making the Case for Play: Building policies and strategies for school-aged children*, which makes over 50 recommendations to Government, local agencies and the play sector, on the future of children's play in England.

This report contains the four detailed research reports:
- **Something Good and Fun**: an analysis of over 100 reports of consultations with children and young people and parents focussing on children's free time activities, undertaken by the Children's Play Council.
- **The Value of Children's Play and Play Provision**: a major review by the New Policy Institute of the most recent literature on play and school aged children.
- **The Planning and Location of Play Provision in England**: a three-tier mapping process, undertaken by the New Policy Institute, describing play policy, development and provision in England, examining how the extent and nature of play services and provision varies in one English region and exploring the reasons behind this variability in four local authorities.
- **The State of Play**: a survey of play professionals undertaken by Children's Play Council.

Section 1

Something Good and Fun

Children's and parents' views on play and out-of-school provision

Issy Cole-Hamilton

Acknowledgements

Thanks go to all the people who contributed reports of their consultation exercises with children and young people and parents; also to Tim Gill, Jessica Lubbock, Mark Dunn, Sabina Collier, Pennie Hedge, Bethany Rawles.

Children's Play Council
February 2002

Something Good and Fun
Children's and parents' views on
play and out-of-school provision

Contents

1	Main findings	3
2	Discussion	9
3	Detailed findings	11
	3.1 Where children go after school	11
	3.2 What out-of-school activities children enjoy	13
	3.3 What children would like more of in their free-time	15
	3.4 Where children play out	16
	3.5 Reasons why children do not play out	17
	3.6 How outdoor play space could be improved	19
	3.7 Consultations about after-school clubs and play settings	20
	3.8 What children do not like about childcare and play settings	22
	3.9 What children would like to change in childcare and play settings	24
	3.10 Children's views about staff in childcare and play settings	26
	3.11 Rules in play and childcare provision	
4	Parents' views	29
	4.1 The consultation reports	29
	4.2 Views on outdoor play opportunities	29
	4.3 Types of childcare used by parents	29
	4.4 Types of childcare parents wanted more of	30
	4.5 What parents look for in provision	30
Appendix 1	Methodology	31
Appendix 2	Location of consultations	33

1   Main findings

"Play is what I do when everyone else has stopped telling me what to do."

A review of over 100 consultations with children and young people of school age and with parents, in England in 2001, shows that:

Where children go
When not at school:
- The majority of children are at home or with friends or relatives.
- Significant numbers of children spend some of their time in formal childcare.
- A small proportion of children use open access play settings and organised clubs or groups.

"I like going to out-of-school club because I can play with friends and have lots of fun."

Where children play
When at home children play out in a variety of places including:
- The streets.
- Local parks and recreation fields.
- Open spaces.
- Play areas.

"When I go out it gets air to my brain so that I can think and stuff."

What children like
Children are most likely to say they enjoy:
- Physically-active outdoor and indoor pursuits.
- Meeting with their friends.
- Quiet activities.
- Being able to choose from a range of activities.

"Sometimes I like to make stuff, sometimes I like to play games, sometimes I like messing about, sometimes I don't like doing anything."

What stops children playing out
But many children are prevented from playing out as much as they would like by:
- Fears for their own safety, in particular, bullies.
- Dirty, unkempt play areas and parks.
- The lack of things for them to do.
- Traffic.

"The parks are dirty and not enough equipment, people leave needles there, it's dangerous."

What children dislike

Children in childcare and play settings are least happy about:

- Bullying and roughness.
- Lack of choice of things to do.
- Lack of suitable provision for disabled children.
- Poor quality buildings, facilities and equipment.

"The staff say you've got two choices, you can either do bouncy castle or football, and then you have to do that all day."

What children think about staff

Children using staffed provision like:

- Staff who listen.
- Staff who are funny, friendly, cheerful, kind and fair.
- Having a say in what they do.
- Staff who can deal with conflicts between children.

"Workers should be kind, responsible, funny, strict when they have to be and have a first aid qualification."

What parents think about play

Consultations with parents about childcare show that:

- Parents are concerned that their children do not play outdoors very much.
- Relatively few parents regularly use formal childcare.
- The cost of childcare is prohibitive for many parents.
- Significant proportions of parents would like their children to be able to use after-school provision and holiday play schemes.

What parents think about childcare

The most important elements of childcare for parents are that:

- The staff are well trained and good at their jobs.
- The children are happy.
- The provision is easy to get to.
- Children are able to make and meet friends.

Many parents also find childcare too expensive or inconvenient to be useful to them or their children.

2   Discussion

> "We want something good and fun. We don't want people telling us what to do all the time, that's what happens all day at school. You need it to be different."

In summer 2001 the Children's Play Council collected 108 reports of consultations with school-aged children and young people and parents about children's free-time activities. These reports came from EYDCP audits, Best Value Reviews, Education Action Zones, Children's Fund applications and other local consultations. While many of the consultations were wide-ranging, this review looks only at the sections concerning children's free-time activities.

The analysis showed that most children either go directly home or to friends or relatives after school and in the holidays. When at home one of the main activities is watching television although some also play outside, meet their friends or do their homework.

The proportion of children going to after-school clubs varies widely between areas, from under 6 to over 50 per cent. Some children go to organised structured activities, some to play centres and some to religious or after-school classes.

When not at school children like to have a variety of activities available to them. They enjoy playing and being with their friends, sporting activities particularly football and swimming, trips to places in interest, and practical activities which include making things such as cooking and crafts.

Children are not always happy with their out-of-school arrangements. Some say they do not have enough to do and are bored, others are concerned about the amount of bullying they encounter, and many are restricted in their outdoor play by difficulties with transport and costs of transport, the broken-down state of their local playgrounds which they considered to be dangerous and unhygienic and their parents' fears of traffic and other possible dangers.

Children have clear ideas of how their free-time opportunities could be improved. In a high proportion of consultations children wanted more outdoor and sport-related activities and places where they could meet their friends.

In some areas children wanted more play centres and staffed activities although they do not necessarily want the adults interfering in their play.

In many of the surveys children were concerned about the lack of opportunities for disabled children and felt this should be rectified.

In some areas children wanted places where they could get snacks and drinks, and cleaner, better toilets were often mentioned.

> "My best thing is playing out. I love it with my friends, I have learned how to climb and jump."

Some of the consultations asked specifically about the play or childcare provision that the children were being interviewed in. The things children liked about these play settings included physically-active pursuits, a range of quieter indoor activities, the opportunity to be with their friends and just being able to play.

However there were things that children did not like about some of the childcare and play settings. These included bullying and roughness, lack of choice of activities and being told what they had to do by the staff. In some areas children were also aware of and unhappy about inter-racial tension.

In general staff in the play and childcare settings were popular. But children were very clear that staff who looked after them should both like children and be kind and caring. Rules in clubs and play centres were generally popular but the children felt strongly that they should be involved in developing them.

Some of the surveys asked children specifically about outdoor play activities. In general children wanted more opportunities for outdoor play and better maintained outdoor spaces. They also wanted more say in what they did whilst outside and to feel safer whilst out on their own or with their friends. They wanted to feel safer from traffic, strangers, dirt and other children.

"Please do something about our area because we are all classed as delinquents but we are not. We want somewhere to go. Thank you." (14 year old girl)

Parents are also not always happy with the facilities available to their children when not at school. Children do not play outdoors as much as they would like and they are concerned that children stay inside, watching too much television.

Parents would like there to be more after-school and holiday provision for their children and are concerned, primarily, that the staff running that provision are well trained and understand the different needs of different children.

The Children's Play Council research shows strongly that, contrary to popular belief, children want more opportunities for outdoor and physically-active pursuits. Play and out-of-school provision is important to them for the range of opportunities for play and other activities it offers, for the friendships it allows them to develop and maintain and for the new and different experiences it offers them.

3 Detailed findings

3.1 Where children go after school

- *Most children go home or to friends or relatives after school.*
- *The proportions of children using after-school provision varies between areas but is generally low. A relatively small proportion of children go to play settings after school.*
- *A small proportion of children use other facilities including sports clubs, organised groups and religious or culturally specific provision.*

Thirty-three reports gave some information about where the children went after school. Of these:

- 9 were carried out in schools;
- 8 were carried out in childcare or play provision;
- 9 were carried out in combinations of settings including schools, childcare and youth projects;
- 1 was a home based consultation.

Information was not available about the location of the remaining six.

Consultations undertaken in play and childcare settings are not representative of children generally but those done in schools are more likely to be. The proportions of children consulted whilst at school or home, who went straight home from school, ranged from 60 to 89 per cent. Amongst the children consulted in after-school clubs and play settings between 6 and 79 per cent sometimes went straight home. Where the research had been undertaken in a combination of settings the proportions of children going straight home ranged from 28 to 79 per cent.

"I'd go round my mum's friends and play with her children."

"I sometimes go and play piano. Sometimes I go swimming. I go to Chinese school every Saturday. I enjoy it because you learn things and at break-time you can go outside. I would choose to go to Chinese school instead of here because you learn things and at break-time you can go outside and you can learn Chinese."

"I play on my PlayStation of course, I do it on Thursday and Monday because Tuesday I'm here, Wednesday I go to Cubs and Friday I swim." (Child with special educational needs.)

"You can go to town shopping or ice skating but it costs a lot of money."

"I go to Brownies and child-minders." (Child with special educational needs)

"I stay at home and go shopping."

The consultations done in schools show that a relatively small proportion of children went to after school clubs or play settings. In three of the consultations around 10 per cent of the children used the clubs but in one consultation of 11 to 16 year olds as many as 55 per cent used the clubs from time to time. Amongst the 33 relevant consultations, 21 mentioned that children used after-school clubs. Only one of the school consultations mentioned that some children went to play settings after school but in that report 30 per cent of the children did from time to time.

"Football clubs and a child-minder because mum and dad are too busy to pick me up." (Child with special educational needs)

"No things for teenagers to do after school – there is nowhere to go, you just hang around the streets." (14 year old girl)

In addition, the 33 consultations showed very wide variations in the proportions of children involved in different types of activities. For example:

- 18 indicated children sometimes went to sports clubs or activities: ranging from 6 per cent to 55 per cent of children;
- 16 indicated that children sometimes played outside with their friends: ranging from 2 per cent to 86 per cent of children;
- 15 indicated that children some-times went to organised clubs and specific activities: ranging from 3 per cent to 34 per cent of children;
- 3 indicated that children sometimes went to religious or language classes;
- and in 5 consultations a small proportion of children felt there was nothing at all for them to do after school. This was particularly true for older children.

Although in ten consultations children mentioned going to child-minders, the proportions were usually relatively low with fewer than 20 per cent of children using child-minders in most cases.

Sixteen of the reports gave some general information about the activities children undertook after school, not only where they went. Of these, nine mentioned the proportions of children who watched television or used computers and in almost every case this was over 70 per cent.

A few of the consultations asked children why they did not use existing out-of-school provision. Reasons included difficulties with transport to the provision, not knowing what was available, the expense, and fear of being bullied.

Four consultations asked children what they did not like about their after-school arrangements. In three reports children mentioned homework; in two, having to wait for their parents; and in one, having to be with brothers and sisters.

3.2 What out-of-school activities children enjoy

Children are most likely to say they enjoy:

- *physically-active pursuits*
- *meeting with their friends*
- *quiet activities*
- *being able to choose from a variety of activities*

Twenty consultations asked children about the activities they most enjoyed when not at school. The types of activities mentioned in the largest number of reports were physically-active pursuits including a range of sports-based activities, meeting friends and quiet activities such as arts, crafts and board games. (See Table 1)

Table 1: Favourite after-school activities (Total number of reports mentioning issue = 20)

Favourite activities after school	Number of reports mentioning activities
Physically-active pursuits	15
Meeting friends	13
Quiet activities	13
Variety	8
Trips	4
Playing	4
Being with family/friends/relatives	3
Shopping	3
Pets	2
Playworkers	2
Outdoor play	2
Religious schools	1

"Friendly staff, they're number one!"

"I like it a lot because it is not like school. The workers look after you but they don't act like teachers telling you what to do all the time. I think that's good. It makes me feel grown up."

"We get to do stuff with our friends and you don't get bossed around like you do at school."

"I love it, it's really good. I just get bored at home so I have to go on at mum to let me come all the time."

"It's dead good round here cos you go on trips and you go swimming and run around. You play football and stuff. I like that stuff and so do me mates." (10 year old boy)

"It's not like school as you get to do all sorts. I like baking the best. We're going to make cakes, will you help me?"

"I didn't want to go – my mum said I had to go because she was at work. But now I really like going. It's good and there's no teacher to nag you and stufff." (Child with special educational needs)

"I enjoy going because I get fed up and bored [at home] and it gives me a chance to play with my friends."

"I enjoy going to stop with nanny because we play cool games."

"I like it because we get to make new friends."

"I like the people here."

"I like coming because it's something to do. I'm the youngest in the family, my brothers are too old." (Child with special educational needs)

"I like playing with other children."

"It's really good and I can learn new things everyday."

"I felt safe because there were lot of people there."

"I like the club, I like to play." (Child with special educational needs)

"It's fun, you play and muck around and stuff." (Child with special educational needs)

"Its better than watching TV." (Child with special educational needs)

"It's wicked. I can make space ships and everything." (Child with special educational needs)

"It's so amazing, it gives you something to do and stops you getting bored." (Child with special educational needs)

3.3 What children would like more of in their free-time

Children would like more opportunities for:

- *physically-active pursuits – both indoor and outdoor*
- *outdoor play*
- *quiet play*

In the 26 reports providing information about what children would like to be able to do more often in their free-time, the most frequently mentioned interests were physically-active pursuits including dance, disco and a wide range of sports-based activities and play, both indoor and outdoor. (See Table 2)

Table 2: Activities children would like after school (Total number of reports mentioning issue = 26)

What would you like to do after school?	Number of reports mentioning issue
Physical activity – indoor and outdoor	16
Outdoor play	10
Quiet play	10
After-school clubs	8
Be with peers	6
Sports centre	4
More play areas	4
Better parks	4
Indoor play	3
Somewhere to get food/drinks	2
Variety	2
Cheap/free	2
Junior/youth children	2
Trips	2

Also mentioned were opportunities to be with friends and other children the same age, and uniformed groups.

"A bike track that was kept nice for us instead of vandals ripping it up." (11 year old boy)

"A park with a pond (with fish and frogs), a climbing frame, swings, slide and football park." (11 year old girl)

"A close swimming pool and proper football pitches." (11 year old boy)

"I would like to have a better park and swimming leisure centre." (12 year old girl)

"A bigger park and a better fishing pond." (12 year old boy)

3.4 Where children play out

When not in the care of adults children play in:

- *parks and recreation grounds*
- *the streets near their homes*
- *local open spaces*
- *school grounds*

Nine of the consultation reports provided some information about where children played in their free-time. In line with other published research the analysis showed that many children play out more frequently in the streets nearer their homes than anywhere else. In six of the nine reports children talked of playing in the streets. Where figures were available the proportions of children varied from 11 to 76 per cent.

Parks, recreation grounds and playing-fields were mentioned in eight of the nine reports, with between 10 and 50 per cent of children saying they played there. Children also played in their own gardens, in their own or their friends' homes, in school grounds, play areas, play centres and in other open spaces. (See Table 3)

Table 3: Places children play out

(number of reports mentioning issue = 10)

Location	Number of reports citing location
Park or recreation field	8
In the streets	6
Own garden	6
House (own or friends')	6
Open spaces	6
School grounds	3
Play areas	3
Sports area	2
Play centre	2

"Now I am older I can go to the local park and play with my friends at football and tennis."

"Playing in our streets behind our house."

"We play on the quarry but not when there was foot and mouth."

"Building a den in my back garden."

"We play around the dustbins – we hide behind them and jump on the lids."

"I play in my garden with my brother with the ball just for fun."

"Playing cricket, tig, roller-skating in the street with my brother and sister and other children."

"We sneak on school fields."

3.5 Reasons why children do not play out

There are many reasons why children play out less than they want to:

- *Unkempt, dirty areas*
- *Fears for their safety*
- *Nothing for them to do*
- *Dogs and dogs' mess*
- *Play paces are too far away*

Sixteen reports provided information why children did not play out as much they should have liked. Children were most likely to mention the poor state of their play spaces as a main reason for not playing there. Rubbish, broken glass, dogs' mess, discarded needles and even abandoned cars were seen as major problems by many. Although mentioned in fewer reports road traffic was seen as an even worse problem in the reports where it was cited, especially in urban areas.

Older children were more likely to say that, whilst there was provision for younger children, there was nothing for them. Most of the reports specifically focusing on children of 9 to 14 years old mentioned that there was little for them to do.

Children were also concerned about their own personal safety, citing a number of safety issues including their fears of older children and bullying, poor lighting and general fears of being out when there were no adults they could refer to. (See Table 4)

"The beck is dirty, it needs tidying up."

"The swings are missing, the council came and took them away, we don't know where to."

"There's nothing good about any of the places in our area."

"All the facilities are not really local."

"And there is loads of land round here with nothing on it."

"It would cost us loads to go ice-skating. If there was something like that here it'd make it a lot nicer place to live."

"There is play ground near us but it is full of broken glass and burnt cars – we don't go there."

"We don't play out because we have not got anywhere to play – mum says we can't play out on the road."

"I'm only allowed in my garden - my dad says I cannot go out cos I might get run down."

Table 4: What stops children playing out? (Total number of reports mentioning issue = 14)

Factors putting children off outdoor play	Number of reports mentioning issue
Rubbish, broken glass, needles	14
General fears for personal safety	10
Nothing to do	9
Dogs and dogs' mess	9
Parents stop them	7
Older children/bullying	7
Broken equipment and unsafe play areas	7
Traffic	6
Nothing	5
Not suitable for age	5
Too expensive	5
Lack of transport	4
Strangers	3
Adults	3
Darkness	3
Distance	3
Other things to do	3
No outreach staff	3
Weather	2
Motorbikes in park	2
Other issues mentioned: don't know what is available, drug use in parks, mud, cultural reasons, hard surfaces, not accessible to everyone.	

"Last year I got pulled by this kid with a gun outside the youth club and he had a gun."

"I've got mugged three times before."

"You can only go once a week cos it costs, and you have to pay bus fares too." (13 year old girl)

"Go to the park - its rubbish." (12 year old boy)

"Not much to do. There's West park and a little park that has been ripped up." (11 year old boy)

"In the park there is only a slide and a climbing frame . Other things are too far away." (Girl aged 12)

" People fighting at night and the police chase them through the woods."

"I had to sweep all glass before playing."

"The football field's wrecked because people go on motorbikes on it and there's rubbish everywhere."

"You can't go out at night at all. Once it gets dark at 6pm that's it, you can't go out."

"Some parks don't even have swings and roundabouts."

3.6 How outdoor play space could be improved

Four reports also offered some thoughts from children about how their play places could be improved. In one consultation over half the children felt that activities should be organised and supervised by adults. More and safer equipment and safer places to play with better lighting and easier roads to cross and cleaner, better kept play areas were also mentioned in other reports.

"There should be a place that we could sit in the warm and talk." (Girl aged 14)

"Somewhere where we could walk to and from our house and play safely without adults supervising us."

"No cars in my street so that I can play outside."

"This is the quarry. I think they are going to build bungalows here but we would like a BMX track."

"A graffiti wall so no one will do it on the sides of houses."

"Make sure you can cross the road by having traffic wardens everywhere."

"Police should come and play with children and talk to adults."

"Elephant rides switched on by litter not money." (Could help reduce litter)

"They should send round a bus. So you feel safe."

"Park with swings and a little stall selling ice creams."

"I should feel safe about where I play and who looks after me."

"You can't go anywhere in the parks, there's gum on them and graffiti. You need a section for little children." (Girl aged 9)

"There should be a park-keeper to look out for smokers and junkies." (Boy aged 10 years)

3.7 Consultations about after-school clubs and play settings

When in childcare and play settings children are most likely to say they enjoy:
- *quiet indoor activities*
- *physically-active pursuits*
- *playing with their friends*

The need for ensuring there is a wide choice of activities for children in after-school clubs and play settings was clear when children were asked about what they liked about the different types of provision they attended. In 43 of 49 reports some of the most popular activities were indoor activities such as arts and crafts, cooking and board games.

Physically-active indoor and outdoor pursuits were also very popular. Particularly popular indoors were dance and drama and outdoor sporting activities including football, swimming and a range of other sports-based activities.

It was also clear that one of the important parts of play and after-school provision was the opportunity it gave children to be with their friends and to socialise. In a small number of consultations children cited the opportunity to have a quiet time as one of the things they liked about the provision. Trips out were also popular. (See Table 5)

"I love it, it's really good [at the club]. I just get bored at home so I have to go on at mum to let me come all the time."

"It's not like school as you get to do all sorts. I like baking the best. Were going to make cakes, will you help me?"

"We get to do stuff with our friends and you don't get bossed around like you do at school."

"We have competitions like drawing. This afternoon we've got a treasure hunt – the staff have organised it for us and brought us sweets."

"We have competitions like drawing. This afternoon we've got a treasure hunt – the staff have organised it for us and brought us sweets."

"I like running around and stuff and also love making frogs. They make you think and I am pleased when I finish them."

"They have equipment here and coaches. The facilties are very good." (Child at the Bangladeshi Centre)

Table 5: Things children like about different types of provision (Total number of reports covering issue = 49)

What children like	Number of reports mentioning issue
Quiet indoor activities	43
Physically-active outdoor activities	36
Physically-active indoor activities	27
Playing and socialising with friends	15
Playing generally	13
Fixed equipment	11
The choice of activities	10
Quiet outdoor activities	10
The staff	8
Trips out	8
Food and snacks	8
Quiet times	3
Other	6

"There are loads of fun activities. They phone up football coaches, drama people. You can play table tennis, pool, computers, chess, go outside, karate – we don't fight each other, we only practice a move, we don't hit each other."

"The best bit in the holiday club is swimming and crafts."

"Playing on the bikes, play indoors, do some painting and things." (Child with special educational needs)

"I like the bit when we do all the sticking and glueing."

"I enjoy going to the after-school club where I am making a boat for my cousin. I wouldn't like it if my friends stopped going. I would like to keep getting experience of things to do when I am older, like ... I want to be a joiner." (A 10 year old with special educational needs)

"We like going outside and playing on the hoops and things."

"Play outside on the bikes." (Child with special educational needs)

"Jumping up and down on the floor."

"Drawing, playing in the hall. Sometimes when there's a parachute I play that or skipping or racing with one of my friends." (Child with special educational needs)

3.8 What children do not like about childcare and play settings

When in childcare and play settings children do not like:
- *Bullying and roughness*
- *Not enough choice of activities*
- *Lack of provision for disabled children*

There were things that children did not like about the childcare or play provision they attended. Amongst those most frequently mentioned were bullying and roughness, particular individual activities, insufficient choice of things to do and swearing and bad behaviour from other children.

The lack of provision and activities which disabled children could join in with was also seen as a problem in some settings. The buildings and facilities were also criticised, with lack of space, unpleasant toilets and poor maintenance being cited. Some children also felt the provision was expensive. (See Table 6)

"We should have more staff."

"Especially cards so people can swap them in the breaks but the staff think that it's like the number one sin in the world."

"We had a room but it got trashed."

"There is nothing to play on and the playground is covered in glass. People use it to take drugs."

"We can't run about inside when there is not much room."

"We are not allowed to play indoor football."

"People call me names and bully me."

"I don't like the big boys going there the same time as me."

"Instead of just having sports we should sit down and play cards – something relaxing – or board games."

"It's boring, we need new stuff, it's really old where the nursery have had it and it's got chocolate all over it." (Child with special educational needs)

What children do not like about after-school clubs and play settings

Table 6: Things children do not like about specific provision (Total number of reports mentioning issue = 34)

What children do not like	Number of reports mentioning issue
Activities and atmosphere	
Bullying and roughness	16
Specific activities	13
Not enough choice or things to do	10
Swearing and bad behaviour	7
Nothing for disabled children	6
Not enough active sporty activities	5
Poor equipment	4
Nothing for older children	4
Being told what activities to do	3
Specific rules	3
Noise	2
Clearing up	2
Not enough chance to play out	2
Buildings and space	
Not enough space	5
The toilets	4
Poorly maintained	5
Nettles and mud	2
The building	2
Too crowded	2
Not safe	2
Other	
Too expensive	5
Not being able to play with friends at home	2

"I'd like to keep doing gymnastics but they say you have to go swimming instead."

"Sometimes they're out of order because if you don't want to do something they put you on time out."

"I'd like to stay at home sometimes and play with my friends who live near me. I don't see them much." (Girl aged 8 years)

"I'd like a club near where I live then I could go there sometimes and be with me mates from home. I like it here but I'd like a change sometimes." (Boy aged 11 years)

"Youth Club bias towards boy and football."

3.9 What children would like to change in childcare and play settings

Children have clear ideas about what they would like to change in childcare and play settings. They would like:

- *More physical activities*
- *More quiet activities*
- *A better choice of toys, equipment and activities*

In order to address some of these difficulties there were a number of things children would have liked to change about the out-of-school provision they used. In particular they would have liked more physically-active pursuits open to them as well as more quiet activities. Food and drink and trips out also featured in a number of reports. Buildings and toilets could be improved and been generally cleaner and children felt the staff should be able to control 'naughty' children better. (See Table 7)

"There should be quiet areas for time out and rest."

"It would be at school so I didn't have to walk all the way, you walk through the school and your there." (Child with special educational needs)

"My brother, he's 13, he doesn't come anymore. Would he like to come? Yes."

"Most of my friends are older than me, they are 12 and they don't come anymore. I don't know why, I think it's because of the age groups and they are too old."

"There should be older groups because at the moment there is 8 to 13 years. My mum works so I would have to stay at home by myself and it gets really boring. And we are in with 8 year olds who can't kick a ball. I'd like a 12 and up group – 12 to 15 year olds."

"I'd get cleaners to come to clean it up a bit more. It's getting dirty and the paper is coming off." (Child with special educational needs)

"I wouldn't mind getting some more games and a computer." (Child with special educational needs)

"The boys go over the top sometimes and it's hard to do what you want to do when they are being so noisy." (Two 10 year old girls)

"Decorating because it's really dirty. I'd have more sports and make it bigger." (Child with special educational needs)

Table 7: What children would like to change in specific provision (Total number of reports mentioning issue = 31)

What children would like to change	Number of reports mentioning issue
Physical activities	20
More quiet activities	14
More choice	8
Have food and drink	7
More trips	7
Indoor play area	7
More for older children	6
More computing	6
More space to run	5
Quiet corners	5
More outdoor play	4
More for disabled children	4
More for younger children	3
Better equipment	3
Stop bullies	3
Separate activities for older and younger children	3
Children's art on show	2
Also mentioned were: children wanting to be able to use all the equipment, the need for family space, more say for children, better funding, celebration of religious festivals, clear rules and rewards for good behaviour	
Better buildings	7
Cleaner	5
Better toilets	3
Also: comfortable seating, more colourful	
Staff in control of naughty children, less interference from the staff, staff, staff who respect children more	
Other	
Cheaper or free	2
Better transport	2

"We'd like somewhere to make loads of noise and not have lots of people telling you to be quiet – I get told that at home enough." (Boy aged 11)

"They have toy weapons. It is like the jungle, it has sand, it has water, there is lots of disturbing things."

"I will change the football ground because they shout and kick the football hard at a person's head and I think they shouldn't do that."

"It is important to go on trips because you get to see other places and have different experiences."

"We would like nice toilets that are clean."

"If they can do some more sports things and things for the older children as they keep putting out Barbies and Action Men." (Child with special educational needs)

3.10 Children's views about staff in childcare and play settings

Children like staff who:

- *Listen*
- *Are funny*
- *Let them have a say in what is happening*
- *Are friendly, playful and cheerful*

Between the 30 reports describing children's views of staff there are a large number of attributes appealing to children. Top of the list was 'adults who listen'. (See Table 8)

There are, however, some things children do not like about some of the staff they encounter. This includes staff who shout, are bad tempered or 'bossy' and, in some cases, staff who tell them off.

In two consultations there was concern that there were insufficient staff in the provision.

"The adults who look after me should agree with each other what they are doing and why they are doing it."

"The staff don't get paid enough."

"They're fun, good to play with, and good at listening." (Child with special educational needs)

"Adults should listen to our opinions."

"You can talk to them about anything." (Child with special educational needs)

"I think that the supervision was very good, if someone got lost they knew what to do."

"Very nice, if I want them to play with me, they play." (Child with special educational needs)

"Kind, gentle, patient and who listen to what I say." (Girl aged 8)

"The helpers always help people: don't go there, they take pins away and tell you to put your shoes on if pins are dropped."

"They don't tell you off, only if you have done something really wrong." (Child with special educational needs)

Table 8: Specific provision: What children like about the staff (Total number of reports covering issue = 30)

Children like	Number of reports mentioning issue
Adults who listen	8
Funny	5
Having a say and involved in what they do	4
Friendly	4
Cheerful	4
Playful	4
Helpful	4
Deal with conflicts	3
Facilitate integration	3
Calm	3
Staff should like children	2
Know safety, first aid, etc	2
Know about aiding disabled children	2
Kind	2
Fair	2
Also mentioned were: staff who understand, are confident, are able to relate to children, empower children with skills and knowledge, agree with each other, give equal treatment to all children, can 'teach', are trustworthy, respect children, are clean, healthy and do not smoke, have their own children, are well trained, are responsible, join in, are sporty, are fun, are polite, caring, patient and gentle and who look after the children.	

"They just say what we want to do and they have exciting activities on offer. The week before they write it down what we want to do."

"The helpers always help people: don't go there, they take pins away and tell you to put your shoes on if pins are dropped."

"All the helpers are friendly."

"When we do something wrong, they don't shout at us, they talk, or send us to the corner."

"Skilful teachers, wonderful, kind, generous, nice, caring." (Child with special educational needs)

"They don't tell you off, only if you have done something really wrong." (Child with special educational needs)

3.11 Rules in play and childcare provision

Six consultations asked the children what they felt about rules in their play or childcare provision. In general, rules were thought to be useful and important and that:

- adults should enforce the rules (mentioned in 4 reports);
- children should be involved in making the rules (mentioned in 4 reports);
- the rules should be fair to all (2 reports);
- there should not be too many rules (1 report).

However, in two of the reports some children felt they should be able to do as they pleased with no rules.

Children also had views on the types of rules that should exist. These included:

- no hitting or fighting (4 reports);
- no name-calling (3 reports);
- respect for all (2 reports);
- safety (2 reports);
- no swearing (1 report);
- no bullying (1 report);
- know when stranger present (1 report);
- caring for the environment (1 report).

"We want the rules to be fair."

"We make the rules so if we break them they say - well you made them!"

4 Parents' views
4.1 The consultation reports

In addition to consultations with children and young people the Children's Play Council collected 27 reports of consultations with parents of school-aged children. These reports were mainly from Early Years Development and Childcare Partnerships and focused on parents' childcare needs rather than children's play. The 27 reports included responses from around 10,000 parents. A small number did, however, look at parents' views about what the childcare should provide for their children and one report of a survey commissioned by the Children's Play Council in 1999 asked parents specifically about their children's opportunities to play out.

4.2 Views on outdoor play opportunities

The Opinion Poll, conducted by NOP for Children's Play Council in August 1999, showed that 80 per cent of parents believed their children had fewer play opportunities for outdoor play than they had had as children and that the children's development was suffering as a result. For example:

- 68 per cent worried that their children's development was suffering because of poor outdoor play opportunities.
- 78 per cent said the main reason their child did not play out was their own fears for their child's safety.
- For 52 per cent their fear of traffic danger was a major influence.
- 75 per cent felt that children watched too much television and spent too much time on computers.
- 32 per cent said the main reason their children did not play out was lack of local parks and playgrounds.
- 24 per cent said playgrounds were dirty and equipment unsafe.

- 27 per cent thought the main reason for the trend was that working parents do not have the time to take their children out to play.

4.3 Types of childcare used by parents

Thirteen reports gave information about the types of childcare used by parents. From the larger, statistically analysed consultations, it was clear that the majority of school-aged children rarely use formal childcare. Where children are in the care of others this is most frequently their family friends and relatives. As children get older, parents become even less likely to use childcare. After-school clubs were generally used by around 10 per cent of parents although in one area 67 per cent used them.

The proportions of parents sending their children to holiday play schemes was typically also around 10 per cent although in one area it was 27 per cent and in another 43 per cent. There was no specific mention of children going to open access play settings in any of the reports.

Eleven consultations investigated the reasons why parents did not currently use childcare. The most commonly cited reason with the largest proportions of parents commenting, was the cost of childcare. Between 20 and 30 per cent of parents in three consultations giving statistics thought childcare was too expensive. The fact that the provision was not open for sufficient hours or at convenient times was also an important deterrent to use, with nearly 10 per cent of parents in three consultations identifying this as an issue. Lack of information about what was available, difficulties in getting to provision and lack of places were also mentioned. In two consultations parents of children with special educational needs were concerned that there was no provision suitable for their children.

4.4 Types of childcare parents wanted more of

Of the 19 consultations asking parents what provision they would like to be able to access, 15 mentioned after-school clubs and 14 mentioned holiday play schemes. Where figures were available, around 35 per cent (ranging from 13 and 50 per cent) of parents would have liked more access to holiday play schemes and similar proportions would have liked to be able to send their children to after-school clubs. In three consultations parents would have liked their children to have greater access to local leisure facilities and to homework clubs and in one area there was a view that young people should have access to services specifically run by young people for young people.

4.5 What parents look for in provision

Eleven consultations asked parents about the elements of childcare provision important to them. The most frequently mentioned was that the staff should be well qualified and good at their jobs. That children should feel happy and the provision should be near home were mentioned in three reports. In one survey of 2,200 parents 96 per cent wanted to feel their child was being well cared for, 96 per cent that their child would learn at the provision, 93 per cent that their child would be able to make friends and 88 per cent that their child's cultural background would be respected.

In another survey of 486 parents, more than 75 per cent wanted to be sure their child was well cared for, that the staff were qualified and good at their job and that the buildings and environment were suitable.

Parents of children with special educational needs wanted to be sure that the staff were interested in and able to meet any specific needs their child might have.

Appendix 1: Methodology

The Children's Play Council Research Project

Methodology
Between May and July 2001 the Children's Play Council contacted all the EYDCPs in England, the Health Action Zones that were working with children, Education Action Zones, and local authorities known to have undertaken Best Value Reviews of children's play and asked them for copies of any reports written about consultations with children and young people about children's free time. We also included other consultations we were aware of, linked to the Children's Fund.

The 108 reports received were analysed for common themes and interests of children and young people and parents. The analysis was as systematic as possible given the different ways in which information was collected and reported.

The consultation reports
In total well over 13,000 children and young people had taken part in 93 consultations[1] which had been undertaken in a range of settings and using a mix of methodologies. The numbers of children in each consultation varied widely, ranging from small groups of five or six, to one major consultation of over 2,700 children and young people.
- 10 consultations included fewer than 20 children;
- 6 consultations involved 21–49 children;
- 11 consultations involved 50–99 children;
- 15 consultations involved 100–199 children;
- 14 consultations involved 200–500 children;
- 4 consultations involved over 500 children.
(Information was not available about the numbers of children in the remaining 33 consultations but it was apparent that they varied in size.)

The larger consultations, of over 200 children and young people, were almost all conducted using written questionnaires although four did involve a mix of methodologies. All the consultations undertaken by young people trained as researchers (young consultants) involved groups of fewer than 20 consultants and the smallest consultations were more likely to have been group discussions or interviews. Other, less conventional methods included poetry and writing, oral description, observation and photography.

Of the 84 consultations from which information was available:
- 33 were written questionnaires;
- 14 were based on interviews;
- 14 employed a mix of methods;
- 8 had been undertaken by young consultants;
- 7 had involved focus groups.
- 1 had been a children's conference;
- 6 involved other methods.

---

[1] The remaining consultations had been with parents

Information was available from 76 of the consultations about the location in which the research had taken place.

- 22 consultations had used a mix of locations including schools and childcare and play settings;
- 16 consultations had been done in schools;
- 13 consultations had been done in after-school clubs;
- 11 consultations had been done in play settings;
- 6 consultations had been done in unspecified types of childcare;
- 2 consultations had been done at children's homes.

Six consultations had involved other locations including parks, play events and children's conferences and early years settings.

Most of the consultations had involved children of school age and few had separated out the responses of children of different ages. The ages of the children were given in 69 of the reports. In total:

- 17 reports included the views of children under 5 years old;
- 40 reports included the views of children from 5 to 7 years old;
- 56 reports included the views of children from 8 to 11 years old;
- 39 reports included the views of children from over 11 years old.

Fifteen consultations explicitly sought the views of children and young people from specific groups. These included children from different black and minority ethnic groups, disabled children and those with special educational needs, refugee children and children in traveller families.

The focus of reports

The consultations taking place in schools focused on children's free-time needs and the kinds of out-of-school activities they were involved in. Consultations that had taken place as part of EYDCP audits tended to look at both children's free-time activities in general and at their views of the provision they attended. Questionnaires relating to specific types of provision came from both childcare and free play settings. A small number of consultations were specifically about play and the local outdoor and indoor play facilities.

Appendix 2: Location of consultations

Geographical distribution of consultations with children and parents

Consultation reports were received from the following areas:

Barnsley
Bath & North East Somerset
Bedfordshire
Birmingham
Blackpool
Brent
Brighton and Hove
Bristol
Bury
Cheltenham
Cheshire
Cornwall
County Durham
Dorset
East Cleveland
Essex
Hackney
Hammersmith and Fulham
Herefordshire
Kensington and Chelsea
Kent
Kingston upon Hull
Kingston-upon-Thames
Kirklees Metropolitan Council
Lambeth
Lancashire
Leeds City Council
Leicester
Leicestershire CC
Lewisham
Luton
Manchester
Middlesborough
Norfolk
North Tyneside
Northamptonshire
Nottingham City
Plymouth
Ravensbourne
Reading
Redcar and Cleveland
Rochdale
Rotherham
Salford

Sheffield City Council
Shropshire
Somerset
Southend
Southwark
Stogumber
Stoke on Trent
Sunderland
Surrey CC
Tameside
Worcestershire

Section 2

The Value of Children's Play and Play Provision

A systematic research review

Cathy Street

NOVEMBER 2001

The Value of Children's Play and Play Provision: A systematic research review

CONTENTS

SECTION A: INTRODUCTION **39**
Objectives and scope..39
Overview of review findings...41
Structure of the report 43

SECTION B: BACKGROUND...**45**
The UN Convention on the Rights of the Child............................45
Out of School Care National Standards 50
The National Childcare Strategy 50

SECTION C: THE VALUE OF PLAY: THE INDIVIDUAL CHILD **53**
Overview..53
Health benefits and play..57
Education benefits and play 60

SECTION D: THE VALUE OF PLAY: SOCIALISATION AND CITIZENSHIP ..**69**
Overview..69
Where and how children play – their use and experience of place.........................70
Specific groups of young people 76

SECTION E: GOVERNMENT INITIATIVES AND PLAY CASE STUDIES **79**
Overview..79
Examples of projects incorporating play within government initiatives.................79
Case studies of Play Projects..84

SECTION F: ONGOING RESEARCH AND UNPUBLISHED DATA................**89**

SECTION G: CONCLUSIONS **91**
The benefits of play...91
Suggestions for the way forward...91

APPENDIX 1: DATABASE SEARCHES AND KEY WORDS..........................**93**

APPENDIX 2: STUDY METHODOLOGIES **95**

REFERENCES **99**

SECTION A: INTRODUCTION

OBJECTIVES AND SCOPE

The review presented here was undertaken by the New Policy Institute throughout the Summer and early Autumn of 2001. This project is part of the Children's Play Council's work for the Department of Culture, Media and Sport (DCMS) which is primarily aimed at establishing how play and play initiatives can help to support wider government policies and objectives.

The agreed objectives of the review were to:

- Assess the published data relating to the UK's progress in meeting Article 31(2) of the UN Convention on the Rights of the Child, regarding the rights of children and young people and the provision of opportunities for their cultural, artistic, recreational and leisure activities.

- Create an up-to-date record of the evidence that exists to substantiate the arguments for play, on the basis of a wide-ranging review of the literature.

- Establish an initial consensus on the benefits of play and the value of play provision than can link specialists, both practitioners and researchers, and non-specialists, including civil servants both within the DCMS and elsewhere in the government.

After further discussions between the New Policy Institute and the Children's Play Council, it was agreed that the review would also:

- Identify a small number of exemplar play projects that have been developed to support the Government's policy objectives.

A focus on school-age children

This study is chiefly concerned with the value of play for children of school age. This is mainly because the benefits of play, and the consequences of play deprivation amongst this older age group, are under-researched (NPFA, 2000). Much of the existing literature appears focused on the pre-school age group, or to have examined the specialist applications of play therapy for children who may have physical or emotional difficulties.

Furthermore, there are concerns that within the education system, children are under increasing pressure, with the opportunities for free play being increasingly squeezed out or downgraded in learning value (Carvel, 1999; Macintyre, 2001). There are some anxieties that the particular emphasis of the National Curriculum may erode the child-centred principles of early childhood education based on play as a key means to learning (Wood, 1999) and that play is increasingly seen as 'non-productive and insignificant', a stance which is influencing children's views towards play (Sherman, 1997).

Such shifts are particularly important given the increasing numbers of four year old children beginning formal schooling in the UK – a trend which is at odds with many other European countries. Overall, as society becomes more complex and competitive, there is concern that spontaneous play is being replaced with structured activities both at home and within school (Rogers and Sawyers, 1988; Mental Health Foundation, 1999a).

Such a process is being exacerbated by a loss of space (NPFA, 2000); the increasing commodification of leisure (McKendrick and others, 2000a), the heightened parental fears for the safety of their children (PLAYLINK 2000; McNeish and Roberts, 1995; McKendrick and Bradford, 1999) and a growing sense of increased control over children's lives (Petrie, PLAYLINK Portsmouth Conference, 2000).

Set against this is the increasing awareness of children as 'consumers' (McKendrick and others, 2000a), new interest in social studies of childhood and of childhood identities (Holloway andValentine, 2000), and of children's marginalisation in planning processes, especially those affecting access to their local environment (Adams and Ingham, 1998; Woolley and others, 1999; Spencer and Woolley, 2000)

It is within this context that a more in-depth and robust understanding of the benefits of play is now needed. Whilst there is a popular view that play is 'natural' or 'good' for children, more specific information about both immediate and long-term benefits needs to be elucidated – or alternatively, gaps in current knowledge identified. Similarly more information is needed about how children's play is adapting to the current climate, how provision is meeting their needs or not, or has the potential to do so in the future.

The definition of play

For the purposes of the review, *'play'* has been defined as activities which children choose to undertake when not being told what to do by others. The activities are freely chosen, personally directed and may take place with or without adult involvement. They may take place in the home; the street or local community; the school premises including the playground and the countryside. Such activities may be undertaken by the child on their own or with peers.

In reviewing the literature, it should be noted that much of the material is of a qualitative nature rather than quantitative. As such the approach taken has been to try and establish evidence on the *types* of benefits that play brings, rather than the *scale* of those benefits.

It was also agreed that the report would attempt to provide a 'bigger picture' of what the available information on play tells us about the current state of evidence supporting play and about other relevant issues which may need to be considered rather than simply summarising the research findings item by item. For this reason, some of the material presented goes beyond the definition of freely chosen play and discusses closely related areas of research including the effects on children of physical activity and of arts education. The literature presented is largely drawn from the UK, with a more limited focus on international data.

Wherever possible, in order to give some indication of the basis of the research findings cited in the text, some information about the study sample or methodology is given. It should be noted however that in some areas, as a number of the researchers themselves acknowledge, much of the work has been largely descriptive.

Consultation

In undertaking this work, the New Policy Institute has consulted with or requested information from a wide range of organisations, government departments and university departments working in the fields of play, playwork, recreation and leisure, human geography and services for children.

These include:

Government departments and units: the Department for Education and Skills (DFES); the Department of Health (Quality Protects, Sure Start and National Healthy Schools staff); the Children and Young People's Unit and Early Excellence Centre; the New Opportunities Fund; the Health Development Agency; the Countryside Agency.

Specialist play and leisure organisations: the Institute of Leisure and Amenity Management (ILAM); Joanna Ryan, Kidsactive; Jan Cosgrove, Fair Play for Children; Jean Elledge, National Centre for Playwork Education – West Midlands; PLAYLINK; Steve Macarthur, Islington Play Association; Camden Play Service; Birmingham Playtrain.

National charities: the Child Accident Prevention Trust; Education Extra; Barnardos; the Children's Society; the Royal Society for the Prevention of Accidents (ROSPA); the Daycare Trust; Kid's Club Network; the Child Psychotherapy Trust; YoungMinds; Young Voice; the Gulbenkian Foundation; NACRO.

University departments and research bodies: Polly Morton, Action for Sick Children; Helen Woolley, Department of Landscape, University of Sheffield; Gill Valentine, Department of Geography, Sheffield University; Stephen Rennie, Playwork Team, Leeds Metropolitan University; Peri Else, Sheffield Leisure Department; the National Foundation for Educational Research (NFER); the Audit Commission; the ESRC; the Centre for Family and Household Research, Oxford Brookes University; Fred Coalter, Centre for Leisure Research, University of Edinburgh; Sarah Holloway, Department of Human Geography, Loughborough University; the Local Government Association; NACRO; John McKendrick, School of Social Sciences, Glasgow Caledonian University; School of Education, University of Leicester.

Independent play consultants: Haki Kapasi, Inspire; Rob Wheway, independent play consultant.

OVERVIEW OF REVIEW FINDINGS

The information gathered from the contacts made with a range of specialist organisations working in the play field and with university departments, many of which made useful suggestions of areas of literature to be included in the review, suggest quite widespread activity in both research and service development where play may be a component of what is provided.

This is backed up by the array of recent literature identified in this project. In particular, within the academic fields of geography and urban studies, research interest is apparent in children's use of and access to urban spaces, their use of commercial play spaces and what is called the 'commodification' of childhood (defined 'as making a consumable product of an everyday experience and, at the macro-level, as the net effect of ever greater realms of life becoming consumable products' (McKendrick and others, 2000a).

Alongside this, a variety of studies have examined the issue of risk, both from the perspectives of children and their parents, and how this may curtail their access to play provision located outside the home and, at a wider level, may impact on children's levels of physical activity and on their independent mobility. Another reasonably frequent line of inquiry has focused on children's participation in the planning of provision and their access to and experience of their local environment.

The quality of provision, guidelines for promoting safety, ensuring inclusion in play and encouraging access for children with disabilities, have been the subject of other published reports. Studies examining the growth of structured out-of-school provision, including learning or study support, the changing role of schools and the impact of such provision on children, and the place for play within the National Curriculum, are a further developing focus of investigation.

All of these areas provide some valuable information in terms of where and how children and young people are spending their leisure time, how they play and their views towards what is on offer. It also identifies a number of quite widely agreed upon trends in terms of play opportunities unsupervised or organised by adults becoming more restricted, or the process of 'domestication ... the increasing control and supervision of play to get rid of its physical dangers and its emotional licences' (Sutton-Smith in Goldstein, 1994).

Data Limitations

Unfortunately, and in line with deficits identified in another recent analysis of the literature on play (Coalter and Taylor, 2001), the New Policy Institute review again suggests that, whilst there is widespread recognition of the importance of play in child health and development, in terms of **evidence** about the specific benefits of play to, in this case, school-age children, considerable caution is needed. This is because:

- Much of the literature is still focused on the pre-school and younger age group, with less attention on adolescents.

- There remains a lack of systematic outcome analysis, most especially on a longitudinal basis.

- The definitions used for play are often imprecise and the boundaries between play, sport, learning and education remain poorly defined; as Coalter and Taylor note, there are 'unresolved disputes as to whether positive outcomes are necessarily related to *play-specific* processes or more generic processes' (e.g. social interaction).

- Analysis of the growing area of out-of-school provision and the benefits thereof appears especially problematic in terms of blurred distinctions between organised childcare and play provision – and often a lack of clarity about the actual aims of such services.

- The sample sizes used in a number of studies identified during this review appear to be quite small and often very local in their focus, which raises questions about how applicable the findings may be to other areas.

- Data about young people from minority ethnic groups, those with disabilities and those with other special needs (for example, excluded from school or homeless) remains generally sparse.

- With regard to specific projects where play is one of the core components of provision, evaluation data is often hard to come by – the struggle to keep up with actually running the project and the need to continually search for funding, means that many projects have not been able to attend to such information gathering.

STRUCTURE OF THE REPORT

The report is divided into five main sections. Following this introduction, the second section presents a brief background overview of the policy context surrounding play provision. This particularly refers to the UN Convention on the Rights of the Child which contains a number of Articles that are highly relevant to the opportunities for children and young people to play. The recently introduced Out of School Care Standards are also likely to be of increasing relevance in terms of opportunities for play given the rapid expansion of out-of-school provision recently witnessed in the UK (Kids' Club Network, 2001a; Smith and Barker, 1997).

The third section focuses on the individual child and the benefits of play, specifically in the areas of health and education. The section begins with a general overview of the literature on play and child development, including for children under the age of five years. The focus then shifts specifically to children of statutory school age and examines recent (largely 1995 onwards) published literature about this age group. Included in the discussion of potential education benefits are a small number of studies which have examined the views of teachers and children towards play within the school day.

The next section takes a broader perspective on play and looks at the literature on play and its effects on socialisation and citizenship. The literature reviewed covered a broad sweep of quite diverse areas including children and young people's access to their local environment; their invement in urban planning; where and how they play, and the factors which impinge on this.

Section E describes an array of government policy initiatives where play has been identified as one means by which at the local level projects may realise national aims such as supporting young people excluded from school. Two concluding smaller sections contain details of some unpublished university research projects on play recently completed or now being undertaken by students of play work and allied disciplines. The report then concludes with some analysis of the implications of the studies cited and of the gaps in currently available information.

The material that follows is essentially based on the following:

- An overview of a number of existing reviews identified by the Children's Play Council, including *Best Play* (NPFA, PLAYLINK and Children's Play Council, 2000); *Cross-National Perspectives on the Principles and Practice of Children's Play Provision* (Candler, 1999); *Research into Children's Play* (NPFA, 1999); *Realising the Potential: The Case for Cultural Services – Play* (Coalter and Taylor, 2001) and *The State of Play – a Survey of Play Professionals in England* (Children's Play Council, 2001).

- A review of key books on play published subsequent to these reviews including *Out of School Lives, Out of School Services* (Petrie and others, 2000); *The Excellence of Play* (Moyles, 2000) and *Just Playing?* (Moyles, 2001).

- A search of published data held within the Library and Information Services of the Children's Play Council and the National Children's Bureau.

- Database searches of a range of specialist health, education, social policy and leisure and sport libraries.

- Internet searches of specialist websites relevant to these fields.

- Information gathered by e-mail in response to requests for data placed on the Play-Children e-mail noticeboard.

- A review of recent press cuttings relevant to the topic of play and children.

- The collation of a range of play project descriptions and project evaluation reports.

SECTION B: BACKGROUND

The provision of play opportunities for children is dependent at the national level upon a number of key policies and pieces of legislation. These provide the context for promoting child-focused services, for encouraging children's access to a wide range of opportunities including play, for meeting children's needs and for ensuring that what is provided is appropriate and of high quality.

This section briefly describes and assesses progress in implementing firstly the UN Convention on the Rights of the Child, secondly, the recently introduced Out of School Care National Standards and thirdly, the National Childcare Strategy, all of which mention play specifically within the articles, standards and/or recommendations they set out.

THE UN CONVENTION ON THE RIGHTS OF THE CHILD

The United Nations Convention on the Rights of the Child (1990) sets out 54 articles that identify a range of principles and standards for the treatment of children. The Convention was adopted by the United Nations General Assembly on 20 November 1989, and came into force on 2 September 1990. By 1994, the Convention had been ratified by 154 countries, including the United Kingdom.

A number of the Convention's articles are specifically relevant to children's access to and experiences of their local environment and their access to play (Adams and Ingham, 1998; Wheway and Millward, 1997; Guddemi and Jambor, 1992; Candler, 1999; NPFA, 2000; Petrie and others, 2000). These include:

- Article 3, which states that all actions taken concerning the child should take account of his or her best interests.

- Article 12, which states that children have the right to express an opinion on all matters which concern them and that their views should be taken into account in any matter or procedure affecting them.

- Article 13, which gives children the right to obtain and make known information and to express his/her views unless this would violate the rights of others.

- Article 15, which sets out the right of children to meet with others and to join or set up associations, unless doing so violates the rights of others.

- Article 24, the child's right to the highest level of health possible.

- Article 31, which sets out the right of the child to rest and leisure, to engage in play and recreational activities appropriate to the age of the child and to participate freely in cultural life and the arts.

In addition, Article 23 recognises the rights of children with disabilities – 'a disabled child has the right to special care, education and training to help him or her enjoy a full and decent life in dignity and achieve the greatest degree of self-reliance possible'.

Implications of the UN Convention and the right to play

Analysis by the National Playing Fields Association in partnership with the Children's Play Council and PLAYLINK (*Best Play*, NPFA, 2000) suggests that arising from the UN Convention, playworkers have developed a set of values and principles about children and play which are set out in the National Strategy for Playwork and Training. These are that:

- Children's views must be taken into account.

- That it is the responsibility of the community to ensure that all children have access to rich, stimulating environments that are free from unacceptable risk, which allow children to explore through freely chosen play.

- Children's freedom to play must be preserved.

- That all children, irrespective of gender, background, cultural or racial origin, or individual ability, should have equal access to good play opportunities.

- That children should feel confident that the adults involved in play welcome and value them as individuals.

- The child's control of their own activity is a crucial factor in enriching their experience and adults need to recognise and support this.

- There should be no task or product required of the play by those not engaged in it.

- That an appropriate level of risk is fundamental to play allowing children to develop confidence and abilities and that it is the responsibility of play providers to respond with 'exciting and stimulating environments that balance risks appropriately' (NPFA).

- That adult encouragement and responsiveness must be available when needed and appropriate.

Drawing together other analyses of the implications of the Convention highlights three main areas which need to be addressed in terms of a child's right to play:

- *The provision of space:* 'space is a basic resource that children need in order to play. It is by this measure that we can begin to judge how seriously a community is attending to the needs of its children' (Guddemi and Jambor, 1992).

- *Consultation with young people:* is an explicit requirement underpinning the UN Convention; however in order for this to happen, children and young people need help in making their views known and structures need to be put in place to promote their participation in planning processes (Adams and Ingham, 1998).

- *Integration of all children:* in particular, those with disabilities, is highlighted by Guddemi and Jambor – 'play is the right of all children', which thus requires the provision of play settings which provide 'comfortable and equitable opportunities for integration of children with and without disabilities'.

Analysis of progress in implementing the UN Convention

General concerns about implementation of the UN Convention are outlined by Michael Freeman in his recent article 'The future of children's rights' (Freeman, 2000). This argues that the needs of many children are currently neglected, including disabled children, gay children, girl children and street children.

Within this debate, Freeman highlights the 'backlash against children's rights', also 'the tendency to assume that now that we have a Convention, we have reached the finishing line'. With regard to a number of the specific articles, Freeman then goes on to make recommendations for how these could be clarified, strengthened or gaps plugged, in particular in terms of how children can express their views. An earlier paper by the Institute for Public Policy Research (Lansdown, 1995) also presents a similar view of very variable progress in implementing the Convention.

The following provides a summary of progress in the UK in implementing Article 31 of the UN Convention, based on the three implications discussed previously:

Provision of space

Although now quite dated, Guddemi and Jambor (1992) provide some data with regard to how many countries had either standards or guidelines obligating the developers of family housing to set aside space for children's play. Their analysis is based on the findings of a three day meeting of the American Affiliate of the International Association of the Child's Right to Play and suggests only limited progress in this area by the early 1990s. They mention that only one country, Norway, had introduced a legal requirement to address children's needs in local municipal planning, and for young people to participate in the development of those plans.

Within the UK, information from the National Playing Fields Association indicates a steady reduction in play space, including playing fields, open spaces and playgrounds – NPFA estimates that over the last 20 years one field per day has been lost (Kids' Club Network, 2001a). Other studies paint a similar picture of reducing space (Coalter and Taylor, 2001).

Participation and consultation

Data from Save the Children is cited by Adams and Ingham (1998) which suggests that there is still a considerable way to go in terms of involving young people in planning for their local environment. They note that 'planning decisions affect everyone, including children. However, provision for the needs of children and young people does not feature prominently, and the way younger members of the community are included in consultation varies widely.'

This theme is also apparent in a number of pieces of research which have examined young people's experiences of town and city centres and their involvement in planning urban development (Davis and Jones, 1997; Wheway and Millward, 1997; Woolley and others, 1999; Spencer and Woolley, 2000; Matthews and others, 2000). Most recently, the Kids' Club Network report *Looking to the Future for Children and Family: A Report of the Millenium Childcare Commission* (2001a) suggests that whilst there are now more examples of children being involved and consulted in service developments – for example, children's play zones and safe play areas – these are examples of innovative good practice rather than standard practice.

Petrie's recent analysis of out-of-school provision (Petrie and others, 2000), which is based on an in-depth analysis of a wide range of services for different user groups and interviews with both professionals and families, reaches similar conclusions. She suggests that 'congenial and realistic ways of consulting them need to be found. Perhaps more importantly, we may need to recast how we think about children: not as needy recipients or consumers of services, but as participants, with other children and adults, within services.' This theme is echoed in recent work by Moss (2000) who notes that in Britain, 'the surveillance, control and regulation of children are dominant'.

With regard to the right to play, recreation and culture, Petrie notes that providing these rights within the UK remains largely the private responsibility of parents, notably mothers, rather than wider society. Also that services which are provided purely for children's neighbourhood play on an open-door basis (where children can make their own decisions about activities and whether or not to attend) are declining, and with them, the ability to have a choice in the services available within their locality.

This ultimately means that both parents and children cannot make an informed choice – they have to use what is available, even if it may not be particularly suited to their needs. This in turn has implications in terms of children's opportunities to engage in freely-chosen play.

Integration and children with disabilities

Petrie's analysis of out-of-school services for disabled young people, including play provision (Petrie and others, 2000), indicates that problems persist in this area, not least because access to provision has to be limited in many ways, often due to insufficient funding. Due to places being limited, providers were often found to ration the number of sessions children could attend. Petrie explains that this can result in discontinuities in terms of children meeting different children on different occasions (hardly helpful to the formation of peer relationships) and highlights that at the level of public policy this is a challenging issue in that 'the attendance of non-disabled children is much less likely to be rationed'.

Petrie also makes the important point that whilst a local authority might recognise disabled school-children as having the same right to play as others, 'in practice, their access to a place within out-of-school services was more limited than that of other children because they were more expensive to provide for than others, in particular because of the need for a higher staffing ratio'. Considerable variability is also noted in terms of whether play provision included equipment suitable for the needs of disabled children (for example, large-scale toys and padded surfaces).

An important conclusion of the study was that disabled children's autonomy is much more circumscribed than that of other children, which in turn imposes limitations on their parents. On a more positive note, the study also notes that 'the services visited had much to offer disabled children and fulfilled many of the intentions of their providers. In allowing children the opportunity to play, often to be physically active and, for many, to interact with their peers, they may be seen to be empowering children whose experience may otherwise be very restricted.'

The analysis of the growth of commercial playgrounds by McKendrick and colleagues (2000b) also raises questions about the extent to which integration of children with disabilities is being achieved in the area of play. This study notes that whilst many commercial playgrounds market themselves as providing a 'non-discriminatory environment' and clearly have much to offer disabled children, parental concerns about the suitability of such resources are evident and affect the use of such resources.

The study concludes, 'on one level, these centres have clearly opened up leisure arenas and areas of the city from which disabled children were previously excluded. Both disabled and non-disabled children share these opportunities. However, as participation statistics reveal, relatively fewer disabled children capitalise upon these opportunities, and among those who do, they are capitalised upon less frequently.'

Integration of children from ethnic minority groups

Within the study of out-of-school services by Petrie and colleagues, a variety of comments are noted about children's experiences of racism and of inadequate awareness and training of staff to deal appropriately with this behaviour. The study also found that 'few of the ethnically mixed projects addressed the needs of children as members of minority ethnic groups. Service providers seemed to demonstrate little awareness that the UK has a plurality of ethnic groups and cultures; many were unaware of the distinctive requirements of parents from different groups...'. An important conclusion drawn from the study is that sometimes children are excluded from a service because insufficient work has been undertaken to make it acceptable to the local community.

Discussion

These findings suggest that in terms of public policy development to implement the UN Convention Article 31, a more active approach to service provision is needed, to be underpinned by structures which give young people a voice in the planning process and a coherent and stable source of funding. This appears to be particularly true for disabled children, where under-resourcing of services appears to be most acute and where access remains limited. There is also a need for research focused on out-of-school play services for disabled children since this has been largely neglected in the research field.

With regard to the integration of children from minority ethnic groups, progress in ensuring their right to play, a key recommendation made by Petrie and colleagues is detailed consideration must be given to the development of non-racist policy and practice and to the support of staff in carrying this through.

OUT OF SCHOOL CARE NATIONAL STANDARDS

The National Standards are a set of outcomes that providers of out-of-school care should aim to achieve. Ofsted inspectors will register and inspect provision against the National Standards and as such these standards reflect an important development in policy focused on provision for children and young people.

Standard 3, Care, Learning and Play, is of particular relevance in terms of children's opportunities for play. This states that the registered person must 'plan and provide activities and play opportunities to develop children's emotional, physical, social and intellectual capabilities'.

The standard suggests that the staff should consider providing learning and play opportunities for children through a wide range of planned and free play activities both inside and outside, including visits and outings.

Time, space, staff and resources must be organised in order to give children a mix of active times where children can take part in energetic play, and quiet times when they can rest and relax in a quiet area. The level of staff interaction with children must also be carefully balanced. There must be time given for children to play and learn independently, initiating their own activities and exploring freely, and time when activities are more directed and involve the staff.

Standards 9 and 10 and Annex A are also relevant to the play arena. Standard 9 requires staff to actively promote equality of opportunity and anti-discriminatory practice for all children; provision should be carefully organised and monitored to ensure all children have access to the full range of activities. Standard 10 highlights the need for staff awareness that some children have special needs or disabilities and are proactive in ensuring that their needs are met.

Annex A sets out the alternative criteria applicable to Open Access schemes and notes that 'children attending open access schemes have a right to play in a safe and suitable environment. This is best achieved where staff with appropriate training and experience in playwork actively plan to ensure that children are not put at risk. Staff plan a programme of activities and take account of children's own preferences and choices.'

Analysis of progress

Advice from Ofsted indicates that, as yet, no information is available concerning progress in implementing the National Standards, including Standard 3. Data from the first batch of inspections, which is currently under way, is likely to be available later in 2002.

THE NATIONAL CHILDCARE STRATEGY

Within the National Childcare Strategy, which was launched in May 1998, the role of play is acknowledged as important, especially in the early years which should be a time for children 'to have fun and gain the confidence to learn through play, through exploration and through a developing sense of their own selves in relation to others' (Children and Young People's Unit, 2001).

The Strategy consists of a range of measures to increase the range of childcare services, to raise quality and to make these services more affordable. A key part of the strategy has been to integrate early education and childcare and to put in place a framework for inspection and training. By releasing considerable amounts of start-up funding through the New Opportunities Fund, the strategy has also sought to increase the amount of out-of-school childcare provision and therefore to improve access.

An expansion of the Strategy was announced early in 2001 (Children and Young People's Unit, 2001), so that current aims are to:

- Create childcare places for 1.6 million children by 2004, with a threefold increase in the budget.

- Direct funding to disadvantaged areas, by establishing up to 900 neighbourhood nurseries, developing 50,000 out-of-school hours childcare places and recruiting 25,000 child-minders.

- To invest a further £16 million to support children with special educational needs and disabilities.

Analysis of progress with regard to play provision

An evaluation of progress in implementing the National Childcare Strategy with regard to the provision of play opportunities is currently being undertaken by the DfES. Information arising from this evaluation should be available shortly.

With regard to other work appraising progress in implementing the Strategy, analysis by Megan Pacey, Policy Officer of the Daycare Trust (2000), has highlighted concerns that the Strategy is driven by the need to provide opportunities for parents to work or study and as such, key groups of families could miss out. These include children of unemployed parents and children in refugee families. Pacey's work also raises concerns about access to provision by parents who are students and families living in rural areas where services are 'scarce and difficult to access'.

Key texts

Adams, E. and Ingham, S. (1998) *Changing Places – Children's participation in environmental planning*

Coalter, F. and Taylor, J. (2001) *Realising the Potential: The Case for Cultural Services – Play*

Children and Young People's Unit (2001) *Tomorrow's Future: Building a Strategy for Children and Young People*

Freeman, M. (2000) 'The future of children's rights', *Children & Society*, 14

Guddemi, M. and Jambor, T. (eds) (1992) *A Right to Play*, Chapter 3

Kids' Clubs Network (2001) *Looking to the Future for Children and Family*

Lansdown, G. (1995) *Taking Part – Children's participation in decision making*, IPPR

McKendrick, J and others (2000) 'Enabling play or sustaining exclusion? Commercial playgrounds and disabled children', *The North West Geographer*, 3

Moss, P. (2000) 'From Children's Services to Children's Spaces', *NCVCCO Annual Review Journal*, 2

Ofsted (2001) *Out of School Care: Guidance to the National Standards*

Pacey, M. (2000) 'Childcare for All: An Appraisal of the National Childcare Strategy', *NCVCCO Annual Review Journal*, 2

Petrie, P. and others (2000) *Out of School Lives, Out of School Services*

Wheway, R. and Millward, A. (1997) *Child's Play: Facilitating Play on Housing Estates*

SECTION C: THE VALUE OF PLAY: THE INDIVIDUAL CHILD

OVERVIEW

This section begins by providing a summary of the literature outlining the importance of play. To the extent that it is generic, it applies to all children, not just to those of school age. Much of this material has traditionally focused on individual benefits – however more recent works have taken a different perspective and looked more at the benefits to society in general.

> *'Play is an essential part of every child's life and vital to processes of human development. It provides the mechanism for children to explore the world around them and the medium through which skills are developed and practised. It is essential for physical, emotional and spiritual growth, intellectual and educational development, and acquiring social and behavioural skills.'* (Charter for Children's Play 1998)
>
> *'Play is used as a broad term which covers a wide range of activities and behaviours which may serve a variety of purposes according to the age of the child.'* (Bennett and others, 1997)
>
> *'Play looks deceptively simple ... but there many different kinds of play ... Play touches on every aspect of development and learning...'* (Rogers and Sawyer, 1988)
>
> *'All children play. Play is a universal process, most evident in the young. Like the processes of eating, sleeping and procreation, play is easily recognised but not well understood. Every major reference to children since the dawn of time has recognised its crucial role in childhood. Without play there are no arts, no sport, no games. It is argued that it is the most powerful tool of all in developing understanding of the social and physical environment.'* (Rennie, in Barrett, 1991)

Defining play

As the above quotes illustrate, there is widespread acceptance of the positive effects of play and there is a considerable amount of literature on the various dimensions of play, giving different definitions and taken from a variety of perspectives. These include child psychology and child psychotherapy, human geography, anthropology and studies of children's folklore.

However, as Coalter and Taylor (2001) note, 'because of the comprehensive and complex nature of the claims for the developmental/learning outcomes of play, it is generally accepted that a single definition is neither necessary nor sufficient to capture such multi-dimensionality'. This theme is also the starting point of the review of the forms and possible functions of play by Pellegrini and Smith (1998), who also suggest that 'one of the most commonly agreed upon definitional criteria for play is that it does not seem to serve any apparent immediate purpose'.

Unfortunately it is this variety, and the notion that it is the 'means rather than the ends' which are important, which lie at the root of some of the problems in providing robust evidence as to the value of play – or in actually agreeing what data is appropriate to be considered (Cattanach, 1998, whose paper raises concerns about 'mechanistic' views towards play).

This is despite the fact that its importance in childhood, in particular during the pre-school period, is widely accepted and has been extensively written about – again however, with much of the focus being on the pre-school and younger end of the child population.

Historical theories of play

Some writers have recognised two basic viewpoints towards the importance of play – one that says it is a **preparation for the future** and the other, that it is **an adjustment to the present** (Sutton-Smith, in Goldstein, 1994). Others have identified play as reflecting different developmental stages which children pass through, whilst others have identified different basic forms of play – for example, Moyles, who identifies physical play, intellectual play and social/emotional play. In much of the literature, the idea of play evolving into gradually more sophisticated forms as the child matures is evident.

According to Bruce (1997), historically play was originally seen as a break from work; another early theory saw it as the way that children 'let off steam from the pressure that work builds up inside them'. Gradually however, from the 1920s onwards, interest in childhood play grew and it became increasingly seen as helping children to learn. Sigmund Freud's work was a significant influence highlighting the emotional aspects of childhood play, with play being recognised as one way in which children could learn to control their feelings and to deal with anxieties and conflicts.

Bruce notes that 'as it was gradually realised that emotional and social development are helped by play, those interested in young children began to understand that play also helps children to think'. Piaget's theories of how children take in and make sense of experiences, took the understanding of children's play a stage further in the 1940s, with much greater attention then shifting to the importance of play in encouraging cognitive development.

Rogers and Sawyer's analysis of the importance of play in children's lives (1988) suggests that play is an important element of children's **motivation and therefore participation in society**. They suggest that:

- Children cannot be passive recipients of play and that since they are actively involved, this encourages autonomous thinking.

- Play provides the opportunities to develop the skills of active environment building.

- Play provides children with the chance to turn passive experiences – things that have been done to them – into activity. It provides a repertoire of experiences.

With regard to the importance of play **helping cognitive development**, they note that:

- Play is an active form of learning that unites the mind, body and spirit.

- Play provides the opportunity to practice new skills and functions.

- Play allows children to consolidate previous learning.

- Play allows children to retain their playful attitudes, a learning set which contributes to flexibility in problem-solving.

- Play develops creative and aesthetic appreciation.

- Play enables them to learn about learning – through curiosity, invention, persistence.

- Play reduces the pressure or tension that otherwise is associated with having to achieve or needing to learn.

- Play provides a minimum of risks and penalties for mistakes.

From the literature on play, Rogers and Sawyer also identify four other areas where play is important: in encouraging children to develop problem-solving skills; in supporting their language development and literacy, in developing their social skills and in expressing their emotions.

With regard to problem solving, they cite research from the early 1980s comparing children allowed free play to solve a problem, those given a demonstration and those given no activity at all. This suggested that the children in the free play group consistently outperformed the other groups – although caution is noted in such data given the differences unaccounted for in terms of children's behavioural styles and personalities. With regard to the development of language and literacy, they note that 'children's first attempts to read and write frequently occur during play'.

In terms of the acquisition of social skills encouraged through play, they suggest that this is probably the least controversial and widely agreed upon area. They explain that it is through pretend play that children learn to understand more than one viewpoint, and the views of others; that play encourages group co-operation, social participation and impulse control where the games/play involves rules. (Again however, no evidence is actually presented.)

In *Best Play* (NPFA, 2000) the importance of play in a number of areas of children's lives is summarised, namely that:

- Play has an important role to play in learning – 'play complements schooling by providing an opportunity for children to review and absorb and to give personal meaning to what they learn in formal educational settings'; play is important particularly in the way that it helps children to acquire 'not specific information but a general (mind) set towards solving problems'.

- Play is central to the development of good physical and mental health; the physical activity involved in most play provides exercise, encourages co-ordination and develops skills for the growing child. With respect to mental health, 'many of the attributes enhanced by play are found to be helpful to developing resilience...' (to stressful life events).

- Play offers opportunities for testing boundaries and exploring risk.

The National Playing Fields Association summary also suggests that play has a number of benefits which develop over time, including that it helps to foster children's independence and self-esteem; develops children's respect for others; increases children's knowledge and promotes children's creativity.

Key texts on play and child development

Bruce, T. (1997) *Helping Young Children to Play*

Bennett, N. and others (1997) *Teaching through play*

NPFA (2000) *Best Play*

Rogers, C. and Sawyer, J. (1988) *Play in the lives of children*

Moyles, J. (2001) *Just Playing? The Role and Status of Play in Early Childhood Education*

More recent perspectives on the importance of play

In addition to individual benefits to the child, both *Best Play* and *Realising the Potential: The Case for Cultural Services* include discussion of the wider benefits of play which go beyond the individual child and relate more to the family and local community. These issues are explored further in the following section. These reports also discuss the adverse consequences of play deprivation, which could from one perspective, prove the benefits of play.

With regard to the adverse effects of play deprivation, the National Playing Fields Association report notes that children could be affected in the following ways:

- They could have poorer ability in motor tasks.

- They could show lower levels of physical activity.

- They could show a poorer ability to deal with stressful or traumatic situations.

- Their abilities to assess and manage risks could be curtailed.

- Poorer social skills could result, leading to difficulties in negotiating social situations such as conflict.

The report gives details of some research undertaken in Zurich in 1995 (Huttenmoser and Degen-Zimmermann, 1995) which suggested that a lack of play opportunities, coupled with parental concerns about motor traffic, resulted in considerable isolation of some families; that parents tended to accompany their children more often which impeded their opportunities to make friends with other children and to become independent of their parents. When starting at kindergarten, such children, who had been deprived of the opportunity to play freely near their home showed less advanced social and motor development than their peers who had been able to play out freely.

Again caution is needed in that whilst interesting, the study was based on a small sample of families. A number of other factors such as cultural differences amongst the mothers, and their ability to speak German, may also have been an important influence on the study findings.

HEALTH BENEFITS AND PLAY

Literature on this dimension of play suggests that there are two main areas of benefit:

- The physical activity involved in energetic play is traditionally recognised as of benefit to children in terms of providing exercise. This aspect is especially topical given the current widespread concerns about children leading more sedentary lifestyles and increased rates of obesity (Dietz, 2001; Crespo and others, 2001). It also links to the concerns about the increasing restrictions placed on children in terms of the opportunities for them to explore freely and to play away from home (McKendrick and Bradford, 1999; PLAYLINK, 2000).

- Play can enhance the mental health of children and young people. Again this is relevant given current concerns about greatly increased rates of mental health problems among young people (Meltzer and others, 2000).

Physical activity and mobility

The adverse physical consequences of decreasing mobility among children and young people, and a decline in active outdoor play, are explored in the work of Wheway and Millward (1997). They note that this shift has had a measurable detrimental effect on children's physical health and that low levels of fitness have been identified by bodies such as the Sports Council and the Chartered Society of Physiotherapy.

In addition, Wheway and Millward cite other research undertaken by the Policy Studies Institute (Hillman and others, 1990) which suggests that decreased mobility may adversely affect children's social and creative health – that independent mobility has been found to be important in promoting self-esteem, a sense of identity and the ability to take responsibility for oneself. This data was gathered by the Policy Studies Institute through a survey of children and parents from 10 schools (5 primary and 5 secondary) from five areas of England and replicated an earlier Policy Studies Institute survey undertaken in 1971. In addition, the 1990 study also included a survey of a similar sample of schools in Germany.

Caution is needed in interpreting research data on the benefits of sport and physical activity as supporting the need for play, since clearly such activities may not be the same. Nevertheless, research has shown that there are strong links between health status and physical activity, sport practice and level of fitness, including during childhood and adolescence (Ferron and others, 1999). Research has also indicated the potentially negative long-term consequences of a sedentary lifestyle and is increasingly suggesting that involvement in physical activity is a protective factor against stress, depression and risk-taking behaviours such as drug use (Ferron and others).

The study by Mulvihill and colleagues (2000), which draws on the extensive 1998 work by Biddle, *Young People and Health Enhancing Physical Activity – Evidence and Implications* for the then Health Education Authority, states that physical activity is widely recognised as an important health behaviour in childhood, providing benefits for both physical and psychological well-being. Physical benefits include positive effects for blood pressure and on preventing obesity. Psychological effects include enhanced psychological well-being, reduced symptoms of depression and anxiety and increased self-esteem.

The study also notes that young people in the UK have become more sedentary over the last fifty years and that among primary school children, levels of physical activity are declining. Previous research also indicates a further decline as children grow older, especially among girls. However in terms of more interpretive studies to understand this trend, Mulvihill reports a noticeable deficit, with the majority of studies in the UK focusing on children's involvement in sport rather than in physical activity more broadly defined. The few studies that do exist however, suggest that physical activity is viewed positively by children, and in a 1998 study of children aged 8 to 10 years, that the concept of 'being well' was commonly associated with being physically active and doing things.

In order to address this deficit in interpretive information, Mulvihill and colleagues undertook an in-depth qualitative study across five sites in England to examine the factors influencing children's involvement in physical activity. Sixty children and 38 parents were interviewed. The study found very positive attitudes among the children interviewed towards physical activities, although their involvement in such activities is influenced by perceived enjoyment and of it being fun.

Crucially the study found that parents appear to play a central role in determining levels of physical activity and that a lack of facilities and play areas was a concern for many parents, which in turn affects the levels of physical activities engaged in by their child. Such findings clearly support the need for opportunities for physical play to be properly considered within the planning of local parks and recreational resources and indicate that such provision would be viewed positively and thus likely to be used by children.

In terms of other research identified on the health benefits of play, Moyles (2001) makes reference to physical play promoting a feeling of general well-being, and cites the findings of Wetton (1988) that 'children who are physically healthy are more able to function properly in intellectual and social interchange'. However, no supporting data of Wetton's findings for this assertion is presented.

Physical activity and its effects on brain development

Most recently, new work on the effects of physical activity is also indicating that more sedentary lifestyles among children may be adversely affecting their academic performance and that by increasing levels of physical activity, academic performance can be stimulated (Berliner, 2001). This research, which is still in its infancy, is based on the premise that increased physical activity increases blood flow to the brain, which when coupled with learning tasks, causes the formation of dendrites and thus increases the neural pathways within the brain.

A variety of school-based projects which have introduced more physical activity into the school day have reported positively on the effects of these changes in terms of children being more alert, gaining better scores in government SATs tests and in some schools, less truancy and bad behaviour (Berliner, 2001) – results which are likely to attract more detailed research attention in the future and which may have an important contribution to make to the play arena.

American research more specifically focused on play but based on animal subjects has reported a 'strong positive link between brain size and playfulness' (Furlow, 2001). One study, prompted by the observation that play seemed confined to the most intelligent animals, examined the behaviour and brain size of marsupials and found that playful species had bigger brain sizes for their body size in comparison to less playful species.

Such findings have lead to a variety of theories that play has a vital role in particular phases of brain development and in promoting cognitive development – that 'play creates a brain that has greater behavioural flexibility and improved potential for learning later in life'. Again this is an area of increasing research interest that may in time produce robust data concerning the effects of human play activity.

Mental health

Finally, in terms of promoting the mental health of children and young people, research by the Mental Health Foundation (1999a) highlights the importance of children being able to play and take risks and to use their initiative. It is also essential for them to have opportunities to practise making and consolidating friendships and to deal with conflict – the basic skills needed in order to become 'emotionally literate', which increases their resilience to mental health problems (Mental Health Foundation, 1999b).

The *Bright Futures* report, which is based on an extensive gathering of over 1,000 pieces of evidence drawn from professionals, parents and young people, refers to earlier work undertaken by the Foundation (*Listening to Children*, 1998) where young people talked of the importance of personal achievement for their well-being. The growth of out-of-school care and the importance of play in these settings is also highlighted. This may 'provide children with opportunities to take part in recreational activities which may otherwise be denied to them – commonly involving children in creative artwork, physical activities, music, sport and drama'.

This suggests another aspect of play in supporting mental health, that of providing enriching experiences that may help to develop children's emotional and social skills and may reduce the risk of them developing mental health problems later on. This theme is also to a limited extent picked up on in Gilligan's review of factors that may promote resilience (2000) where mention is made of 'spare time experiences' (identified by Gilligan as including cultural pursuits, the care of animals, sport, help and volunteering, and part-time work, though interestingly, not specifically play) in helping to foster feelings of self-esteem and self-efficacy.

Despite these general positive points however, again no detailed research on how play may contribute to the mental well-being of school-age children was identified during this search of the literature. Much of the focus of existing studies has been on the use of play therapy techniques with children experiencing emotional and behavioural difficulties – not therefore play as defined for the purposes of this review.

This omission is also reflected in recent DfES guidance on promoting children's mental health within school settings (DfES, 2001). Here no mention is made of the potentially valuable role of play save for a brief reference to playground interventions which may help children with emotional and behavioural difficulties engaging with other children at playtimes and of the use of role-play, games and stories to enhance students' understanding of others within a curriculum using materials to promote positive behaviour.

Summary of review findings – health and play

- In the health field, much of the existing research has been focused on levels of physical activity and on sport. Such activities may not be the same at all as play freely chosen by the child and therefore considerable caution is needed in interpreting the benefits identified in these studies in terms of play. Nevertheless research indicates positive views among children and young people towards undertaking physical activities – but that a lack of local play facilities may be one reason why children are unable to participate.

- New research on brain activity based on animals is suggesting that play may activate higher cognitive processes and that there may be links between brain building and play. Other research, on physical activity levels, is also examining the effects on brain formation. Both are likely to stimulate further research which may shed valuable light on the importance of play, but as yet the data is limited.

- In the mental health field, the importance of unsupervised play enabling children to take risks, to think through decisions and to gain in self-confidence, has been emphasised (Mental Health Foundation, 1999a). The increasing restrictions on children's free time are thus a cause for concern and require further research in terms of their effects on children's mental health. Overall research focused on the role of play in promoting mental health among school-age children is lacking, with much of the existing data focused on the use of play therapy with children already experiencing mental health difficulties.

- No literature on play and the health benefits for disabled children and children from ethnic minority groups of school age was identified during the literature review. This is an important omission given the particular concerns about the mental health needs of these groups (Bhui, in Johnson and others, 1997) and the research findings presented later in this review, that these groups of young people experience more restricted access to their local environment, including to play and recreational provision (Jones, 1998; Howarth, 1997).

- There is a reasonable body of data concerning the use of play for helping children who are sick and requiring hospital care to feel less anxious about treatment – although again, this often refers to specialist adaptions of play or play therapy which are not freely chosen or personally directed; as such, this literature is not discussed here.

EDUCATION BENEFITS AND PLAY

Literature concerning the benefits of play in supporting education has tended to focus on:

- Play and its contribution to learning, including the development of cognitive and problem-solving skills.

- The role of play and break periods within school and on behaviour within class – this area has attracted growing interest, possibly in connection with heightened awareness of the incidence and adverse consequences of bullying (Katz and others, 2001) and a widespread perception that there has been a decline in children's play – that 'children don't know how to play any more' and will therefore behave in a difficult or aggressive/unacceptable way during break periods (Bishop and Curtis, 2001; Blatchford, 1998b)

Play and learning

In existing research, play is recognised as a major route to learning, particularly in children's early years (NPFA, 2000). Play can support and consolidate learning from both informal and formal school settings and is widely seen as having an important role in children's cognitive development, although it must be noted that much of the existing evidence relates to the pre-school age group.

According to Bennett and colleagues (1997), early childhood education is underpinned by a long tradition that emphasises the central role of play in early learning and development. A direct link between play and learning is assumed – 'play is considered to be such an educationally powerful process that learning will occur spontaneously'. However, as Bennett points out, whilst the case for play may be strong ideologically, it is debatable whether it provides a coherent framework to guide education practice. A particular problem in the current climate of 'back to basics' and target-setting is that play is hard to evaluate and may not produce any tangible outcomes and yet teachers have to provide evidence of learning and attainment.

This theme is also picked up on in Macintyre's recent work *Enhancing Learning through Play* (2001) in which it is noted that in the current pressure for children to achieve a range of key competences 'there is likely to be less time for either free or structured play, fewer opportunities for children to decide what they would like to do and to determine their own pace of learning. To achieve the targets the children must conform to an "outside" notion of what education in school is for, and to someone else's idea of what they should learn. They must, in following that agenda, confront someone else's problems rather than setting and solving their own.'

To a large extent, Macintyre suggests that the value of play in education is in question because of differing views as to what exactly education in school is for – to pass exams (which suggests the need for direct instruction) or a more enabling, exploratory form of learning (where play may have a greater role in helping children to explore and to learn from their activities).

Having suggested that there are significant questions about the impact of play on formal learning, within the school setting, two specific areas of research interest have focused on the positive outcomes of school playtimes: firstly, the impact of play periods on social learning and the formation of friendships and peer networks; secondly, the effects on children's attention span in ensuing lessons.

Play and Social Learning

There appears to be an extensive amount of work that, although largely descriptive and somewhat limited in terms of systematic evidence, discusses the role of break-time within schools as a time for learning social behaviours and forming social networks. For example, Smith's analysis of playtime (Blatchford and Sharp, 1994) suggests that it is during these periods that children practise and develop important physical and cognitive skills, including practising language, role-taking activities and problem solving. Of key importance is the social learning that takes place during playtimes and of peer interactions.

This theme is taken up in Blatchford's book *Social Life in School* (1998a). This indicates that break-time has an important role to play in terms of providing a 'forum for enjoyment and activity, play and games, socialisation into adult roles, and cultural transmission; the development of friendships, social networks, social skills and competence; the opportunity for independence and freedom from teachers and classrooms; and the management of conflict, aggression and inter-group relations. It can also be a site of harassment, cruelty and domination.'

In another work on play in schools, Blatchford ('The State of Play in Schools', 1998b), again highlights the importance of the social dimension of break-time in school, that this time is important to pupils and is 'of value to pupils throughout the school years, though the nature of the value changes from primary to secondary'. He points out that as children are far more likely to be driven to school than to walk, interactions at break-time are of increasing importance since for a growing number of pupils, this may be the main opportunity for them to interact and develop friendships and social networks.

In reviewing what he terms the 'positive aspects of break-time', Blatchford describes the earlier work in 1980 by Youniss on peer relationships and their value for social and cognitive development. He refers to the positive views among pupils towards break-time revealed in a longitudinal study undertaken at the Institute of Education with pupils aged 7, 11 and 16 years, that break is an important time for socialising with friends, having a break from work, for playing games and for having some independence from adults. He also describes earlier research by Sluckin in 1981 on the culture children may develop in break-time which is separate and distinctive from the school culture. Such a development, which is complex and rule-bound, has been recognised by some researchers as an important process for cultural transmission and socialisation into adult roles. It may also have a valuable role to play in the 'acquisition and development of a distinctive children's culture' (Blatchford).

Overall, however, the theme which runs throughout much of the literature on play and break times is that of managing difficult or disruptive behaviour or bullying, and as such, the positive contribution that break-time might make to children's development appears to have been overlooked. As Blatchford acknowledges, part of the reason is that the largely descriptive nature of the data 'means that the social value of break-time cannot be proved as such'.

This deficit is also picked up on by Pellegrini and Smith (1998) who note that whilst there have been many experimental enrichment studies involving the effects of play on children's social skills such as role-taking, and that many of these studies show positive benefits, considerable caution is needed. This is because such 'laboratory-based experimental manipulations of play tell us how certain variables *may* affect behaviour; they may not tell us about the ways in which these behaviours develop in nature'.

This situation is gradually changing as schools recognise that a positive break-time experience will impact on school life as a whole and a number of initiatives have focused on improving and developing these experiences, including environmental improvements, staff training experiences and support to facilitate peer relationships. Research on these more recent developments may in time add to the understanding of how play can contribute to children's education.

Play and its effects on children's ability to concentrate

A number of studies have examined the impact of play periods, in particular physical activity during break-time, on children's attention span in the ensuing lessons and a variety of claims have been made as to the effects which emerge. These are discussed by Pellegrini and Smith (1998), and have been more recently reviewed by Coalter and Taylor (2001). Some of these studies have suggested that break-time maximised primary school children's attention to school tasks when they returned to the classroom, whilst others found higher levels of restlessness and distractability.

As Pellegrini and Smith highlight, considerable caution is needed in interpreting these results given that they reflect examples of experimental deprivation studies (in this case, depriving children of opportunities for locomotor play) and as such, the studies 'can be criticised on the grounds that more than one thing is involved when we deprive children of play. So when children are deprived of social play, they are often deprived of other forms of social interaction as well.'

These researchers conclude that the role of play in children's development remains controversial and unresolved and that more systematic research is needed before sound conclusions can be drawn. This is also echoed by Smith in Blatchford and Sharp's work (1994) where it is noted that 'what children learn through playing may not be so great in a purely cognitive sense; certainly it has proved difficult to establish that play is anymore effective than instruction or classroom learning'.

Folklore studies and studies of children's oral culture

This quite distinct area of study examines children's play traditions and games and how these have evolved over time. In the UK, folklore studies have struggled to establish themselves as an academic discipline (Bishop and Curtis, 2001), although they are widely accepted in other countries. The underlying rationale is that analysis of the games engaged in by children provides a valuable insight in to other aspects of society at a point in time – the structure of games change over time to suit the social climate.

Whilst within the academic world there may be a lack of agreement as to the value or indeed validity of this area of work, some recent folklore studies of the free play of children in middle childhood appear to provide some valuable information which challenges the view mentioned previously, that there has been a decline in children's play.

Based on detailed case studies which explore the many aspects of children's play traditions and which examine children's actual play activities in the playground, and with an emphasis on children's own perceptions of play, according to the researchers working in this field, such studies provide a valuable source of data on the 'vibrancy, creativity and variety of free play activities'. The use of detailed case analysis also provides information on how children use play spaces, including the school playground, and 'the ways in which children learn and adapt games and rhymes in multicultural and monocultural settings' (Bishop and Curtis, 2001).

The views of teachers and children towards the value of play

A recent area of concern evident in the literature on play and education, has been the potentially adverse consequences of the National Curriculum in undermining the principles of a play-based curriculum for younger school children (Wood, 1999; Keating and others, 2000; Wood and Bennett, 1997; Bennett and others, 1997). Several studies have examined this area and whilst they raise questions about the rhetoric and reality of play within reception classes, they clearly indicate that teachers value play within the curriculum. Especially for children at this younger end of the school population, play is considered to be important because of the children's stage of development.

Wood's study, which was supported by the Economic and Social Research Council, examined the experiences of nine teachers who were committed practitioners in the use of play in the reception class. Whilst this is clearly a small sample, the study gathered 'comprehensive accounts of their theories and approaches to classroom practice' and from this it was clear that all of the teachers valued play and integrated it into their teaching provision. In different ways, all of the teachers were found to be experiencing pressure from the National Curriculum in terms of content and assessment procedures and yet to be managing to accommodate play within the school day – although in some cases, this now meant more structured rather than free play activities.

Perhaps most importantly in the current debate about play, the study findings indicate that the top-down influence of the National Curriculum was not seen as the main constraint on providing good-quality play experiences. Instead the following were identified – space, resources, some aspects of the daily school timetable and most especially, large class sizes and the lack of classroom assistant support, all of which were seen to impact on the quality of children's activities and on their learning.

In terms of the value of play, language development and socialisation were most frequently mentioned by the teachers, and 'there was a broad consensus that play was as valuable, if not more so, as formal, teacher-directed activities'. Various examples were provided by the teachers of how they used free play experiences and exploration to enhance learning of the more structured subject areas, including experimentation with emergent handwriting. In addition, the integration of play into the curriculum was seen as a valuable way of fostering positive attitudes towards learning and schooling and in developing a sense of self-worth and self-efficacy in children.

In assessing a child's progress, 'play was considered to have a revelatory function which could provide evidence of a child's developmental stage, needs, interests, knowledge and skills'. Nevertheless, the teachers often found it difficult to find time for sustained periods of interaction or observation during play and there was a shared concern about the quality of learning through play, something which is also picked up by Bennett and colleagues (*Teaching through play*, 1997). In wishing to use play for assessment purposes, Wood's nine teachers often struggled with the difficulty that children often played to their own agenda, which 'reinforced the view that learning through play is notoriously difficult to assess because of its open-ended, free-flow nature'.

Furthermore, the teachers found it 'difficult justifying the importance of play to parents who think that, if the children are playing they cannot be working, and therefore are not learning'. In Wood's earlier discussion of this research project (with Bennett, 1997), similar issues are noted.

In the work by Keating and collegues (2000), the value of play was also a clear theme among the sample of adults interviewed for the study, who were drawn from ten primary schools based in the North-West of England. Play was seen as a 'powerful and productive learning medium'; a way of stimulating and extending learning, a 'building block' or 'foundation' upon which to develop future learning and 'a means of promoting the child's whole development'.

Again the tensions of balancing play within the demands of the curriculum and the requirements for assessment were evident in the study findings – which had resulted in play being regarded across the sample as a reward for the completion of work. It was suggested that written tasks provided more attainable and accessible evidence, also that 'the strong current focus on standards … seemed to be resulting in play being perceived as inferior and secondary learning'.

Keating and colleagues also gained a strong impression of play being now viewed as an organisational tool for keeping children occupied when the teacher was engaged elsewhere. Crucially they suggest that a form of vicious cycle could be encouraged by current uses of play – 'with the more able children finishing their work and thus having the opportunity to play, which then leads to enhanced social and cognitive development, and thus they finish their work more quickly, gaining more time for play, and thus the cycle repeats itself. The reverse could then be true for the less able child, who has less time for play and therefore does not experience the situations which allow developments in a range of areas and thus the downward cycle is perpetuated.'

Clearly such a 'vicious circle' is an extreme example of the potential use of play and as such, is unlikely to go unchecked in classrooms. However, as the researchers conclude, there needs to be more research in this area and work is also needed to develop shared meanings for 'play'. It would also seem fair to conclude from this study, and that of Wood's previously discussed, that the actual contribution of play within early years education, and the reasons why teachers value play, needs more extensive research. This is especially relevant in that what constitutes good practice and what is an appropriate curriculum for children at the younger end of the school population in particular, are matters of current debate.

With regard to the views of children towards play within school, many of the studies cited earlier (for example, Smith, in Blatchford and Sharp, 1994; Blatchford, 1998a; Blatchford, 1998b) have highlighted that children have a positive view towards break-time in school and in particular like the time afforded for socialisation and meeting their friends. Other work, which has looked at some of the difficulties and problems which can emerge at playtime, has examined how involving children in decisions about playtime can bring about benefits (Blatchford, 1993).

As mentioned, there is an acknowledged problem with proving the value of playtime. Nevertheless these study findings are briefly mentioned here since, at the most simple level, they are important in terms of the UN Convention and the principles of listening to children discussed in Section A. As such, this is another area where more systematic research is required.

Several studies have also looked at children's views towards play and work in school and how they define these (Robson, 1993; Sherman, 1997). In Robson's work, based on children within three primary schools, and Sherman's study of 50 children drawn from five schools in a large city area, there were clear indications of children differentiating between play and work which seemed to reflect the views of adults – 'that school is a place for work, and that play is not concerned with learning' (Robson) or 'an attitude about the trivialness of play seems to have already reached these five year olds' (Sherman).

Arts and Culture

Finally, moving into a slightly different arena of play, the role of art within education and of encouraging access to cultural activities has been an area of recent research interest (Kids' Club Network, 2001a, citing the findings of NFER 2000).

Whilst clearly different from free play chosen by children, the NFER study into arts education in secondary schools reveals some valuable benefits of children being exposed to more creative processes and less structured forms of learning. The NFER research, which is based on among other things, an in-depth study of two longitudinal cohorts of pupils and an extensive survey of over 2000 Year 11 young people, notes that increasing evidence suggests that art education can support child development by encouraging:

- A heightened sense of enjoyment, excitement and fulfillment.

- The development of creative and thinking skills.

- The enrichment of communication and thinking skills.

- Advances in personal and social development.

- Effects that transfer to other contexts such as learning in other subjects.

Analysis of the pupil perspectives on their experiences highlighted the sense of satisfaction in achieving something and of the arts being a release from the stresses of everyday life and from other lessons. A number of pupils also talked about the arts increasing their awareness and understanding of other people's feelings.

Teachers reported a therapeutic value to these experiences, suggesting they had a calming effect on the pupils. Teachers also talked of improved social skills, of the development of the skills of group work such as co-operation, negotiation, leadership skills and listening. Developments in skills of interpretation and in feelings of self-worth and self-esteem were also noted – although one important conclusion noted is that the study revealed 'virtually no statistical evidence that engagement in the arts boosts general academic performance at the age of 16'.

Summary of review findings – education and play

- In the education field, much of the literature has focused on the value of play in the learning of social skills and the formation of peer relationships and friends. As researchers in this field acknowledge, even though the information which has been gathered is generally positive, caution is needed since many of the studies are quite descriptive in their approach.

- Studies which have examined the effects of play periods on children's attention span in ensuing lessons suffer from the fact that these are examples of experimental deprivation studies and thus deprivation of play may not be the only factor influencing the results which are in any event contradictory.

- Analysis of teachers' perspectives on play in reception classes indicates that teachers value play within the curriculum. Play is seen as important in terms of language development and socialisation and can also reveal valuable information about a child's developmental stage, needs and interests. There is a tension in meeting the demands of the National Curriculum, however other factors play a role in constraining play opportunities in school, most especially large class sizes. The increasing use of play as a time management tool by teachers, and the reasons why they value play, require more extensive research.

- A small body of literature suggests that children's views towards play are being influenced by the current trend in society to devalue play as a medium for learning. However much of the literature highlights children's positive views towards playtime at school, in particular from the point of view of socialisation and making friends.

- In two quite separate areas, firstly folklore studies of children's play and secondly, research into the effects of exposure to arts and cultural learning activities, it appears that there is some useful recent data emerging which may support the importance of play activities in children's learning.

- No literature on the benefits of play and education for children with special educational needs, disabled children and children from ethnic minority groups was identified during the review, a deficit which should be addressed as a part of any future research in this area.

SECTION D: THE VALUE OF PLAY: SOCIALISATION AND CITIZENSHIP

OVERVIEW

Throughout the literature reviewed so far, a common theme is that play provides social benefits for children and young people in allowing them to mix with their peers, to exercise free choice (to some degree at least), and, in doing so, that their self-confidence and feelings of self-worth are promoted. At this level, the assumed benefits are largely individual.

However, as mentioned in the previous section, some of the recent literature on play takes another perspective – with some proponents of the importance of play arguing that it brings wider benefits to the community as a whole. By encouraging the use and development of local community facilities, play provision can have a strategic use in bringing more widespread social benefits, including greater social cohesion and the building of community networks.

Whilst highlighting the need for caution since other factors such as the work of professionals and non-professionals with children and their families may be an influence, Coalter and Taylor note that of the suggested outcomes of 'successful' play for the wider community include:

- Fostering inclusion and tackling social exclusion by engaging marginalised families and communities.

- Tackling anti-social behaviour and juvenile offending.

- Supporting families and communities by providing a focus for informal networks of support, and by allowing children autonomy within an environment which parents feel secure about.

- Offering opportunities for exploring cultural identity and difference.

These benefits assume that children have access to their local environment and the facilities therein, and that by having such access, a sense of 'ownership' and social inclusion is fostered – a point picked up on by Coalter and Taylor (2001) who note 'the fundamental rationale for public provision of play is to facilitate the social inclusion of children – most of the presumed outcomes of play have implications for social inclusion...'

The literature which is reviewed in this section therefore focuses on the information available on children's access to their environment in the broadest sense, their favourite places, not only their current use of play and recreation facilities. Their participation in planning is also considered (a central principle of the UN Convention), also the restrictions which may impact on children's play opportunities and lead to their expressed preferences being unmet or ignored. Finally, the section reviews a number of studies that have looked specifically at the circumstances of young people from ethnic minority groups.

With regard to the contribution of play in tackling anti-social behaviour and offending, it should be noted that very limited literature was identified and this largely focused on diversionary activities and non-school skill programmes. In such studies, as Coalter and Taylor (2001) note, 'it is often difficult to identify the precise contribution of "play". As such, these studies are not reviewed here.

Key issues

Overall a number of predominant issues emerge from this part of the review which have significant implications for children's opportunities for play.

There is also an impression that these issues have gained in significance in recent years and link to the concerns mentioned earlier, about children and young people leading increasingly sedentary and potentially solitary lifestyles. Some of the trends discussed in the literature could be argued to mitigate against the social inclusion benefits of play provision.

Predominant issues within the literature include the following:

- A number of studies from the fields of urban geography and urban studies raise concerns that children and young people have been 'conceptualised in urban planning as problems and the result has been their marginalisation and increasing exclusion from a hostile urban environment' (Davis and Jones, 1997; Woolley, Dunn and others, 1999). Several describe young people expressing views that their voices are unheard in this arena (Jones and others, 2000; Matthews and Limb, 2000).

- What some researchers have termed the commercialisation of playspace and the 'commodification' of childhood (McKendrick and others, 2000) raises, among other things, issues about access and about whether certain forms of play provision can actually sustain exclusion.

- The recent considerable growth of organised out-of-school provision and the focus on providing 'care' and on boosting academic attainment through study support, is influencing both the nature of recreational provision and the level of control parents exert over their children's play activities. Play in this context, whilst clearly provided, and its value realised (Education Extra, 2001a) is clearly of a more structured variety than the more purist definition of play which is chosen and directed by the child.

- Adult, in particular parental, fears about safety, especially traffic safety, are significant influences on children's independent spatial mobility and on an increasing tendency for parents to escort their children to and from more structured and supervised leisure activities or to prevent their children from playing outside unsupervised (Jones and others, 2000; PLAYLINK, 2000; McNeish and Roberts, 1995; Mayall, 2000).

WHERE AND HOW CHILDREN PLAY – THEIR USE AND EXPERIENCE OF PLACE

Findings from the literature suggest a variety of venues where children and young people like to play, amongst which, public outdoor places are an important venue for meeting friends and retaining some social autonomy away from adult supervision (Matthews and Limb, 2000). These researchers note that 'although there is evidence for a retreat from the street by urban children, for a substantial number of young people the street remains an important part of their everyday lives. Less than one-third of young people report that they never use the street as a social venue.'

In line with a number of other studies, the study by Matthews and Limb, which was based on 9 to 16 year old children in three contrasting localities and which included a questionnaire with over 1,000 respondents, picks up on seasonal variations in the use of such outside space, with use not surprisingly perhaps being higher in the Summer. One finding which perhaps is not expected however is that the use of the street by girls often rivals that of boys – although often girls will use the street for chatting and talking with friends, whereas boys are more likely to use the street as a venue for informal sport. Importantly the study also found that:

- Traffic is considered by young people to be the greatest danger and that 'safe streets are those close to home or relatives, away from traffic, where other people are around' – which suggests that perceived environmental factors are restricting the mobility of young people.

- The major reason identified for being on the street is that children have nowhere else to go, and that certainly for less affluent children it may be the only social forum, 'especially as a large proportion cannot afford to participate in other leisure or recreational opportunities or choose not to do so'.

- Shopping malls are frequently used by older teenagers as a place for meeting up with friends on the basis that they provide free, warm and safe places – although many of the young people described a sense of being watched or treated with suspicion by mall security guards. Again, their use appears to reflect the lack of appropriate venues for this age group.

Wheway and Millward's 1997 study of play on 12 housing estates, which involved observations of over 3, 000 children, to some extent mirrors some of these findings, namely that roads and pavements continue to be the most popular location for outdoor play. They also comment that this finding varies little from the survey undertaken by the then DfE in 1973. They note that one of the surprising findings was that most children spent time playing where they could see and be seen, often in open view of houses. Part of the reason identified for this were parental restrictions, however the children themselves seemed concerned about their safety in isolated locations. Play in back gardens also featured in this study as a favoured location.

In terms of public play facilities, Wheway and Millward suggest that the most well used play areas were the ones that were open and visible – these promoted a sense of security. However another trend identified in the study was for children to be on the move between a number of places – which these researchers suggest highlights the importance for children to be able to move freely around their physical and social environment – an important activity in itself, which the researchers defined as 'going', and which they note is 'crucial to an understanding of how children use their environment. The interviews showed that they have very definite ideas on preferred play spaces. What is clear is that they travel from one to another, trying them out, and meeting different friends. The travelling to and from, constitutes a significant amount of any time spent outdoors.'

Such a finding is clearly important in terms of the concerns highlighted earlier about the reduced independent mobility experienced by many children, possibly due to the range of factors outlined at the start of this section. Furthermore, the study found that when asked for their regular and favourite place to play, the children consistently referred to green open spaces and if there was one available, an equipped play area.

However in terms of usage, other factors such as parental permission and proximity to home, and the feeling of security provided by a location, emerged as important influences. The actual layout of the estate roads also appeared important in terms of children not having to cross busy roads – a situation appreciated by parents and children alike.

In drawing conclusions from their findings, Wheway and Millward note among other things the following:

- that in terms of location, 'estates which stimulate the highest level of outdoor play are those with the greatest variety of places and the slowest traffic' and that those which stimulate the highest range of play activity and satisfaction among parents and children are those with footpath networks, cul-de-sac layouts, public open spaces and play areas;

- the majority of play is physically active and involves moving around locations;

- children strongly desire play areas including green spaces such as parks and trees;

- older children's recreational needs are not well catered for;

- the front street remains the most frequently used location for outdoor play and for children to be able to exploit this environment properly, traffic speeds need to be reduced.

The study by Callaghan and Dennis for the Children's Society (*Right up our street*, 1997) based on a sample of around 60 4 to 11 year old children drawn from three schools in rural Cleveland also revealed very positive preferences towards playing in parks, the street and green and open spaces generally. These researchers report that in their study, the girls' choices of preferred play location tended to be nearer to home and to be focused on social gatherings, whilst for the boys, the locations were often found to be further way. Age was also a significant influence on experiences of different forms and arenas of play, with younger children tending to stay closer to home and to play with siblings as opposed to peer groups.

Children's participation and access to their local environment

A range of literature within the fields of environmental psychology, geography and urban studies, has highlighted that children have been marginalised in the decision-making processes and, as a consequence, feel that urban areas have no spaces for them (Davis and Jones, 1997; Woolley, Spencer and others, 1999; Spencer and Woolley, 2000). This in turn can have adverse consequences for their use of public spaces – research, based on an extensive survey of over 1,300 children in six neighbourhood clusters, suggested that there has been a decrease in the independent use of public space by children since the 1970s (O'Brien and others, 2000).

Such research findings obviously have implications for public play provision and are also of relevance in terms of progress to date in meeting the requirements set out by the UN Convention to take account of children's views and to promote their participation. They also raise fundamental public health issues.

The research study by Davis and Jones, which involved semi-structured questionnaires with a sample of over 400 9 to 11 year olds and 13 to 14 year olds in four state schools in a major UK city, is an example of one of these studies which examines the problems arising from the failure to consult with and involve children and young people in the planning of their environment, to take account of children's needs and aspirations. This argues that 'the conceptualisation of children in transport and environmental planning as "a problem" has resulted in an urban environment which is extremely hostile to their needs and aspirations. As problems, children are tidied away behind railings, in parks, in gardens and – best of all – indoors.'

The researchers argue that it is as a result of the urban environment becoming more dangerous, that children find themselves increasingly constrained – and that in particular, 'opportunities for independent mobility and access, associated with the development of important life skills, have declined as traffic levels have increased'. This they suggest should be a major agenda for public health and for environmental modification so that children 'can begin to travel, play and participate in urban life without fear'. Without action, the alternative is a 'more physically inactive, less independent and less healthy young population', also that by allowing such marginalisation, young people are in danger of social exclusion.

Davis and Jones note that the findings of their study support the findings of Wheway and Millward that the majority of primary school children's outdoor play was active and that 'hanging out' was a valued activity. However for many, dirt, lack of safety and traffic noise were perceived to be major problems.

They conclude that 'the views of children and young people are worth listening to, if urban planners are to create environments in which young citizens can participate. If they continue to be, as at present, marginalised in planning and policy making then the high (to some worryingly high) numbers who spend most of their out-of-school time watching television and playing computer games, and being driven to leisure activities in parents' cars, will continue to increase.'

The growth of commercial playgrounds and supervised activities

Interest in the growing commercialisation of play provision and of the considerable expansion of out-of-school provision, is evident in a number of areas of the literature, with both developments having implications for children's opportunities for free play – in particular because such provision usually involves parental choice and often has a cost implication which also requires adult agreement.

According to McKendrick and colleagues (2000a), 'the growth of commercial playgrounds in the UK is adult-led and can be attributed to the conjunction of a umber of discrete trends that rendered their development viable'. These include the proliferation of the service and leisure industries, the availability of land and buildings and the growing recognition of children as consumers. The trends already mentioned of greater control over children's play activities, driven in part by parents concerns for safety and concerns about the quality of facilities within the local environment, are other likely factors (McKendrick and others, 2000b). Another important influence has been a major change in family life which has taken place over the last few decades – that of leisure as a shared family experience (McKendrick and others, 2000b).

In other analysis of this form of playspace, which can include a range of play environments, McKendrick and colleagues (2000) note that it is 'overly simplistic to suggest that these new developments are testimony to the new-found consumer power of children. Children play a marginal role: in the production of these play environments; in contributing to parents' information field prior to decision-making, and in the visit decision-making process.' It is this aspect of commercial play provision that goes against the definition of play as something chosen and directed by the child.

Furthermore, commercial playgrounds, 'largely based on pay-for-play, raises the possibility that they will not cater for *all* groups' and could therefore potentially be a cause of exclusion – a finding confirmed by McKendrick from other research which systematically examined patterns of participation and found that non-car owning and large families were under-represented among users (although other findings confounded expectations in terms of family structure and family work status – where it was found that children of lone parent families and those with fewer working adults, were as likely to visit as children from two parent families and those in work-rich households).

With regard to the trend towards increasingly supervised leisure and recreational activities in out-of school hours, a number of studies have highlighted the significant expansion of out-of-school clubs, often to provide childcare for working parents or to promote study support (Smith and Barker, 1997). Data from Kids' Club Network suggests that since the launch of the National Childcare Strategy in 1998, this expansion has increased and that since 1997, the number of clubs has doubled to reach 7, 000.

By 2004, there are set to be up to 12,000 clubs, one for nearly half of all schools in the UK (Kids' Club Network, 2001b). Whilst acknowledging the support offered by such clubs, the wealth of activities they can offer and the positive views of the children and young people who attend them (Kids' Club Network, 2001c) such a trend clearly has implications for opportunities for free play.

Restrictions on children's play – parental concerns and environmental factors

A range of recent studies have highlighted that parental concerns about safety in the local environment, and in particular, the dangers posed by traffic, are resulting in children's independent mobility and their opportunities for free play being restricted (PLAYLINK, 2000; Matthews and Limb, 2000; Wheway and Millward, 1997; Jones and others, 2000; McNeish and Roberts, 1995).

For example, in the McNeish and Roberts study for Barnardos, a range of findings from a survey of 94 parents and 62 children, identified via a range of Barnardos' projects from across the UK, highlight the fears of parents and the ensuing effects:

- 60 per cent reported being very worried when their children were playing out.

- Danger from strangers was reported to be the biggest worry (66%), followed by danger from traffic (60%), drugs (49%), bullying (36%) and danger from dogs (27%).

- Most thought their neighbourhood was unsafe for children, with 31% rating it very unsafe and 39 per cent fairly unsafe.

- Play facilities were reported as generally poor, with 35 per cent saying there was no playground in their neighbourhood. Most children played in their garden or yard (44%) or on the street (33%).

- The lack of facilities and parental anxieties were found to be affecting children's play experiences – 44 per cent of the parents reported that their children never or hardly ever play out without adult supervision.

- These fears were also diminishing the independence of children to walk to school.

Furedi's analysis of parental fears (PLAYLINK, 2000) highlights similar widespread concerns. He cites the findings of a 1998 MORI poll of more than 500 parents which found that almost 80 per cent would not let their children play unsupervised in the park during their Summer holiday for fear of danger. A NOP poll the following year reported a similar figure.

The findings of the study by Huttenmoser and colleagues referred to earlier in the report (page 56), also highlighted the role of parental concerns about the safety of their neighbourhood, about traffic safety and how these impacted on the children's opportunities for playing out, making friends and social networks, and their abilities on starting nursery school. Such studies, whilst small-scale, are thus important in providing valuable information on parents' perceptions of their environment and on the safety of their children, which in turn, may provide some important pointers to aspects of the environment which require attention if opportunities for free play are to be promoted.

On this basis, another study based in Germany, does provide some interesting data about how environmental factors could be improved which may in time serve to reduce parents' fears about letting their children out to play. In a recent study of 278 children who had experienced a pedestrian or cycling injury, von Kries and colleagues (1998) undertook an in-depth risk analysis on the basis of the numbers of streets with 30 kph speed limits, the numbers with traffic lights and pelican crossings, and the provision of playgrounds in the vicinity of the children's homes.

The study involved a detailed case control design and attempted to minimise bias by checking data with national results. From their results, the researchers conclude that 'it appears that increasing the number of streets with a speed limit of 30kph, increasing the density of pelican pedestrian crossings on streets with a speed limit of 50kph or above, and increasing the number of playgrounds is likely to be effective in reducing the risk of traffic injuries to school age children'.

Whilst encouraging, some caution is needed with the study findings in that as the researchers acknowledge, the study did not measure traffic density, nor could it account for socio-economic/ social class variations due to Germany's data protection laws, both of which could have some influence on the data.

With regard to children's fears of their local environment and how this influences their mobility and access to local facilities, the McNeish and Roberts study just described, notes that the children were very aware of their parents' fears. Several other studies have highlighted that children and young people share the concerns of adults about traffic (Woolley, Dunn and others, 1999), and that, in one study of 349 young people aged 13 to 14, drawn from three locations in the Midelands, that these fears meant that the young people were less likely to travel unaccompanied, even in their local areas (Jones and others, 2000).

SPECIFIC GROUPS OF YOUNG PEOPLE

Children from ethnic minority groups

A number of studies focused on ethnic minority groups, indicate that their use of public open space and their use of play and recreational facilities, is more restricted than for other groups, as a result of a range of complex environmental and family factors (Woolley and ul-Amin, 1999; Howarth, 1997; Ravenscroft and Markwell, 2000; Kapasi, 2001).

Generally this is an area of research that has received only limited attention, certainly up until recently. However, a general theme evident in the studies which have been identified is that young women in particular experience considerable restrictions on their access to public recreational facilities (Jones, 1998). Several recent studies have highlighted factors that may help to improve access to play provision for this group.

In examining the experiences of a sample of 214 young women aged between 11 to 14, of who just under half were of Asian origin, Jones found that the girls of Asian origin experienced more problems encountering hostile urban environments than the non-Asian girls, and that fears about assault and racial and sexual harrassment resulted in a more home-focused style of life. The Asian girls also reported restrictions on their physical activity and frustration about their lack of freedom.

Specific areas of concern for the Asian girls included fear of unaccompanied travel, of rape or attack, as a result of which Asian girls were much more likely to travel with relatives. It also appears that parental restrictions on Asian girls increase when they become teenagers.

In Kapasi's recently updated work on Asian children playing, (*Asian Children Playing*, 2001) concerns about safety are also apparent, in particular, physical safety and supervision within play settings where both sexes attend. The study, which undertook questionnaires, interviews, focus group meetings and field visits to play projects in six areas of the country, also found that one problem in accessing play projects is that the daily lives of Asian children do not conform to those of white and African-Caribbean children, which meant that often the projects were open at times when they could not attend. Travel limitations were another factor identified limiting access for young Asian girls in particular.

The study findings pose some fundamental questions about the level of integration of Asian children into play projects, and about racism, on the basis of observations of play behaviour in mixed play provision. These found that Asian children played separately from non-Asian children. In addition, some of the children indicated a clear sense of not being understood. As Kapasi discusses, this highlights the need for effective staff training to challenge racism and also, the importance of employing Asian staff.

The study also found a considerable underuse of play provision by Asian girls in comparison to Asian boys. Parental fears about safety were again prominent – with the provision of transport to some girls' groups resulting in increased usage. Community-led groups which ran separate provision for girls and boys were found to be the most successful in working with large numbers of girls – although a number of girls only groups had folded due to a lack of support and resources from local authority providers.

Children with disabilities

Research on the use of play provision by children with disabilities appears to be particularly limited, and very little literature was identified in this review. In the Kapasi study just mentioned, the use of play projects by disabled Asian children is mentioned, to the effect that this group of children are particularly under-represented in their use of such resources and that Asian families with disabled children were found to face 'severe institutional discrimination'.

Identified barriers to access included language difficulties, racist attitudes of service providers and a lack of information about support services. There was also an assumption that 'disabled Asian children were looked after by extended families', which clearly denied their right to participate as an equal member of the community.

With regard to other research concerning children with disabilities, the recent study by Petrie and colleagues (2000) discussed in Section B, raises concerns about problems with access to play provision by children with disabilities, often due to funding limitations leading to places being restricted. Recent research by Kids' Club Network (2001) also notes that provision for disabled children in kids' clubs is inadequate; a 1997 survey undertaken by the Network found that only 21 per cent of clubs provided places for disabled children, although more encouragingly, 78 per cent of club co-ordinators reported providing a service for 'all' children and 70 per cent of clubs had disabled access.

Earlier research (Petrie and Poland, 1998) highlighted the importance of play provision for disabled children as a means of making friends, and work by McKendrick and colleagues (1998) highlighted that in a survey of parents with children attending special schools, three quarters of the parents felt that play providers did not cater for the specific needs of their disabled children. The majority of these parents also indicated that they wanted their children to play more often with children who were not disabled.

In terms of commercial play spaces, McKendrick and colleagues found that most centres have easy wheelchair access and provide a suitably wide range of opportunities. However the researchers note that the often multi-storey layout and the physically demanding nature of much of the play equipment, may serve to restrict play opportunities for physically disabled children. In addition, the crowded nature of many of the centres does little to encourage integrative play. Nevertheless, the study also concluded that 'despite the problems which many soft-play areas present, disabled children reported enjoying themselves'.

Summary of findings – socialisation and citizenship

A variety of factors are impacting on children's opportunities for free play and for socialisation, including:

- Trends towards increasing commercialization of playspaces and the growth of organised out-of-school provision, both of which reflect a shift towards more organised, adult-led forms of activity.

- Limited progress in involving young people in planning for their environment and indeed, some suggestions that young people are being conceptualised as 'a problem' and further marginalised, which in turns creates a perception of a hostile environment with no spaces for them.

- Parental safety fears, in particular fears about traffic, are leading to parents exerting more control over their children's activities and opportunities to play out.

- For children from ethnic minority groups, a range of factors are serving to limit their use of play provision, including fears of assualt when travelling, racism and concerns about safety; girls especially are restricted by these concerns.

- For children with disabilities, there are concerns about a lack of suitable resources – however in this area particularly, good research data is lacking.

- Despite all of the above, information on children's play preferences indicates a strong wish to play outdoors, in green and open spaces which are visible to those around them.

- The provision of roads with reduced speed limits and a cul-de-sac layout enhance the chances of physically active outdoor play – to which end the limited available research on the positive effects of reducing speed limits (von Kries, 1998) warrants further attention.

- An overwhelming argument running through this literature is of the importance of effectively consulting with children and young people, in listening to their views and aspirations and in involving them in planning, particularly in urban areas.

SECTION E: GOVERNMENT INITIATIVES AND PLAY CASE STUDIES

OVERVIEW

Examination of a range of projects and strategies arising from national social and economic initiatives such as *Sure Start* and *Quality Protects*, various DfES and Children and Young People's Unit initiatives and a number of Home Office or Youth Justice Board projects to reduce offending, truancy and exclusion in disadvantaged neighbourhoods, suggest that in a number of different ways, play is being used within projects to support children and families or to engage older teenagers.

Funding for provision has come from a variety of sources including the New Opportunities Fund (NOF), the Department of Health, the Single Regeneration Budget (SRB), from Early Years Development and Childcare Partnerships (EYDCPs) and from a range of voluntary sector organisations. A notable tendency is for many of the initiatives to be based on short-term projects or to be highly targeted, which obviously raises questions about general accessibility to, and longer-term sustainability of, such provision.

Some of the examples given below clearly fall into the category of more structured activity or sport rather than free play. They are included however to give as wide a picture as possible of current activity where play may be a component of what is provided. Some are also more clearly aimed at improving educational standards rather than recognising the value of play activities in their own right.

EXAMPLES OF PROJECTS INCORPORATING PLAY WITHIN GOVERNMENT INITIATIVES

(1) Summer Activities for 16 year olds – DfES initiative

The Summer Activities for 16 year olds came about through the need for intervention at specific transition stages in learning. It is aimed at young people in England coming to the end of compulsory education who are thought to be indifferent to further learning and who are not involved in any other activities during the Summer break.

Young people in this position are more likely to lose contact with education, employment and training and to be unemployed at age 21. The aim of the programme, whose projects are based entirely or predominantly on outdoor adventure activities, with a residential element, is to re-engage uncommitted young people so that they further their education and to enhance their personal and social skills. Objectives for young people are to: develop self-esteem, develop confidence, become good team workers, develop leadership skills and to broaden their horizons.

Thirty-two organisations from all sectors, led pilots in 2000 offering some aspects of the scheme to 1,400 young people, using up to £1 million of DfES money. In 2001, 47 second-phase pilots operated, one within the boundaries of every Connexions service. Between 2002–04, a three year national roll-out is planned; this will be funded by NOF under the generic title Activities for Young People. The Connexions Service National Unit will oversee the implementation.

Evaluation of the first phase of the programme involved project monitoring, a survey of participants and in-depth case studies of eight projects (Hutchinson and others, 2001). This revealed that the average project size in terms of young people attending was 50; the smallest was attended by 7 and the largest by 232 young people. The projects offered a range of activities, including IT related activities, community and environmental projects, work experience, football coaching, music and drama activities.

Young people were recruited onto the programme in a number of different ways, including direct mailing to young people identified by schools, by youth workers inviting those they were working with to attend, by local radio and newspaper advertising. The number who attended was fewer than expected; this was thought to be due to the short lead in period and problems setting up some of the partnership arrangements.

Key findings of the first evaluation revealed:

- A moderate but significant increase by the end of the programme in the number who said they wanted to attend school or college.

- That for 41 per cent of the young people, the programme had either a big impact or had completely changed what they intended to do.

- That 45 per cent thought that the programme had improved their group working, communication and problem-solving skills (although a significant minority thought that their skill levels across various attributes had decreased at the end of the programme).

- That for 85 per cent of the young people, the Summer activities programme had made them more determined to achieve future plans. These effects were also reported to last over time since they were still evident when young people were followed up by telephone later in the Autumn.

In terms of good practice, evaluation of the first pilots suggests that it is important for there to be clarity of expectations between young people, their families and those running the projects; that young people should be involved as much as it practical in the design of the programme and in having some responsibility for organising some element of the programme and that it is important to offer a range of activities which provide 'something for everyone'.

(2) Playing for Success – DfES initiative

Playing for Success is a national initiative established by the DfES in partnership with the FA Premier League, the Nationwide League and their clubs and the LEAs. The aim of the initiative is to raise educational standards, in particular in urban areas, through the creation of Study Support Centres in professional football clubs. The Centres are managed by experienced teachers and use the medium and environment of football to support work in literacy, numeracy and ICT; they also provide facilities for homework.

The programme has been particularly focused on under-achieving young people in Years 6 to 9 and has proved to be extremely popular with pupils, parents and schools. Pupils volunteered to attend and were offered individual support, with a focus on them becoming more self-reliant and trying things out for themselves. Most pupils attended over 80 per cent of the course and almost half attended all available sessions.

The evaluation findings are based on data obtained from questionnaires completed by 1,200 pupils, 450 parents and 70 teachers (Sharp and others, 2001). Pupils' attitudes were obtained at the beginning and end of their time at the Centre. The evaluation responses suggest that the football setting was attractive to all young people, irrespective of gender or ethnicity. The young people were felt to respond positively to what was on offer and that they also benefited from the opportunity to meet people and make new friends. In terms of educational achievement, substantial and significant progress in numeracy and in ICT skills were found.

(3) Youth Inclusion Programme (YIP) – Youth Justice Board

This programme seeks to reduce offending, truancy and exclusion in disadvantaged neighbourhoods by providing targeted assistance and support though a variety of activities to 13 to 16 year olds. In each of the selected areas (YOTS), YIP projects are required to work with a core group of 50 young people in this age group who are known to be at risk of offending, truancy or exclusion; they can work with a wider group of young people if they wish but the focus of assistance must be on the core 50.

The objectives of the YIP are to:

- Reduce arrest rates in the target group by 60 per cent.

- Reduce recorded crime in the area by 30 per cent.

- Achieve at least one third reduction in truancy and exclusions of the young people concerned by 2002.

Each project receives £68,500 from the Youth Justice Board for each year that they are fully operational, plus a further £6,500 per project is paid direct to local evaluators. In return, projects must match grant funding with minimum local (partnership) funding in cash or in-kind of £75,000 per full year.

YIP projects can be based on a wide range of interventions that are intended to be multi-focused or to tackle offending behaviour tendencies. What is offered will depend on local needs and circumstances, but in all cases, a variety of activities will be offered. Whilst it is intended that the activities on offer should be fun, the programme guide also notes that they must be underpinned by social, educational or diversionary objectives.

Possible interventions include: family link centres in schools, utilising their computer facilities, which may include language support for ethnic minority students, after-school and holiday clubs; skill centres aimed at providing excluded young people with training and qualifications; mentoring; sports and other forms of recreation; environmental work such as clean-up projects and the development of recreation areas; arts work such as drama, film-making and graffiti art.

Each project is intended to build up to an average of 10 hours provision for each targeted young person per week, although projects can be flexible in this in that it is recognised that some young people may need more intensive assistance than others.

The Youth Inclusion Programme has recently been evaluated and there are now 70 operational projects, at various stages of maturity. Although the programme cannot be expected to show immediate dividends (since it aims to encourage a significant behaviour change in young people, to avoid offending behaviour), a recent interim evaluation report encouragingly shows that the programme is having a positive impact on its objectives with, for example a 30 per cent reduction in arrests after a young person's engagement in the project, and falls in crime of between 14 and 32 per cent, with the largest decreases being for burglary, theft and handling offences.

(4) Splash Summer Schemes

Another Youth Justice Board initiative, Summer holiday 'Splash' schemes were started in Summer 2000 in some of the most deprived estates in the country, with an aim of providing constructive activities for 13 to 17 year olds. In a similar vein to YIPs, the aim is diversionary and the activities on offer highly varied.

Splash projects often combine life and educational classes (e.g. drugs awareness or sex education) with a range of recreational activities such as video making, team sports and drama.

Findings from the first year of the schemes suggested that they played an important role in reducing youth offending in the areas where they operated. According to figures released in a press release by the Youth Justice Board, (29/08/01) in areas where a Splash scheme ran, there was a 36 per cent reduction in domestic burglary and an 18 per cent reduction in 'youth crime'.

(5) NACRO crime prevention and diversionary projects – various funding bodies including the Department of Health (including the Opportunities for Volunteering Grant) and SRB in partnership with NACRO

NACRO, a national charity working to reduce crime, runs a variety of activity-based projects for young people, often focused on disadvantaged areas of the country such as inner-city housing estates. The activities offered currently involve around 5,000 young people and 350 volunteers across the country.

NACRO also provides outreach work for disaffected young people to help them develop their skills and to make decisions about their future training and employment options; school exclusion projects, which work to support reintegration back into school or to help young people into training or employment, and projects for young offenders, which may include anger management programmes or helping them to deal with drug misuse. NACRO is also heavily involved in a number of YIP programmes mentioned previously.

NACRO's activity-based projects cover a wide range of activities, both leisure-based and more structured. Some are focused on specific groups of young people such as those at risk of drug misuse. Activities include: after-school holiday provision; football projects; residential experiences; art work; new technology.

Project examples

(i) DEAL (Drugs, Empowerment, Action, Learning) is one example of a NACRO diversionary project to prevent young people becoming involved in drug taking. It also offers help to those who are already involved to tackle their addiction. The aim of DEAL is to provide young people with challenging and engaging activities at little or no cost to themselves, and to help them to improve their self-confidence and relationships.

Set up in 1997, the age range catered for by DEAL is 8 to 19 years, and on average, the project works with around 200 young people each year. Approximately one quarter of these have an addictive drug habit. The project is funded by and runs on a partnership basis which includes the DH, SRB, NACRO, a local community association, a youth information and activities centre, a drug treatment day centre and the local health authority. The project employs four members of staff and relies heavily on adult volunteers from the local community; a wide range of arts, music and drama-based activities are offered.

(ii) Four Football Community Link Projects are currently in operation around the country. These projects use football as a way to increase young people's self-confidence and the channel their energies in a constructive way. The projects, wherein one paid staff member works with the local community to set up and run football clubs for young people aged up to 16, also aim to increase the skills and confidence of adult volunteers and to foster good community relations. The clubs provide affordable and accessible opportunities for football coaching and participation in local tournaments, regardless of skill or ability. Over 2,000 young people and over 250 volunteers are now involved in these projects nationwide.

Evaluation of these projects has highlighted positive effects both in terms of young people's expressed views towards them and in a reduction in the numbers of offences and incidents of nuisance behaviour committed by young people in the areas where projects have been operating (NACRO, 2000).

(6) Integrated learning and care – Education Extra extended study support (initially DfES-funded and now NOF)

The charity Education Extra currently runs a small number of schemes which aim to provide integrated care and learning provision or what is now termed 'extended study support' for 11 to 14 year olds. These operate after school and often use school premises to provide a wide range of activities, including play and leisure pursuits that the children and young people are free to choose. These include arts activities such as jewellery making, dancing and sports.

Eleven schools from across England and Wales participated in the original pilot projects that try to support the needs of the children and their parents who are typically working, and the schools. The projects aim to provide an environment which is as much like home as possible (the 'home base') and yet to also provide access to out-of-school learning and enrichment activities to support the school curriculum. The projects have paid great attention to how they provide activities for this older age group of school children who do not want to be 'cared for' in the same way as younger children and who wish to take more responsibility for how they spend their time. As such, the projects consulted with the children and many of the activities now offered are in response to student suggestions.

The 11 projects supported by Education Extra have evolved in different ways to reflect local needs and interests; some have a main focus on pastoral care, others on active learning; some charge a small fee per session, whilst others are free; some are open to specific school year groups. Feedback from the participating pupils and school staff has been positive, with improvements in pupil self-esteem and confidence being noted.

Most recently, Education Extra has highlighted the importance of play provision within schools; it notes that in some areas, the school may be the only appropriate setting in which to provide positive play opportunities (*Extra Special,* Issue 84, Summer 2001a) and that 'play can be a medium for raising achievement by engaging communities with children's learning'.

The charity is currently developing a new project for refugee children using play and a further project where art will be a key component of what is offered. With regard to children's access to the arts, Education Extra has also been extensively involved in work to encourage more museums and galleries to work with schools (*Alive with Learning – Study support in museums and galleries*, 2001b). Evaluation of the pilot projects has reported positive results in terms of stimulating enthusiasm and creativity among the children who have participated.

(7) Other arts initiatives

(i) 'Making it Happen in Art' – Quality Protects/Department of Health funded initiative

Under the Quality Protects initiative, a team has been established to focus on leisure, culture and the arts in the lives of young people in public care. Based on short-term programmes of activity, one of the first projects, the *Galleries programme* was piloted throughout the Summer 2001.

Across the country, a range of museums and galleries offered workshops with groups of young people. Different dimensions of art were covered, including conventional and digital photography and working along artists and sculptors working in a range of different mediums.

This programme culminated in an exhibition of the art produced by the participants. Currently no evaluation data is available; the Department of Health is however working on guidance materials aimed at local authorities who may wish to provide such programmes in the future.

(ii) 'Arts in Pupil Referral Unit' (PRUs) – charity-supported projects

Since 1996, the Gulbenkian Foundation has supported a range of arts and drama projects based in a range of PRUs across the country. Some of the support has taken the form of covering the costs of local dance companies or artists to allow them to offer workshops for the young people within the units.

The aim of such provision has been to encourage the wider adoption of arts-based programmes in such settings and to provide avenues through which to encourage young people to participate in activities and to enhance their self-confidence and motivation. Feedback from some of the participating PRUs indicates that participation in the arts activities brought generally positive results for the young people. For some, this meant better grades in their examinations than had been expected and improvements in students' skills, understanding and motivation.

CASE STUDIES OF PLAY PROJECTS

(1) Children in Temporary Accommodation Play (TAP) Project, Sheffield

Established in 1998, the aim of the play project has been to provide a means of reducing stress within families living in temporary accommodation by providing play opportunities for children, and also to support them in developing a range of skills.

Often when children and families are homeless, a time when they are in greatest need of support, they have difficulty accessing mainstream services. This adds to the pressures of being homeless and can exacerbate the stress and ill-health they suffer. With regard to play, provision for homeless families (even down to basic provision of space) is the exception rather than the rule. In an attempt to try and improve this situation, the post of Homeless Children's Development Worker was created by the local authority with initial joint finance funding for three years.

To support the work, a joint planning group was initially set up, made up of the main partners of the project – the Housing Services Assessment Support Team; Sheffield Health; Social Services; Shelter's Homeless to Home project; South Yorkshire Housing Association; North British Housing Association; Young Children's Service Area Team, and the Community Recreation and Play team who managed the project.

Since early 1999, the TAP project has provided the following:

- The establishment of regular holiday play schemes on three housing sites, offering 5,866 play sessions to homeless children (with each session lasting up to 3 hours on each occasion).

- Several short-term projects responding to particular needs such as parent and toddler groups; a library group; an after-school club; Christmas parties and regular 'Teddy Bears' Picnics', wherein parents and toddlers go out to various parks and call at a supermarket on the way back. These outings not only encourage parents to socialise but resolve some of the practical problems which face lone parents carrying shopping and pushing prams to and from supermarkets some distance away.

Some initial findings from the pilot project revealed that homeless children present a range of specific needs which need to be carefully considered when planning provision. These include limited concentration spans; limited self-worth; an inability to recognise the value of routine, and poor ability to co-operate. As a result, the work is stressful and challenging.

The project has been staffed by one full-time worker, assisted by casual workers from the Play and Recreation Team and many volunteers such as health visitors and education welfare officers giving freely of their time.

Further funding is now being sought, to allow the project to become a mainstream service and to enhance what is offered by the project in terms of the accommodation used for the play sessions and the numbers of full-time project workers. Play space at the three sites has generally been difficult to find – for example at one site the play provision is based in two rooms shared with the health visitor and doctor; these are also used for laundry and occasional storage.

(2) Projects supported by Islington Play Association: the Finsbury Park Homeless Families Project and PALACE (Play and Learning Creative Education)

The Finsbury Park project is an example of an outreach play project. Established in 1999 with original funding from the SRB and the local Early Years Development and Childcare Partnership (EYDCP), the project first began work with the under-5s age group but quite quickly expanded this as it became apparent that the over-5s needed support too.

The project, which does not charge the families who use it, operates over four days per week, offering two-hour sessions in a range of specific hostels. In the holidays, the project organises a range of schemes and trips out.

The project sessions are provided in the daytime for younger children and in the after-school hours for children attending school. Spare communal spaces are used within the hostels (for example, disused dining rooms) which the project team decorate and attempt to make as child friendly as possible. The project will also work with families in accommodation where there is no space; here support is offered to link families into other play projects or to give advice on local play facilities.

Over the last year, the project has worked with over 200 children.

PALACE is a play project that works with children with disabilities, ranging from dyslexia through to severe cerebral palsy. PALACE caters for the age range 0 to 18 years, with most of the children and young people attending falling in the 13 to 14 years age band. Average attendance at any one time is between 15 to 20 young people.

Based in old day nursery premises, the project has been established for 11 years and was originally started by a group of parents experiencing difficulties accessing services for their children. It has been funded by Islington Play Association, the local EYDCP and a range of charitable funds over this time and is currently applying to the New Opportunities Fund for funding.

Parents pay £10 per annum membership which provides unlimited access to the project. Until recently, the project was open three days a week; a recent increase in funding has allowed PALACE to now operate six days a week, from 10am to 6pm. In addition, the project has recently started to offer some holiday schemes.

The project works with the children in a variety of ways, both individually, in groups and with families. Specific groups are provided for non-speaking children and those with complex needs. The overall aim is to work in a holistic way, which incorporates teaching, therapeutic play and play to enhance communication.

No longer parent-run, but with an emphasis on being parent-led, the project employs a range of specialist staff on a sessional or part-time basis. These include a physiotherapist (19 hours per week), an osteopath (19 hours per week) a Shiatsu therapist (6 hours per week) and a music therapist.

(3) The Hip-Hop Scheme within the Hamara Family Project, Walthamstow

The Hamara Family Project has been established for 12 years and provides a range of services for disabled children and young people. The Project is part of the range of provision supported by Barnardos' London and South East Region. Currently the project is working with 182 young people aged between 0 to 19 years and their families. Seventy per cent of these are boys, which may reflect the high number of children with autism referred to the project (60 children – 33 per cent). Fifty-three of the children involved with Hamara are Asian, 43 are Black, 51 are White and 15 are from other backgrounds. The number of referrals received by the project this year reflects a 20 per cent increase on last year.

Within the range of services offered by the Hamara Family project, a number of play-based activities are offered. These include:

- An integrated play scheme during the school holidays as funding allows.

- The Hip Hop scheme which works to promote the inclusion of disabled children in mainstream out-of-school activities (Hamara Integrated Play and Holiday Opportunities Project).

- A holiday club for young people of senior school age.

The Hip Hop scheme works to assist children with disabilities to access and integrate into mainstream play schemes and to participate in activities they would not otherwise be able to attend. A key aim is to promote the inclusion of disabled children. The scheme builds upon previous play scheme provision offered by Hamara but with possibly a greater focus on inclusion in mainstream services than the previous project which utilised the facilities of a local special school.

Parents cover the costs of actually attending the mainstream playscheme, with Hamara providing a playworker to support the child for 13 weeks. During this time, the service is reviewed to ensure that the child is happy and that any adaptions take place that will allow the child to stay there without support or with reduced support. This project is currently in the pilot phase. The response to date from parents, staff, children and some of the local out-of-school facilities, has been extremely positive. The recent securing of funding from the New Opportunities Fund means that Hip Hop will shortly expand to include providing support workers to allow some children to attend after-school clubs.

The holiday club is another recent development within the Hamara project. With funding from the Social Services Special Carers Grant, this offers secondary school-aged children the opportunity to go on outings with other children during the holidays. Evaluation by Barnardos indicates that the club has proved to be extremely successful with both young people and their parents.

Plans for the future include the building of a Children's Centre as a community resource for all children. This will include a sensory room, a soft play area and a 'safe' outside play area. A particular challenge facing the project workers is to forge links with adult services as more of the children currently attending the project move towards adulthood – Hamara has worked with many of families for over ten years, who therefore see Hamara as a significant part of their support network.

(4) The Building Bridges Project, supported by Camden Play Service

A number of play projects supported by Camden Play Service focus on children with specific needs. These include children with physical difficulties (the Rollercoaster project), children in temporary accommodation (the TAP project) and Building Bridges, which works to support children excluded from school.

Building Bridges, which has been established for three years, operates on three days a week from a voluntary sector play centre, offering sessions between 10am to 2pm. The main age group catered for is 5 to 13 years, and depending on the needs of the children, the project sessions work with up to 7 children at a time. Some of the children have learning difficulties and challenging behaviour; all are referred to Building Bridges by the Local Education Authority (who is responsible for paying for the children's places within the project), with many also being known to social services and health agencies.

The project is staffed by a full-time co-ordinator, a teacher on a twice weekly basis and four project workers for the holiday provision. All of the other workers as employed on short-term contracts as and when required, again depending on the level of needs of the children in attendance. The project offers what it describes as a 'very structured' play programme since the workers have found that the children respond well to short, focused pieces of activity. A key aim is to use play as a means of helping children to learn to manage their own behaviour.

The Building Bridges staff also offer family work and general advice and support to parents (for example, advice on welfare benefits); in-school liaison and support to return and/or reintegrate children back into school and holiday schemes. The project has developed and expanded it play provision and work with excluded children in recent years. When it began, it offered a part-time curriculum alongside the local Pupil Referral Unit (PRU). When the PRU moved to full-time provision, Building Bridges moved to current form of play-based sessional support.

The project has not been externally evaluated.

(5) The Kids and Co Group, Hollybush Family Centre Project, Hereford

Hollybush Family Centre was set up in 1992 with funding from the local social services department, largely in response to the provisions set out in the 1989 Children Act. Offering a variety of groups and support services to families with young children, one of its approaches is to help parents who missed out on experiences of play as a child, to have a chance to play and in doing so, to learn how to play with and relate positively with their child. Throughout the week, the centre offers a range of more structured groups, alongside more informal drop-in sessions. Discovering the importance of play is a key theme of the work undertaken.

Located on a large council estate, the centre is based in a one-floor building with a surrounding garden; inside, there is a soft play room, a messy room for craft activities and a ball pool donated by a local business.

Referral to the Hollybush Centre is by professionals, typically health visitors, GPs and social workers. The centre aims to support up to 150 families, both from urban and rural areas, and raises money from local charities for parents' activities.

The centre also runs a women's group to raise self-esteem, is developing work with lone-parent fathers and offers intensive group work with parents who have learning difficulties, in order to help them be successful parents.

SECTION F: ONGOING RESEARCH AND UNPUBLISHED DATA

The Playwork Department at Leeds Metropolitan Department

Recent studies have examined differences in play between different ethnic minority groups, for example, Christian and Hindu children and between children resident in the UK and their country of origin. Other research areas include play and traveller families and computer aided ways of enhancing play for children with disabilities. The team are shortly to publish work on good practice in playwork.

Contact details for further information: Steven Rennie, Leeds Metropolitan University.

The Daycare Trust

Will be undertaking research into childcare for older children later this year.

Contact details: Megan Pacey, Policy Officer, e-mail: mpacey@daycaretrust.org.uk

Department of Human Geography, Loughborough University

Currently examining children's use of the internet and cyberspace.

Contact details: Sarah Holloway.

Department of Landscape, University of Sheffield

Currently undertaking research for the Department of Transport, Local Government and the Regions entitled 'Improving Urban Parks, Play Areas and Green Spaces'. The study, which will be completed in Spring 2002, seeks to identify innovative management of these spaces and who uses them or not, and why. Data collection is by means of focus groups, including young people but not specifically children.

Contact details: Helen Woolley, e-mail: landscape@sheffield.ac.uk

John McKendrick, School of Social Sciences, Glasgow Caledonian University

Currently consolidating a range of earlier works on commercial playgrounds. Also writing a book on children's geographies for older school-age children.

Contact details: John McKendrick, e-mail: j.mckendrick@gcal.ac.uk

David Ball, School of Health, Biological and Environmental Sciences, Middlesex University

Professor Ball has recently completed an extensive analysis of risk within outdoor playgrounds within the UK for the HSE. The research also reviews international research in risk factors. This report will be available shortly.

SECTION G: CONCLUSIONS

THE BENEFITS OF PLAY

The review of the importance of play for all children earlier in this report paints a picture of strong support for play in a number of different dimensions. Throughout a substantial body of literature, which examines in some depth the various theories of play, and which is drawn from a range of different disciplines, including child psychology and child psychotherapy, human geography, anthropology and studies of children's folklore, a range of benefits are set out. Traditionally these have focused on benefits to the individual child; more recently, the focus has been on benefits to society as a whole.

Running alongside this, at a practical level, the process of consultation undertaken by the New Policy Institute with a range of professionals working in play organisations and projects, children's charities and university departments, has indicated not only a strong belief in the value of play but also concern about some of the trends identified in the review. These include: restrictions on children's access to their local environments; the loss of free time; and, particularly for children with disabilities or from ethnic minority groups, shortages of appropriate play provision. From the case studies however, it is clear that there is considerable activity at the project level and that under a number of national policy initiatives, opportunities for play and recreation, albeit on a fairly structured basis, are emerging.

What remains problematic however, as the summaries at the end of each section of literature reviewed highlight, is that the *evidence* for the benefits of play is complex, often inconclusive and there are a number of areas where data is seriously lacking and research is needed.

With regard to the data on health for example, there is a lack of clarity between play, physical activity and sport. In education, as a number of the researchers themselves acknowledge, the effects of play are hard to prove, although teachers appear to value play and there is renewed interest in the positive effects of break-time. There is also some emerging research on play and brain development. And from the point of view of the social benefits more generally of play provision, again the effects are hard to disentangle and there appear to be a number of trends quite clearly working against the provision of free play opportunities and a move towards more organised and supervised activities.

SUGGESTIONS FOR THE WAY FORWARD

If the value of play is to be more firmly rooted in the current policy environment, the findings of this review would suggest that action is needed in a number of areas:

(1) Building up the knowledge base, based on the established consensus of those working in the play field

The lack of research *evidence* should not lead to the value of play being diminished or dismissed – more, that there needs to be greater recognition of the complexities and subtleties of play. As such, it seems important that amongst those actually working or researching in the play field, efforts should be made to develop what is already known about the positive benefits of play into a more comprehensive and current knowledge base. As Coalter and Taylor note, 'existing information and research is not widely known, even in the playwork profession'.

(2) Evaluation of play projects

From the case studies identified during the review, it is apparent that there is valuable information which requires much wider dissemination than currently undertaken. As the Introduction noted, part of the problem here appears to be the result of funding limitations. Addressing this deficit in evaluating projects would help to build up the knowledge base as just described.

(3) Further research

Many of the suggestions presented here pick up on recommendations made in earlier works such as those by Coalter and Taylor (2001). They are also based on a range of suggestions put forward by some of the individuals and organisations, which the New Policy Institute consulted in undertaking this review.

There is a need for:

- Research which is more clearly defined and focused on play, including the views of teachers towards play as a learning medium.

- Longitudinal data and data covering a wider geographic spread.

- Research on the access to, and use of, play facilities by disabled children in particular, from the perspective of their use of free time.

- Research which clearly separates out the pre-school group from older children.

- Research which looks at innovative ways of bringing care and free play together within the context of the overall expansion of out-of-school services.

- Further research which looks at the environmental factors amenable to manipulation such as traffic speeds and urban layout.

- Research from the parents' perspective in terms of what sort of play provision they want for their children.

Caution is needed however in that given the subtleties and complexities of play as just outlined, attempts to quantify the benefits of play are likely to be unsuccessful. As such, it needs to be acknowledged that the sort of data likely to be of most use will be of a qualitative nature, and may focus on the user perspective. This in itself would be highly valuable in terms of helping the UK to make progress towards implementing Article 31 of the UN Convention – which as discussed earlier, remains an area of only limited success to date.

APPENDIX 1: DATABASE SEARCHES AND KEY WORDS

Databases searched: ILAM; NFER and NfER/CERUK; Institute of Child Health; CPC Information Service; Institute of Education; Library at the School of Education, University of Leicester; Action for Sick Children; London School of Hygiene and Tropical Medicine; Regard (ESRC Research database).

Also manual and online searches of:

Key journals such as the British Medical Journal, Developmental Psychiatry, Childhood and Journal of Child Psychology and Psychiatry (1995 onwards), British Journal of Educational Studies (1995 onwards).

Research briefs and summaries of the DfES; Health Development Agency; ESRC; Joseph Rowntree Foundation; Nuffield Foundation; PSSRU at Kent; World Health Organisation; ROSPA; Child Accident Prevention Trust; Disability Rights Commission. .

With regard to the UN Convention on the Rights of the Child, a number of internet sites were searched including the Childwatch International Research Network (www.childwatch.uio.no).

E-mail contacts were also made via a number of specialist play organisations, for example Fairplay, notifying their members of the review and inviting information of any relevant data sources.

Key words:

CHILDREN – children and play; school-age children and play; children and participation; children's rights; children and social inclusion; children and leisure; children and social learning; children's cognitive development; children and access to services; children's views on play; children's learning; bullying; friendships; activities; play and children's health; children's culture; children and outdoor activities; children's space.

PLAY – play locations; theories of play; trends in play; play and safety; playgrounds; importance of play; play and environmental influences; play initiatives; play projects; play planning; play and the UN Convention; play and social inclusion; play and disabled children; play and children from ethnic minority groups; play and mental health.

EDUCATION: play and school; play and the curriculum; play and the National Curriculum; teachers' views towards play; play and learning; problems with playtime.

APPENDIX 2: STUDY METHODOLOGIES

Harland and others (NfER, 2000) *Arts Education in Secondary Schools: Effects and Effectiveness*

Evidence for the project was collected through in-depth case studies of arts education in five secondary schools; secondary analysis of data from another NfER project; a survey of Year 11 pupils and schools; interviews with employers and employees. The schools selected had reputations for good practice in the provision of arts education and reflected a variety of settings and institutions (e.g. urban and rural, different sizes and different socio-economic contexts).

The data was collected over three phases, 1997, 1998 and 1999. Data was collected from two longitudinal cohorts of pupils (identified by teachers as making good progress in an area of the arts), teachers and education management staff. Data was also collected via video and observation of arts activities. Across the three phases, a total of 219 interviews (up to three per pupil) were conducted. One limitation noted by the researchers about this phase of the project was that the sample was heavily skewed in terms of gender, with boys amounting to only 30 per cent of the sample. This was partly due to the inclusion of an all-girl school in the sample, but also because teachers tended to nominate more girls than boys.

The survey of Year 11 pupils was designed to examine the proposition that studying or engaging in the arts has a positive effect on general academic achievement in GCSEs. The survey involved a pupil questionnaire exploring a wide range of issues to do with their views towards and participation in the arts. Twenty-two schools out of an initial sample of 40 participated in the study, with 2,269 questionnaires being completed. Overall, the researchers note that despite a slight bias towards girls, the sample achieved broad representation in terms of gender, ethnicity and social class; it was drawn from a random sample of schools and contained a valuable mixture of different schools and teaching approaches therein.

Huttenmoser and Degen-Zimmermann (1995) Lebensraume fur Kinder

Study design included telephone interview of all parents of five year old children in the city of Zurich (1,729), a written questionnaire completed by 926 parents and an in-depth study of 20 families, 10 where children could play freely near their home and 10 who could not.

Limitations of the study appear to be the small sample size and the possibilities of factors other than the availability of safe play provision outside the home affecting the results – for example, differences in television viewing and the ability of the mother to speak German which would be likely to influence the degree of integration of the family into their neighbourhood.

Keating and others (2000) Well, I've Not Done Any Work Today. I Don't Know Why I Came to School. Perceptions of Play in the Reception Class

Study sample was based on 10 primary schools in the north-west of England. These were selected at random, but avoided church-funded/aided schools. Focus on what the research team identified as the five major stakeholders in the Reception Class – the headteacher, the reception class teacher, the classroom assistant, the parent and the child.

The data was gathered via semi-structured, informal, individual interviews. These were recorded and transcribed. Supplementary notes were made as required.

Five researchers undertook the interviews and care was taken to ensure that the same issues were raised. To allow for the fact that the interviews were informal and interactive, it was agreed that the researchers would act as a guide during the interview to ensure some continuity between the interviews.

McKendrick and others (2000) Enabling play or sustaining exclusion? Commercial playgrounds and disabled children

Paper is based on findings from the ESRC Research Project The Business of Children's Play. The aim was to review the commercial provision of play space for children aged between 5 and 12 in the UK. The study was based on Greater Manchester and used a multi-method, multi-stage research design involving questionnaires to review patterns of participation and family leisure preferences. Two surveys were conducted, one with families using commercial playgrounds and one with parents of school children from four schools in Manchester selected to reflect different economic areas of the city and different educational needs. In total, 872 families were surveyed. In addition, the study involved interviews with 30 families, observational studies of children at play, case studies and whole family interviews.

The methods were used to build up a detailed picture of family views towards the use of commercial playgrounds and what they provide. A particular strength of the study appears to be the gathering of data from different perspectives, including those of children themselves and how these may differ from their parents/carers.

Mulvihill and others (2000) A qualitative study investigating the views of primary-age children and parents on physical activity

Study was based on six sites across England, three of which were urban and three rural/suburban areas. The study aim was to examine the factors influencing children's involvement in physical activity. Sixty primary school children aged between 5 and 11 years took part in paired interviews and 38 parents were interviewed in groups. The schools were selected to reflect socio-economic diversity and differences in ethnic groups within the school population.

The approach adopted in the study was qualitative and exploratory, with the use of open-ended questions to encourage respondents to exert an influence over the choice of issues covered and to discuss their understandings of physical activity in an informal and interactive manner. A version of the 'draw and say' technique was used with the children on the basis that drawing is an activity which this age group feel comfortable with and provides a starting point for discussion.

The researchers acknowledge that 'as a result of the purposive sampling procedures employed, and the exploratory nature of the investigation, it is not appropriate to offer a record of the frequency with which views were expressed or to make claims about the typicality for an age group as a whole'. Instead the aim was to identify the range of views, recurrent themes and some of the issues which may arise out of children's views towards involvement in physical activity. Some bias may also have resulted from the use of teachers to select the children for interview – teachers may have been encouraged to select active children by virtue of the project's stated interest.

Petrie and others (2000) *Out of School Lives, Out of School Services*

This qualitative study incorporated a variety of research methods, with an aim to provide analysis on families' uses of out-of-school services. A range of specific user groups were identified via a range of service providers and organisations selected on the basis of information supplied by local authorities and others working in the field.

Services were selected to reflect the user groups under consideration, namely young people aged 10 to 13 (15 services/39 families studied); disabled children (6 services/18 families studied); children of African/African-Caribbean background (6 services/18 families studied) and children of Asian background (6 services/18 families studied).

The services selected were from the private, public and voluntary sectors. For each, regular visits were made for the purposes of observation and interviews with staff and with users. The study incorporated ethnographic fieldwork, which involved extensive and in-depth visits which covered young people's activities, interactions between staff and young people, between older and younger service users and any problems experienced by staff and children. Interviews varied from full-length semi-structured interviews through to a series of more brief conversations, depending on the abilities of the children to communicate. A thematic analysis of the data obtained examined the reasons given for using services and satisfaction with them.

The study also included a telephone survey of three London boroughs. A stratified random sample of 27 services was obtained, representing different forms of organisation. Basic background data about the service was obtained from short interviews with staff on site. Telephone interviews were conducted with a sample of 185 parents, randomly selected, and again explored their use of a particular service and their satisfaction with it.

Two identified weaknesses of the study noted in the appendix are that the disabled children from whom the sample was drawn, were mostly referred and paid for by social services, and overly-represent the severely disabled end of the spectrum of disability. Secondly, that whilst the telephone survey achieved a 69 per cent response rate, economically disadvantaged parents may be under-represented in that 12 per cent of those sampled did not have a telephone or their telephone line was dead when the researchers attempted to contact them.

Robson, S. (1993) 'Best of all I like Choosing Time': Talking with children about play and work

Study based on three primary and nursery school, two in suburban areas and one in an urban, inner-city area. The ages of the children studied ranged from 4.6 to 5.6 years and all had been in school for at least one term prior to the study.

In all three schools, the researcher spent time with the children during a variety of activities. This was followed by tape-recorded discussions in a quiet area, with 24 children either individually or in groups of 2 or 3 (which the children selected on the basis of their friendships). These covered a range of areas and were essentially steered by the children.

Sherman, A. (1997) Five Year Olds' Perceptions of Why We Go to School

Study involved a series of visits and interviews with five schools in a large city area.

Fifty children from five county council Reception/Year one classes participated. Data was collected face-to-face via interviews that generally took place after a period of familiarisation in the classrooms.

The familiarisation process took the form of weekly visits to each of the schools for ten weeks before the interviews began. During the visits, the researchers participated in all classroom activities, sometimes working in small groups or individually. A journal was kept of these visits.

The interviews with the children were conducted as informal conversations. An outline questionnaire of 20 questions was used to stimulate conversation with each child.

Wheway, R. and Millward, A. (1997) *Child's Play*

Study focused on 12 housing estates built between the 1890s and 1990s and involved over 3,500 observations of children aged under 18 made between the hours of 9.30am and 8pm. In addition, 236 children and 82 parents were interviewed using a standard questionnaire format. Information was also gathered from estate managers, local planners and youth workers.

The research design, a combination of observations and interviews, deliberately followed closely that used in an earlier Department of the Environment Study (DoE 1973) in order to allow some comparisons over time to be made. It should be noted however that the DoE study focused on 15 relatively modern housing estates which reflected the thrust of housing policy at the time – more recent housing trends have been to renew older stock and to create smaller estates.

Wood, E. (1999) The impact of the National Curriculum on play in reception classes

Study based on nine teachers drawn from a novice–expert range, from a newly qualified teacher to one with 20 years' experience. The research design incorporated a variety of methods, including narrative accounts, semi-structured interviews, teacher group meetings and video sessions of play. Whilst clearly a small sample, the study provides comprehensive and in-depth data from a group of teaching professionals with a wide span of experience. Wood also argues that 'research that represents teachers' voices can present valuable insights into the situated nature of their knowledge about teaching and learning in relation to educational policy'.

von Kries and others (1998) Road injuries in school age children

Study examined all school age children between 6 and 14 in Dusseldorf (population of 570,000) who had suffered a road injury between January 1993 and March 1995. Study was a case control design with controls matched by age and sex. Criteria for inclusion were residence in Dusseldorf and sustaining an injury within 500 metres of home. Random sample of 174 children were selected for interview.

Study bias was minimised by checking data with national figures. Study limitations noted included an inability to control for socio-economic variables; study also unable to account for variations in traffic volume.

REFERENCES

Adams, E. and Ingham, S. (1998) *Changing Places – children's participation in environmental planning*, The Children's Society

Barrett, N. (ed.) (1991) *Leisure Services UK*, MacMillan

Bennett, N., Wood, L. and Rogers, S. (1997) *Teaching through play*, Open University Press

Berliner, W. (2001) 'Mind games', *Guardian* 14 August, Education, p. 4

Bishop, J. and Curtis, M. (eds) (2001) *Play today in the primary school playground*, Open University Press

Blatchford, P. (1993) *Playtime in the Primary School: Problems and Improvements*, Routledge

Blatchford, P. (1998a) *Social Life in School*, Falmer Press

Blatchford, P. (1998b) 'The State of Play in Schools', *Child Psychology and Psychiatry Review* 3(2), pp. 58–67

Blatchford, P. and Sharp, S. (eds) (1994) *Breaktime and the school*, Routledge

Bruce, T. (1997) *Helping Young Children to Play*, Hodder and Stoughton

Callaghan, J. and Dennis, S. (1997) *Right up our street*, The Children's Society

Candler, P. (1999) *Cross National Perspectives on the Principles and Practice of Children's Play Provision*, Faculty of Health and Community Studies, De Montfort University

Carvel, J. (1999) 'Play is out, early learning is in', *Guardian* 23 June, p. 5

Cattanach, A. (1998) 'The Role of Play in the Life of the Child', *Child Psychology and Psychiatry Review*, 3(3), pp. 113–14

Children and Young People's Unit (2001) *Tomorrow's Future: Building a Strategy for Children and Young People*, CYPU

Children's Play Council (1998) *The New Charter for Children's Play*, Children's Play Council and the Children's Society

Children's Play Council (2001) *The State of Play: a Survey of Play Professionals in England*, Children's Play Council

Coalter, F. and Taylor, J. (2001) *Realising the Potential: The Case for Cultural Services – Play*, Report prepared for the Local Government Association, Centre for Leisure Research, University of Edinburgh

Crespo, C., Smit, E., Troiano, R., Bartlett, S., Macera, C. and Andersen, R. (2001) 'Television Watching, Energy Intake, and Obesity in US Children', *Archives of Pediatric Adolescent Medicine*, 155, pp. 360–4

Davis, A. and Jones, L. (1997) 'Whose neighbourhood? Whose quality of life? Developing a new agenda for children's health in urban settings', *Health Education Journal*, 56, pp. 350–63

DfES (2001) *Promoting Children's Mental Health within Early Years and School Settings,* DfES

Dietz, W. (2001) 'The obesity epidemic in young children', *British Medical Journal*, 332

Education Extra (1999) *Student Care and Learning in After-School Hours, Extra Special,* Issue 61, Education Extra

Education Extra (2001a) *Taking Play Seriously, Extra Special,* Issue 84, Education Extra

Education Extra (2001b) *Alive with Learning: Study support in museums and galleries*, Education Extra

Elbers, E. (1996) 'Citizenship in the Making – Themes of citizenship in children's pretend play', *Childhood*, 3(4), pp. 499–514

Evaldsson, A. and Corsaro, W. (1998) 'Play and games in the peer culture of preschool and preadolescent children', *Childhood* 5(4), pp. 377–401

Ferguson, A. (1999) *Research into Children's Play: An Executive Summary,* National Playing Fields Association

Ferron, C., Narring, F., Cauderay, M. and Michaud, P-A. (1999) 'Sport activity in adolescence: associations with health perceptions and experimental behaviours', *Health Education Research*, 14(2), pp. 225–33

Freeman, M. (2000) 'The future of children's rights' *Children & Society*, 14, pp. 277–93

Furlow, B. (2001) 'Play's the thing', *New Scientist*, 9 June

Gill, T. and Lubelska, A. (1996) *Managing Play Services*, Children's Play Council

Gilligan, R. (2000) 'Adversity, Resilience and Young people: the Protective Value of Positive School and Spare Time Experiences', *Children & Society*, 14, pp. 37–47

Goldstein, J. (ed.) (1994) *Toys, Play and Child Development*, Cambridge University Press

Green, J. and Hart, L. (1998) 'Children's views of accident risks and prevention: a qualitative study', *Injury Prevention,* 4, pp. 14–21

Grudgeon, E. (1993) 'Gender implications of playground culture' in Woods, P. and Hammersley, M. (eds) *Gender and Ethnicity in Schools: Ethnographic accounts*, Routledge

Guddemi, M. and Jambor, T. (1992) *A Right to Play,* Proceedings of the American Affiliate of the International Association for the Child's Right to Play, September 17–20

Harden, J., Backett-Millburn. K., Scott, S. and Jackson, S. (2000) 'Scary faces, scary places: children's perceptions of risk and safety', *Health Education Journal*, 59, pp. 12–22

Harland, J., Kinder, K., Lord, P., Stott, A., Schagen, I., Haynes, J., Cusworth, L., White, R. and Paola, R. (2000) *Arts Education in Secondary Schools: Effects and Effectiveness*, NFER

Hillman, M., Adams, J. and Whitelegg, N. (1990) *One false move: A study of children's independent mobility*, Policy Studies Institute

Holloway, S. and Valentine, G. (2000) 'Spatiality and the New Social Studies of Childhood', *Sociology*, 34 (4) pp. 763–83.

Howarth, R. (1997) *If We Don't Play Now, When Can We?*, Hopscotch Asian Women's Centre

Hutchinson, J., Henderson, D. and Francis, S. (2001) 'Evaluation of Pilot Summer Activities for 16 year Olds: Summer 2000', DfES Research Brief No. 260, February

Huttenmoser, M. amd Degen-Zimmermann, D. (1995) Lenstraume fur Kinder, Nationale Forschungsprogramme 'Stadt und Verkehr', (NFP 25)

Johnson, S., Ramsey, R., Thornicroft, G., Brooks, L., Lelliott, P., Peck, E., Smith, H., Chisholm, D., Audini, B., Knapp, M. and Goldberg, D. (1997) *London's Mental Health*, The King's Fund

Jones, L. (1998) 'Inequality in access to local environments: the experiences of Asian and non-Asian girls', *Health Education Journal*, 57, pp. 313–28

Jones, L., Davis, A. and Eyers, T. (2000) Young people, transport and risk: comparing access and independent mobility in urban, suburban and rural environments', *Health Education Journal*, 59, pp. 315–28

Kapasi, H. (2001) *Asian Children Playing: Increasing Access to Play Provision for Asian Children*, Playtrain

Katz, A., Buchanan, A. and Bream, V. (2001) *Bullying in Britain – testimonies from teenagers,* Young Voice

Keating, I., Fabian, H., Jordan, P., Mavers, D. and Roberts, J. (2000) 'Well, I've Not Done Any Work Today. I don't Know Why I Came to School. Perceptions of Play in the Reception Class', *Educational Studies,* 26(4), pp. 437–54

Kids' Club Network (2001a) *Looking to the Future for Children and Family: A Report of the Millennium Childcare Commission*, Kids' Club Network

Kids' Club Network (2001b) *Kids' clubs in the community*, Kids' Club Network

Kids' Club Network (2001c) *Children have their say*, Kids' Club Network

Kids' Club Network (2001d) *Providing for disabled children in your kids' club*, Kids' Club Network

Lansdown, G. (1995) *Taking Part – Children's participation in decision making*, IPPR

Macintyre, C. (2001) *Enhancing Learning through Play*, David Fulton Publishers

Matthews, H. and Limb, M. (2000) 'Exploring the "Fourth Environment": young people's use of place and views on their environment', Children 5–16 Research Briefing No. 9, ESRC

Matthews, H., Taylor, M., Percy-Smith, B. and Limb, M. (2000) 'The Unacceptable Flaneur – the shopping mall as a teenage hangout', *Childhood,* 7(3), August, pp. 279–94

Mayall, B. (2000) 'Negotiating Childhoods', Children 5–16 Research Briefing No. 13, ESRC

McKendrick, J. (2000) 'Conceptualising commercial playspace for children', Paper based on conference presentation 'New Playwork, New Thinking', 2nd Theoretical Playwork Conference, Ely, March 2000

McKendrick, J. and Bradford, M. (1999) 'Organised spaces for leisure: a new departure in the institutionalisation of children's lives?', Paper presented to the British/Norwegian Seminar of the ESRC Children 5–16 and NFR Children, Youth and Families programmes, Trondheim, Norway, 3 September

McKendrick, J., Bradford, M. and Fielder, A. (2000) 'Kid Customer? Commercialisation of playspace and the commodification of childhood', *Childhood*, 7(3), pp. 295–314

McKendrick, J., Fielder, A. and Bradford, M (1998) 'Disability issues and commercial play centres', BoCP Project Paper no. 5

McKendrick, J., Fielder, A. and Bradford, M. (2000a) 'Enabling play or sustaining exclusion? Commercial playgrounds and disabled children', *The North West Geographer,* 3, pp. 32–49

McKendrick, J., Fielder, A. and Bradford, M. (2000b) 'Privatisation on Collective Play Spaces in the UK', *Built Environment*, 25(1), pp. 44–57

McKendrick, J., Fielder, A. and Bradford, M. (2000c) 'The dangers of safe play', Children 5–16 Research Briefing No. 22, ESRC

McNeish, D. and Roberts, H. (1995) *Playing it Safe. Todays children at play*, Barnardos

Meltzer, H., Gatward, R., Goodman, R. and Ford, T. (2000) *The Mental Health of Children and Adolescents in Great Britain Summary Report*, National Statistics

Mental Health Foundation (1999a) *Bright Futures*, Mental Health Foundation

Mental Health Foundation (1999b) *The Big Picture: Summary of the Bright Futures programme, Mental Health Foundation website*, May

Moss, P. (2000) 'From Children's Services to Children's Spaces', *NCVCCO Annual Review Journal*, 2, pp. 19–35

Moyles, J. (2000) (ed.) *The Excellence of Play*, Open University Press

Moyles, J. (2001) *Just Playing? The Role and Status of Play in Early Childhood Education*, Open University Press

Mulvihill, C., Rivers, K. and Aggleton, P. (2000) 'A qualitative study investigating the views of primary-age children and parents on physical activity', *Health Education Journal*, 59, pp. 166–79

NACRO (2000) *Making a difference – Preventing crime through youth activity*, NACRO

NPFA (1999) *Research into Children's Play*, National Playing Fields Association

NPFA (2000) *Best Play*, National Playing Fields Association, PLAYLINK and the Children's Play Council

O'Brien, M., Jones, D. and Sloan, D. (2000) 'Children's independent spatial mobility in the urban public realm', *Childhood*, 7(3), pp. 257–77

Ofsted (2001) *Out of school care: Guidance to the National Standards*, DfES

Pacey, M. (2000) 'Childcare for All: An Appraisal of the National Childcare Strategy', *NCVCCO Annual Review Journal,* 2, pp. 81–8

Pellegrini, A. and Smith, P. (1998) 'The Development of Play During Childhood: Forms and Possible Functions', *Child Psychology and Psychiatry Review*, 3 (2), pp. 51–7

Petrie, P. and Poland, G. (1998) 'Play services for Disabled Children; Mother's Satisfaction', *Children & Society*, 12, pp. 283–94.

Petrie, P., Egharevba, I., Oliver, C. and Poland, G. (2000) *Out of School Lives, Out of School Services*, The Stationery Office

PLAYLINK (2000) Reared in Captivity – restoring the freedom to play, PLAYLINK/Portsmouth City Council Conference 1999

Ravenscroft, N. and Markwell, S. (2000) 'Ethnicity and the integration and exclusion of young people through urban park and recreation provision', *Managing Leisure*, 5, pp. 135–50

Robson, S. (1993) '"Best of all I like Choosing Time": Talking with children about play and work', *Early Child Development and Care*, 92, pp. 37–51

Rogers, C. and Sawyer, J. (1988) *Play in the lives of children*, Washington, National Association for the Education of Young Children

Sharp, C., Kendall, L., Bhabra, S., Schagen, I. and Duff, J. (2001) 'Playing for Success – An evaluation of the second year' DfES Research Brief No. RB291, September

Sherman, A. (1997) 'Five Year Olds' Perceptions of Why We Go to School', *Children & Society*, 11, pp. 117–27

Sluckin, A. (1981) *Growing up in the playground: the social development of children*, Routledge and Kegan-Paul

Smith, F. and Barker, J. (1997) *Profile of Provision: the expansion of out of school child care*, Department of Geography, Brunel University and Kids' Club Network

Spencer, C. and Woolley, H. (2000) 'Children and the city: a summary of recent environmental psychology research', *Child: Care, Health and Development*, 26(3), pp. 181–98

Strandell, H. (1997) 'Doing reality with play – play as children's resource in organising everyday life in daycare centres', *Childhood*, 4(4), pp. 445–63

Towner, E. and Ward, H. (1998) 'Prevention of injuries to children and young people: the way ahead for the UK', *Injury Prevention*, 4 (supplement) S17–25

Von Kries, R., Kohne, C., Bohm, O. and Von Voss, H. (1998) 'Road injuries in school age children: relation to environmental factors amenable to interventions', *Injury Prevention*, 4, pp. 103–5

Wood, E. (1999) 'The impact of the National Curriculum on play in reception classes', *Educational Research*, 41 (1), pp. 11–22

Wood, L. and Bennett, N. (1997) 'The Rhetoric and Reality of Play: Teachers; Thinking and Classroom Practice', *Early Years*, 17(2), pp. 22–7

Woolley, H. and Johns, R. (2001) 'Skateboarding: the City as a Playground', *Journal of Urban Design*, 6(2), pp. 211–30

Woolley, H. and ul-Amin, N. (1999) 'Pakistani teenagers' use of public open space in Sheffield', *Managing Leisure*, 4, pp. 156–67

Woolley, H., Dunn, J., Spencer, C., Short, T. and Rowley, G. (1999) 'Children Describe their Experiences of the City Centre: a qualitative study of the fears and concerns which may limit their full participation' *Landscape Research*, 24(3), pp. 287–310

Woolley, H., Spencer, C., Dunn, J. and Rowley, G. (1999) 'The Child as Citizen: Experiences of British Town and City Centres', *Journal of Urban Design*, 4(3), pp. 255–82

Wheway, R. and Millward, A. (1997) *Child's Play: facilitating play on housing estates*, Chartered Institute of Housing

Youniss, J. (1980) *Parents and Peers in Social Development: A Sullivan-Piaget perspective*, Chicago, University of Chicago Press

Section 3

Section 3

The Planning and Location of Play Provision in England:

A mapping exercise

Andrew Harrop

ACKNOWLEDGEMENTS

We gratefully acknowledge the support of the many people who provided us with information and opinion during the course of this study.

For Part One, thanks to Christine Andrews, John Fitzpatrick, Lesli Godfrey, Leonie Labistour, Maggie Patchett, Wendy Russell and Tanny Stobart.

For Part Two, thanks to members of staff at East Staffordshire Borough Council, Newcastle-under-Lyme Borough Council, North Warwickshire Borough Council, Nuneaton and Bedworth Borough Council, Shrewsbury and Atcham Borough Council, South Shropshire District Council, South Staffordshire District Council, Stafford Borough Council, Staffordshire Moorlands District Council, Stoke-on-Trent City Council, Tamworth Borough Council, Telford and Wrekin Council.

For Part Three, for all their help thanks to Su Barber (Bridgnorth), Nicky Booth (Walsall), Linda Holmes (Coventry) and Rob Preston (Wyre Forest) and to their many colleagues.

Special thanks to Jean Elledge and Alice Field, and our project advisers Haki Kapesi and Steve Macarthur.

THE PLANNING AND LOCATION OF PLAY PROVISION IN ENGLAND:

A MAPPING EXERCISE

CONTENTS

Executive Summary		**108**
Introduction		**118**
Part 1: The National Picture		**122**
1.1.	Objectives	122
1.2.	Survey Response	122
1.3.	Findings	123
1.4.	Conclusions	127
Part 2: The Regional Picture – The West Midlands		**128**
2.1.	Objectives	128
2.2.	Survey Response	129
2.3.	Findings	129
2.4.	Conclusions	139
Part 3: Local Authority Case Studies		**140**
3.1.	Objectives	140
3.2.	Characteristics of the Four Case Studies	141
3.3.	Levels of provision	142
3.4.	Patterns of provision	144
3.5.	Inclusion and Targeting	146
3.6.	Playworkers	147
3.7.	Financial patterns	148
3.8.	Planning, review and evaluation	148
3.9.	Conclusions	149
5.	**Results For The Four Case Studies**	**151**
Case Study 1: Bridgnorth		151
Case Study 2: Coventry		155
Case Study 3: Walsall		159
Case Study 4: Wyre Forest		162
Appendix A: Part 2 Results By Local Authority		**166**
Appendix B: The Part 3 Spatial Mapping Exercise		**178**
Appendix C: Replicating The Work		**180**
Part 2: The Regional Picture		180
Part 3: The Local Authority Picture		181

EXECUTIVE SUMMARY

INTRODUCTION

This report presents the results of a three-part mapping project, which explored how local authorities plan and deliver play opportunities for children aged between 5 and 16. Those three parts were:

- *The national picture*. An overview of the structures and written documents that local authorities have in place for developing play provision.

- *The regional picture: the West Midlands*. A more detailed look at the characteristics of provision, structures and plans within the West Midlands region.

- *Local authority case studies*. An in-depth study of the planning and provision of play in four local authorities, including analysis of needs and the distribution of provision at sub-local authority level.

The main objective of the study was to collect and analyse data regarding the patterns of current provision and the policies and strategies that local authorities are following in making decisions about such provision.

The research was carried out in the summer and autumn of 2001. All findings are snapshots from this period, with information either referring to the situation prevailing at the time of the survey, or where applicable to the 2001/02 financial year.

Scope and Definitions

The scope of the study is play provision for children aged between 5 and 16. 'Play' is understood to be the activities which, for children, are freely chosen, personally directed and intrinsically motivated, taking place with or without adult involvement. Children and young people of all ages 'play'. 'Play provision' is any setting where play (as defined here) is the main or intended activity. For unsupervised play areas, this definition is unproblematic. But the story is different for supervised provision – at least in the context of a high-level mapping exercise, where it is not possible to use a definition that requires observation of the experiences of individual children. We decided to define play provision as any out-of-school provision that respondents judged to be offering opportunities for play.

PART 1: THE NATIONAL PICTURE

The aim of Part 1 of the study was to establish an overview for England as a whole of play planning and provision in local authorities, via an approach to regional play bodies. Information was received concerning 167 out of 367 local authorities, across all regions of England. Apart from the North West and the Eastern regions (where the regional representatives were only able to supply very limited information) and the South East, all regions provided information for more than two fifths of their local authorities.

The key findings from this part of the study are detailed below. All data that is reported is in terms of the number of authorities for which information was available for the issue under consideration:

- *Play officers and services.* Almost half of local authorities have either a play service or officer (two in five have dedicated play officers and one third have play services). A clear majority of unitary authorities have officers and/or services, while few districts and county councils do.

- *Play policies and strategies.* Half of local authorities have either a play policy or a strategy for developing play (two in five have a strategy and one third have a play policy). Four out of five of these authorities have play officers or services. Half of the documents cover both play areas and supervised play provision. A large majority of play plans and policies are developed in leisure departments or related services, but in only a small minority of cases is the work led by a specialist play service.

- *Play Associations and Networks.* Independent play associations or networks were reported as operating in two thirds of authorities. In some areas more than one organisation operates, while in others a single organisation covers several authorities (e.g. a county-wide association). Over two thirds of these organisations promote networking, provide information, and deliver training while only two in five deliver provision themselves. Some of the organisations also have a remit beyond play, for example covering childcare and out-of-school hours provision.

It should be noted that as these figures only include authorities about which regional play experts had information, they are likely to be higher than the results for *all* local authorities (play practitioners tend to know about authorities where there is activity, but often have no available information about areas where there is no activity). But at the very least the results show the *minimum* number of local authorities where activity takes place.

The survey suggests that on the one hand, there are a very large number of authorities with no strategic approach to children's play (around half of authorities for which information was available have neither specialist play employees nor strategic documents for play). But on the other hand, the survey also suggests that a significant number of local authorities *of all types* and *in all regions* take play provision sufficiently seriously to maintain play officers or play services and to develop play policies and play development plans. There is, therefore, a good 'base' of activity in all parts of England from which to build, if policy makers wish to encourage more councils to develop professional structures for the delivery of play.

The number of areas where independent play networks and associations are reported as operating is encouragingly high. A priority for further work should be to investigate the capacity of these organisations to support the development of play, and to assess what resources they need to improve their performance.

PART 2: THE REGIONAL PICTURE – THE WEST MIDLANDS

Part 2 of the study collected detailed information about the planning and provision of play from local authorities in the West Midlands region. Information was collected through a questionnaire, which was first piloted on five authorities and then distributed to the remaining 29 unitary and lower tier authorities. Completed questionnaires were received from 16 authorities (12 of the 21 district councils and four of the ten unitary authorities).

The main objectives of this part of the study were to assemble detailed information about individual local authorities, and to identify patterns and variations across authorities. An additional objective was to provide advice on how to replicate such a data collation exercise in other regions. Key findings from this part of the study are set out below.

Plans and policies

A minority of authorities have play policies or plans: five have either a play policy or strategy, while a further three are preparing one or the other. Some of these documents cover only play areas or only supervised play. Other authorities deal with play in documents such as Cultural Strategies, Early Years Strategies and Local Plans/Unitary Development Plans, although it was not possible to assess how fully play is covered in these cases. Only two authorities reported involving outside organisations in developing their documents.

Unsupervised play provision

The average (median) number of unsupervised play areas is one for every 370 children aged between 5 and 16 and the average (median) level of spending is about £4 per child. In one quarter of cases the local authority is not the main provider of play areas. In other authorities both levels of spending and number of play areas vary considerably, although the two did not always go hand-in-hand. Rather, some higher spending authorities have relatively few, well-resourced play areas, and some lower spending authorities have relatively numerous, under-resourced areas. Detailed analysis of the 12 authorities who are the main providers of play areas suggest they can be divided into the following four groups.

1. *Few play areas, each with high funding* resulting in high/medium spending per child (four authorities).

2. *Few play areas, each with low/medium funding* resulting in low spending per child (three authorities).

3. *Many play areas, each with low funding* resulting in low spending per child (two authorities).

4. *Many play areas, each with medium funding* resulting in high spending per child (three authorities).

It was beyond the scope of this study to identify the reasons for these variations in approach or to assess what impact they have on children's experience of play. This is obviously an area where further investigation would be helpful. It would be interesting to explore further the extent to which the alternative approaches are deliberately chosen and what factors influence councils' decisions.

Supervised play provision

The average (median) number of supervised play settings is one for every 630 children, while the average (median) level of spending is about £5.20 per child. Three quarters of the authorities supplied incomplete information for provision not funded by the council. This finding suggests that despite the expansion of childcare and study support, and the development of EYDCPs, NOF consortium bids, cultural strategies and community planning, many local authorities are not well linked into wider out-of-school provision.

Notwithstanding some discrepancies in reporting, there are large variations in the quantity and characteristics of play provision funded by different local authorities. The highest spending unitary authority spends ten times as much per child as the lowest, while the highest spending district council spends more than ten times as much per child as the lowest. These variations are related to differences in both the number of children to each supervised play setting, and the council's spending per setting.

A quarter of local authorities reported there were local adventure playgrounds. All but one reported that term time provision exists, with around half of councils funding some provision. Holiday schemes are also known to exist in all but one authority.

Measuring and reviewing performance

While play is mentioned in the Best Value Performance Plans of two thirds of the authorities, only four had yet completed any Best Value Reviews covering play. Only two planned to conduct cross-cutting reviews of services for children. Five of the authorities have targets or local performance indicators for play provision and another is currently preparing indicators for a new programme. The most commonly collected information relates to play areas' compliance with NPFA standards and attendance information for supervised play provision.

Partners

Within local authorities, play services or a dedicated play officer lead work on supervised play provision in only one third of cases. In other cases work is usually led by an officer in the leisure department who is not a play specialist, although in two of the unitary authorities responsibility for supervised play lies with Community Education. Management of play areas is most often led by parks services. Schools, parish councils and independent play providers are local authorities' main external partners. Only half of authorities were aware of NOF funding of local play provision, although some did report provision was being funded by regeneration budgets.

Playworkers and training

In four authorities of the sixteen, planning documents set out plans or policies for the training of playworkers, while two set out plans for recruitment.

Consultation with children and parents

Fourteen of the authorities reported consulting parents about local play provision, while 13 reported consulting children. Among the various reasons for consulting parents and children in this way, by far the most frequently mentioned was the planning and development of future provision.

Conclusions

Our conclusions are divided between play areas and supervised play. As far as play areas are concerned, there are some interesting divergences in patterns of provision, firstly between the small minority of councils which are not the main provider and the rest, and secondly between the four 'types' of local authority provision identified above.

These variances suggest a number of important policy questions, which the survey findings raise rather than resolve:

- Do these variations impact on the experiences of children?

- How should local authorities set about resolving tensions between total spending, quantity and quality? Are alternative approaches actively chosen or accidents of history?

- Are planning and review processes really helping local authorities take a fundamental look at existing patterns of need and provision?

As far as supervised play is concerned, the findings also show a great deal of variation in local authorities' activities. Apart from the obvious explanation of variations in responsibilities between authorities, we suggest there are two possible reasons for this diversity:

- First, the longstanding variation in supervised play provision, arising from the discretionary, and sometimes marginal, status of play.

- Second, councils' variable levels of exposure to new government initiatives (for childcare, study support, sport) and the extent to which these have been integrated into (or styled) as play activities.

Finally, the gaps in the answers provided to us show that the quality of information within local authorities about others' provision is often limited. District council leisure departments (even those with dedicated play officers) which have no information about provision, are likely to have little involvement with wider out-of-school initiatives. This suggests that EYDCPs may still have a lot to do to join up the work of providers of out-of-school activities for children.

PART 3: LOCAL AUTHORITY CASE STUDIES

In parallel with the overall West Midlands data collection, four case study authorities were selected for more in-depth analysis. The purpose of this part of the study was to further map the level and characteristics of play provision, in relation to local needs. It also aimed to understand what approaches and strategies are being followed by local authorities, and suggest why these vary. It should be stressed that statements about particular authorities should not be read as judgements on their practice or performance, which are beyond the remit of this study.

The four case study local authorities were chosen because they are geographically and demographically diverse. They are:

- *Bridgnorth* – a large, sparsely populated district, with only a few pockets of deprivation.

- *Wyre Forest* – a semi-rural district centred on the town of Kidderminster with a greater number of deprived communities.

- *Walsall* – an urban area on the edge of the West Midlands conurbation, with a mix of affluent areas and highly deprived areas.

- *Coventry* – a compact free-standing city; with a mix of affluent areas and highly deprived areas.

The discussion of the results of Part 3 of the study is addressed under a number of headings, as follows:

- *The level of provision*. The types and quantities of provision in each area for 5 to 16 year old children, and the basis on which they are accessed.

- *The pattern of provision*. How provision relates to the social, housing and economic circumstances of the children in the locality, as well as an assessment of the key factors which influence provision in each area.

- *Inclusion and Targeting*. The local authority's attempts to ensure the play needs of all children are addressed.

- *Playworkers*. The number of people working on provision, whether they are trained, and to what level.

- *Finance*. The amount of money spent on play provision in each local authority area, in relation to the numbers of school-aged children.

- *Planning, review and evaluation*. Local authorities' approaches to planning, Best Value reviews, evaluation and inspection.

Levels of provision

The key features of provision include:

- *Children per play area*. In three of the four authorities the number of children per play area is similar, with roughly 400 children to every play area. In Coventry by contrast, there are about four times as many children to each area.

- *Children per supervised play setting*. In three of the four authorities the number of children per supervised play setting is similar, with roughly 350 children per setting. In Bridgnorth by contrast, the figure is around four times lower. All four local authorities have more than the average level of provision identified in the Part 2 survey.

Other notable features of the play provision across the four authorities include:

Conditions of access
The majority of supervised provision is paid for by families. Exceptions include Wyre Forest's council-funded clubs and Coventry's play centres. Almost all provision is run on a childcare basis, with children being registered for a whole session. Exceptions include Coventry's play centres and some of Bridgnorth's independent summer play schemes.

Responsibility for delivery
1. Play Areas. Neither of the district councils have control of the majority of local play areas (parishes have responsibility in one, while over half are managed by a social landlord in the other).

2. Supervised Play Provision. In Walsall the delivery of council-funded supervised provision is devolved to independent local bodies. In the two districts responsibility lies within the leisure service, while in Coventry different sorts of provision are delivered by different parts of the council. Wyre Forest is the only authority with a dedicated play section, although Walsall and Coventry both have play budgets (in Coventry this only funds a minority of the council's provision).

Non-council provision
All four areas have independent supervised providers receiving NOF and EYDCP support (although in Bridgnorth they are very few in number) as well as more traditional youth clubs. Schools or school-based community organisations are key deliverers in all four case study areas. Other partners include community organisations, commercial day-care providers, parish councils, a national charity, and a county playing field association.

Term time clubs
All the authorities fund term time clubs, although there is considerable variation in their quantity and style, with some being orientated towards sport, art, study support or childcare. In Wyre Forest clubs have a development remit, running only while the council helps with the launch of independent provision in their place.

Holiday play schemes
There are local authority-funded summer play schemes as well as independent projects in all four case study areas. There seems to be little variation in approach, with an unsurprising overlap between play and more organised activities, such as sport and art.

Other provision
Apart from special needs provision, there are several examples of other types of provision from the case studies. For example Coventry has two council-funded open-access play centres and Bridgnorth has a voluntary sector play bus and children's farm.

Approaches to enhancing levels of provision
The case studies suggested that local authorities have been able to enhance the amount of play provision settings that are available in two ways:

- *Changing the pattern of local authority provision.* Apart from raising overall spending, local authorities have increased the level of their own provision by: making savings through locating provision in multi-use facilities; shifting away from a higher level of provision for a few children towards more dispersed, shorter-duration provision for many more.

- *Playing a development role.* All four local authorities aim to support the development of independent provision. Examples of this include: facilitating a play forum; joint marketing; co-ordinating opening times; offering free training and staff secondments; advising on start-up and funding. The two unitary authorities lead the work of their EYDCPs, passing on NOF funding to individual clubs, while Walsall also provides development and capacity building support for the community organisations it funds through devolved budgets. Wyre Forest has completely transformed itself, from a traditional play service, into a development agency that delivers supervised provision only until it is able to get an independent successor up and running as a replacement.

Patterns of provision

The four case study areas show considerable contrasts in the pattern of provision. As far as play areas are concerned, the following patterns exist:

- *Bridgnorth:* evenly distributed, relative to geography and the distribution of children.

- *Wyre Forest:* almost entirely located in urban areas, with many in deprived areas with social housing. One quarter of children live in areas without a nearby play area.

- *Walsall:* evenly distributed, relative to geography and the distribution of children.

- *Coventry:* play areas are dispersed but the low level of provision means that several parts of the city are some way from an area.

As far as supervised play is concerned, the following patterns exist:

- *Bridgnorth:* widely dispersed provision, but much of it available for limited periods of time; more extensive provision is only available from a few sites.

- *Wyre Forest:* as with play areas, provision is concentrated almost exclusively in urban areas, ensuring provision is available in deprived areas.

- *Walsall:* provision is widely dispersed and evenly distributed, with no particular relationship between distribution and levels of deprivation.

- *Coventry:* provision is widely dispersed and reasonably evenly distributed, with many of both the least and most deprived areas appearing rather better served than communities 'in the middle'.

There are many factors which appear to be causing these differences, including:

- *Factors influencing all provision:* geography and population density; historical patterns; where decision-making resides; decisions about trade-offs between the quality, duration, charges and capacity; decisions about styles of provision (for supervised provision); external influences.

- *Factors influencing council-funded provision:* whether there is a strategy for 'targeting' areas of high social need; whether there is a strategy for maximising 'geographic access'; political constraints.

- *Factors influencing independent provision:* community capacity; development support.

In recent years, two of the authorities have implemented major, plan-led changes to their pattern of provision. It is, however, not clear to what extent local authorities or independent providers, when faced with these many influences, have the capacity to alter patterns of provision, through review and decision-making, rather than unplanned evolution.

Inclusion and Targeting

The study sought information from the case study authorities on their policies for including specific groups of disadvantaged children. Children with disabilities or special needs are supported in all four local authorities, while there are specific policies for low income children in two areas and policies in one authority each for children who are asylum seekers, homeless, travellers or looked after by the local authority. In addition to group-specific policies three of the authorities commented that their geographic targeting of areas of high deprivation was intended to help many of the groups discussed. Dividing between social needs and health-related special needs, a series of comments can be made:

Social needs
All the case study authorities have policies in place to improve the inclusion of disadvantaged children. In three cases these policies focus on where provision is sited, with funding allocations and the selection of individual sites taking deprivation into account. Two of the authorities operate a discount system for people with low incomes, while another has a referrals programme which offers automatic places to children on the at-risk register, and children in homeless or asylum seeker families.

Special needs
Provision is available for children with disabilities or learning and behavioural difficulties in all four areas. In three of the areas there is local authority-funded provision, and in two local authority delivered provision (elsewhere there are voluntary sector services). These two local authorities have programmes which integrate children with special needs into mainstream provision, by allocating them specially trained playworkers.

Playworkers

In three of the four authorities there appeared to be a fairly even split between workers in council and independent provision. In Walsall all workers were in independent provision. Our estimates for year-round workers in the four authorities are: Wyre Forest and Bridgnorth – 35; Walsall and Coventry – 150 to 250. In all cases workers are part time, but as hours worked vary hugely it is not possible to make comparisons between authorities.

Although the response rate from individual play settings was patchy, it was clear from the information we collected that relatively few settings meet the ideal of having at least one qualified playworker. In the three local authorities which provide services, all workers receive some level of training, although in only one authority are all workers expected to have a playwork NVQ. In two of the authorities there are a handful of people with NVQ3s. Limited information was available about the level of training of workers in independent provision, although there are some qualified playworkers in each area.

All the local authorities identified recruitment, retention and training issues as key challenges for improving play provision. Meanwhile, in all the areas, term-time recruitment is difficult both for local authorities and independent providers, because of short, awkward working hours and low pay. Approaches to resolving problems include: creating packages of work at several sites of provision; introducing flexible rotas; and offering competitive pay. For independent providers, the most significant challenge is meeting training needs, with many lacking the capacity to train staff themselves. In the two urban authorities this problem is being addressed through free training from EYDCPs (although levels of take-up was uncertain) while one of the districts has an 'artplay' training programme for potential workers. For local authorities retention is something of a problem, with trained workers moving onto new careers or into independent provision (although in the latter case often staying in the local pool of trained workers).

Financial patterns

Overall local authority spending patterns were as follows:

- ***Play Areas:*** Wyre Forest and Walsall spend similar amounts per child (around £2.70) while Bridgnorth spends half this amount, and Coventry half as much again. In the urban areas variations in spending in part mirror the significant variations in the number of play areas in the two authorities. In the two districts the local authority is not the main funder of play areas.

- ***Supervised Play Provision:*** the two district councils spend considerably less per child than the metropolitan authorities, but Coventry also spends twice as much as Walsall (Wyre Forest £4.10; Bridgnorth £6.80; Walsall £16; Coventry £30). There is some relationship between authorities' spending and the number of play provision settings each operates. But other factors which influence variations in spending are the duration and style of provision.

It should also be noted that the information on supervised play spending was supplied on a different basis by the districts and the metropolitan authorities (the districts' costs are for direct delivery expenses, while the metropolitan authorities also include officer salary and core costs).

NOF- and voluntary sector-funding is available in all the local authorities areas but data on this was not available; neither was information available on the amount raised in charges in each area.

Planning, review and evaluation

The case studies reported different approaches to planning, review and evaluation:

Planning
Within the local authorities the main focus is on 'service-level' planning, with little ongoing co-ordination between departments. Joint planning takes place in response to external pressures (e.g. NOF funding bids) while organisations outside the local authorities have little involvement in planning processes. In recent years the two districts have both implemented plan-based changes in the pattern of their provision, while there have been few major shifts in the urban areas. All the authorities are in a new phase of strategy development. Only in Walsall was this specifically focused on play (elsewhere the focus was on cultural strategy development or Children's Fund bid preparation).

It was pleasing to note that Walsall's decision to embark on play-focused planning was taken as a result of the launch of Better Play and our invitation for them to participate in the research.

Best Value Reviews

In the rural districts, Best Value Reviews are not scheduled to cover play provision for some time. In both urban areas, reviews have been undertaken – in one, a cross-cutting review of all services for children; in the other, supervised provision delivered by Community Education being reviewed alone.

Evaluation and performance

Two of the councils have internal quality assurance programmes. The other two councils measure performance using indicators, although these only measure level of use.

Inspection

In all areas a surprisingly low level of provision is registered as childcare under the Ofsted inspection regime. In Wyre Forest the council had recently registered its provision, in part to set a positive example, while some of Coventry's clubs have registered so parents can claim WFTC. In Walsall the council is encouraging all funded bodies to register.

Conclusions

The case study phase of the study highlights the diversity of practice in both the delivery of play provision and in professional structures and processes.

In terms of equal provision, while there are play areas and childcare-based play settings in all the areas, in most respects there is considerable variation between the authorities. They have different approaches to the quantity, geographic distribution and style of provision. To some extent these variations are linked to the characteristics of the authorities, but the clear contrasts between Coventry and Walsall, and between Wyre Forest and Bridgnorth, indicate that factors such as history and local priorities are also important.

In terms of professional structures each of the four local authorities has a different approach, with only Wyre Forest having a dedicated play service. Both the metropolitan authorities present interesting – although possibly unusual – models, Coventry because of its diverse styles of provision and fragmented management, Walsall because of the devolution of responsibility for delivery. While all have planning and review processes covering play delivery, only Walsall has taken a cross-cutting approach (with both a Best Value Review of all services for children, and plans to develop a play strategy). A key finding from the study was that both the districts had implemented major, plan-led changes to their provision in recent years.

There are several important questions arising from the case studies which could merit further work:

- What relationship should there be between play and other out-of-school-hours priorities and forms of provision? In all the authorities designated 'play provision', and non-directed play within all types of provision, had to co-exist with alternatives. Policy makers need to resolve what status play should have within out-of-school provision in general.

- How can play provision and other out-of-school services resolve their human resources issues? The case studies revealed significant challenges relating to the status, pay, recruitment, and training of playworkers.

- Should local authorities transform themselves, at least in part, from delivers of play provision into development agencies? If so, how should they go about this, and what support might they need from external bodies, including the government?

INTRODUCTION

AIMS AND OBJECTIVES

This report presents the results of a three-layered mapping project, which explored how local authorities plan and deliver play opportunities for children aged between 5 and 16 years old.

The main objective of the study was to collect and analyse data regarding the patterns of current provision and the policies and strategies that local authorities are following in making decisions about such provision.

This remit was largely factual, but we have also provided some commentary on why the considerable variations in provision exist and identified some of the possible policy issues arising. Similarly, where possible, we have commented on the extent to which current provision matches need.

Finally, an additional aim of the work was to advise on how our mapping work could be replicated for other areas of the country.

APPROACH

The study was divided into three parts:

1. *The national picture* – an overview of the structures and written documents that local authorities have in place for developing play provision

2. *The regional picture: the West Midlands* – a more detailed look at the characteristics of the provision, structures and plans within the region.

3. *Local authority case studies* – an in-depth study of the planning and provision of play in four local authorities within the West Midlands, including analysis of needs and the distribution of provision at sub-local authority level.

The national and regional pictures were obtained via questionnaires, with the national questionnaire being completed by regional representatives and the regional questionnaire being completed by local authority representatives.

The case studies were undertaken via face-to-face interviews. In addition, data on individual play services in the four case study authorities was collated and transferred onto geographic maps of their locality.

The research was carried out in the summer and autumn of 2001. All findings are snapshots from this period, with information either referring to the situation prevailing at the time of the survey, or where applicable to the 2001/02 financial year.

SCOPE AND DEFINITIONS

Children

This study focuses on the play needs of children of statutory school-age in England, that is between 5 and 16 years of age.

Play

For the purpose of this study, 'play' has been defined as the activities which, for children, are freely chosen, personally directed and intrinsically motivated, taking place with or without adult involvement. Children and young people of all ages 'play'. As they get older the words they use to describe their activities change and they tend to use terms which describe specific activities rather than the generic term 'play'.

This understanding of 'play' means there can be problems determining its scope. Many parts of children's leisure time, including sport-like games, cultural experiences and learning-related activities can all be 'play' if they fulfil the criteria set out above. So while participation in organised sport with clearly defined external rules, or membership of a youth orchestra, are self-evidently not play, there is a wide middle ground where it is open to question whether actions are freely-chosen and self-motivated. These activities are only play when children are largely free from the direction of adults, so they can decide for themselves how to proceed. Exactly how much adult intervention is acceptable, however, tends to be a subjective judgement.

Play provision
There are difficulties with defining 'play provision'. The obvious approach is to describe play provision as any setting where play – as it is defined here – is the main or intended activity. So if a setting enables children to act freely, without excessive direction, but in a reasonably stimulating environment, it can be described as play provision.

For unsupervised play areas, this definition is unproblematic. But the story is different for supervised provision – at least in the context of a high-level mapping exercise. As the aim of the study was to map play planning and provision without becoming immersed in the details of individual settings it was impossible to use a definition that requires observation of the experiences of individual children.

We identified no entirely satisfactory alternative means of determining what should count as play provision. Ultimately, we decided that any out-of-school provision could potentially count as play provision, and beyond this we relied on the judgement of respondents as to which provision offered opportunities for play (for more details see box).

How to define 'Play Provision' – The Issues

As we were not visiting individual play provision settings we needed to avoid a definition of 'play provision' which was based on observations of the experiences of children. As an alternative we attempted to identify features of play provision which would distinguish it from other out-of-school services, that could be measured without visiting individual settings. There were several possible characteristics, but we reviewed these and concluded that none was entirely adequate.

Traditionally, play professionals have distinguished 'open access' play provision where children are able to come and go freely, from childcare, where they are registered and staff act *in loco parentis*. We concluded that this is not a helpful distinction. Firstly we reject the idea that children can *only* play freely in settings where they can come and go. Furthermore most self-styled play provision, delivered by playwork professionals, is delivered on a childcare basis. If we had only set out to measure the extent to which open access provision was available, we would have found very little to map.

Beyond this distinction, there are several possible indicators that could be used to judge whether settings enable non-directed play. These include:

- *Nomenclature:* is the setting described as 'play' provision?

- *Organisation:* is the setting delivered by a 'play service', 'play association' or similar?

- *Policy:* does the setting have explicit policies for promoting non-directed play (which presumably feed into the ethos of the setting and the practice of employees)?

- *Employees:* are employees trained and qualified playworkers (with understanding and experience of promoting non-directed play)?

We had a number of concerns about using any of the four as proxies for measuring play provision: (1) As terminology, structures and practice vary between local authorities we would not be able to map consistently between areas; (2) We would inevitably include provision that did not offer non-directed play (especially when being guided by nomenclature or organisation boundaries); (3) We would also exclude provision where there is non-directed play (e.g. activity-specific provision, often for older children; recently established settings styled as after-school clubs or childcare, where there is considerable scope for play). We consider that the latter two issues are particularly significant because of the rapid development of out-of-school provision in recent years. At local level, external policy pressures and the availability of funding can have one of two (contrasting) impacts: firstly some existing 'play' provision may now have limited scope for play and instead aim to fulfil childcare, study support or cultural development objectives; and secondly settings that are established as study supported clubs, childcare etc. may actually choose focus on play.

In the future it may well be possible to cut through these definition problems, through the use of play-orientated quality standards. If programmes such as Quality in Play[1] are widely adopted, 'play provision' could simply be defined as settings which are accredited or working towards accreditation. Such a situation is someway off, both because quality standards schemes are not in wide use, but also because play professionals estimate that only a tiny minority of self-styled 'play' settings would meet these schemes' requirements for enabling non-directed play.

After reviewing these issues we decided to use a broad definition of play provision, which was largely reliant on the existing practice and views of the local authorities supplying us with information. We concluded that any out-of-school setting could potentially be included, and beyond this we would collect information about services which were *perceived* by local authorities to be play provision. This approach has many of the shortcomings associated with the measuring provision using the individual indicators discussed above (not least that play provision is viewed differently in each area), but we felt that, in the absence of a robust alternative, our approach had two key advantages: (1) the information is straightforward to collect; (2) relying on local perceptions is more accurate than the alternative of developing unresponsive indicators, that take no account of local conditions.

---

[1] A play-specific variant of PQASSO, promoted by London Play.

Glossary of terms

Unsupervised play areas – the provision of open spaces and play areas which are open without permanent staffing. Play areas usually have play equipment, but this is not essential (e.g. skate parks).

Supervised play provision – play provision where children remain under the supervision of employees. Examples include adventure playgrounds, term time clubs (e.g. after-school clubs, children's clubs), holiday play schemes and play buses.

Setting – a term to describe all possible locations for supervised play provision.

Childcare – any out-of-school hours setting where children are under the supervision of employees *in loco parentis*. In our opinion, the majority of supervised play provision is also childcare of one sort or another.

Play Policies – documents which set out what children and parents can expect from local play provision (i.e. description of entitlement; codes of practice etc).

Play strategies or plans – documents which set out plans for the future development of play provision.

Best Value – the statutory process through which all local government services are subject to internal and external review and audit.

EYDCPs – Early Years Development and Childcare Partnerships, which lead the work of developing out-of-school provision for children within counties and unitary authorities.

Urban and Rural – these terms can be used very differently depending on context (e.g. whether a single ward or a whole local authority is being discussed; the settlement patterns of surrounding areas). But, throughout, when local authorities are described as urban or rural this is based on the Countryside Agency's official designation of rural authorities.

Average (Median) – the mid-point in any distribution of values (e.g. if nine authorities are ranked by the amount they spend in play, the fifth is the median authority).

PART 1: THE NATIONAL PICTURE

1.1. OBJECTIVES

The aim of Part 1 of the study was to establish an overview of planning and support for play in local authorities in England via an approach to regional play bodies.

The objective was to establish which local authorities have:
- Dedicated play services or officers.
- Written policies or strategies for play.[1]
- Local play associations or networks.[2]

This part of the project was intended to provide an overview of activity in each region. Rather than contacting local authorities directly, playwork specialists in each English region were asked to supply information about councils' work using their direct knowledge or close contacts. This approach meant there were inevitably gaps in the data collected, because the regional bodies were unlikely to have detailed information of every authority in their area. But given the knowledge and commitment of the playwork specialists, the assumption was that the information that *was* gathered would provide a useful snapshot of the known 'minimum' level of activity taking place in each region.

1.2. SURVEY RESPONSE

Contact was made with playwork specialists in all English regions (National Centres and Regional Councils for Playwork Education, and one regional play association). In all regions the playwork specialists attempted to collect information, either using existing knowledge or through approaching contacts at regional play events. In two cases (North West and East of England), however, the regional contact was only able to supply very little information. Among the other seven regions, the response rate was good in two regions and acceptable in the other five.

As Table 1.1 shows, information was received concerning 167 out of 367 local authorities, across all regions of England. Of these local authorities, 87 have education and social services responsibilities (71 unitary authorities;[3] 16 county councils). The remaining 61 authorities were district councils.

Table 1.1: Number of English local authorities for which information was provided, by type of authority				
	Unitary authorities	County councils	District Councils	Total
Number of local authorities	71	16	80	167
As a % of all local authorities	62%	47%	33%	43%

Information was supplied for 43 per cent of local authorities including 59 per cent of authorities with education and social services responsibilities. The response rate was variable between

---

[1] We also asked (1) what sorts of play were covered by these documents and (2) which local authority service or department was responsible for producing the documents.

[2] With an additional question about the activities of these play associations

[3] Unitary authorities include metropolitan borough councils, London boroughs and unitary authorities in former shire areas.

regions, with information for close to 100 per cent of authorities available in two regions and virtually no information available in a further two.

Table 1.2: Number of local authorities for which information was provided, by region										
	East	East Midlands	London	North East	North West	South East	South West	West Midlands	Yorkshire & Humberside	Total
Number of local authorities	3	21	31	15	3	19	44	22	9	167
As a % of all local authorities	5%	47%	94%	60%	7%	26%	86%	58%	43%	43%

We consider this rate of response to be satisfactory given the region-level methodology. As the data was supplied by intermediaries who did not necessarily have a relationship with individual local authorities, it is possible that there are some errors in the information reported. But we expect that these are fairly minor, as contributors tended to supply no information when they were unsure about the answers to questions (the information supplied concerning individual authorities often covered only some of the questions). Regional contacts were more likely to have information about local authorities with a reasonable level of play activity, so the results should not be considered representative for all authorities (play practitioners tend to know about authorities where there is activity, but often have no available information about areas where there is no activity). But at the very least the results show the *minimum* number of local authorities where activity takes place.

1.3. FINDINGS

Overview

Key findings for local authorities for which information was available:

- In 117 out of 167, an independent play network or association operates.
- 67 out of 159 have dedicated play officers and 54 out of 158 have play services.
- 52 out of 141 have a play policy and 56 out of 133 have plans or strategies for developing play.

Table 1.3 breaks these figures down by types of local authority, with the columns giving the number of local authorities with a play officer, a play service, a policy document, a planning document and a known representative play organisation. The percentages show the proportion of local authorities which have each (where the percentages are out of those authorities for which information was provided *for that question*[1]).

---

[1] Note, in all cases where percentages are discussed, the denominator is the number of local authorities about which information is available for the question under discussion. Asterisks replace percentages where the sample size is very small.

Table 1.3: Local authorities with play officers, play services, play policies, play development plans, and representative play organisations										
	Officer		Service		Policy		Plan		Play organisation[1]
Unitary authority	48	(70%)	40	(59%)	33	(55%)	33	(58%)	50
County council	2	(*)	2	(*)	2	(*)	2	(*)	8
District council	17	(23%)	12	(16%)	17	(25%)	21	(33%)	59
Total	**67**	**(42%)**	**54**	**(34%)**	**52**	**(37%)**	**56**	**(42%)**	**117**

[1] No data was collected except where play organisations were known.

Table 1.4 provides the same information broken down by region.

Table 1.4: Local authorities with play officers, play services, play policies, play development plans, and representative play organisations										
	Officer		Service		Policy		Plan		Play organisation[2]
East of England	1	(*)	0	(*)	1	(*)	1	(*)	0
East Midlands	6	(35%)	4	(24%)	6	(43%)	5	(38%)	18
London	22	(71%)	21	(70%)	15	(52%)	16	(59%)	21
North East	7	(50%)	6	(43%)	1	(25%)	3	(75%)	6
North West	2	(*)	2	(*)	1	(*)	2	(*)	3
South East	6	(33%)	4	(22%)	8	(44%)	11	(61%)	16
South West	13	(30%)	10	(23%)	11	(26%)	11	(29%)	38
West Midlands	6	(27%)	6	(27%)	6	(27%)	4	(18%)	8
Yorkshire and Humberside	4	(50%)	1	(13%)	3	(43%)	3	(50%)	7
Total	**67**	**(42%)**	**54**	**(34%)**	**52**	**(37%)**	**56**	**(42%)**	**117**

[1] No data was collected except where play organisations were known.

Play Services and Officers

Half of authorities for which information was provided have either a play officer or a play service. While it is encouraging that there are local government officers with specific responsibilities for play in many parts of the country, it is concerning that there are no officers with strategic responsibility for play in so many other local authorities.

Further details from the survey:

- 67 out of 159 authorities were reported to have a dedicated play officer, including a significant share of authorities in each region (between a quarter and a half of authorities, except in London where over two thirds of authorities have play officers). A clear majority of unitary authorities have officers, while they are not nearly so common in either district or county councils.

- 54 out of 158 authorities were reported to have play services. Services are found in all regions and it is again much more common for unitary authorities to have them.

- 45 out of 159 authorities were reported to have both a play service and a play officer, 22 have only a play officer and 9 only a play service. This means that 76 authorities have one or the other (i.e. 48% of local authorities about which information was provided).

Play Policies and Strategies

Half of authorities for which information was provided have either play policies or plans for the development of play. While it is encouraging that these strategic documents exist in many parts of the country, it is concerning that there are no written outputs from play planning and policy development in so many other local authorities.

- 52 out of 141 authorities were reported to have play policy documents, including half of unitary authorities. In London, the South East and the East Midlands over 40 per cent authorities had policies, while one quarter did in the South West and the West Midlands.

- 56 out of 133 local authorities were reported to have plans or strategies for developing play opportunities, again with half of unitary authorities having such a document.

- 69 out of 141 local authorities have either a play policy or a play plan/strategy. 39 have both, while 30 have only one or the other.

Even though play areas and supervised play provision are usually managed separately, half of the documents cover both subjects:

- 58 out of 141 local authorities have policy documents or plans covering supervised play, 42 have documents covering parks and open spaces and 37 have documents covering unsupervised play areas. The documents of 29 of the local authorities cover all three subjects, while 13 local authorities cover two subjects and 24 just one.

Around four out of five local authorities with strategic written documents for play also have a play officer:

- 41 out of 52 authorities with play policies also have a play officer, and 41 out of 56 authorities with play plans or strategies have a play officer.

But, in contrast to this, the survey suggests that the department or service which takes the lead in preparing plans or policies, is in the majority of cases, the leisure department or a related service, *but not* the specialist play service:

- Only 9 play services (out of the 54) were named as the service leading the preparation of documents, suggesting that play services themselves may have only limited influence within local authorities.

- Information on the department(s) leading the writing of policies and plans – available for 67 out of the 69 local authorities where documents were reported to exist – showed a great diversity of practice.[1]

---

[1] But it should be noted that different authorities mentioned different tiers of operation (e.g. education departments as opposed to community education services) so it is inappropriate to make direct comparisons. The total number of services in the list is greater than 67, because in some cases more than one service or department was mentioned. Where one is clearly a sub-division of another, the more senior tier has been excluded, but if two autonomous units have worked in co-operation, both are listed.

Table 1.5: Number of local authorities mentioning a department/service taking the lead in preparing play policies/strategies[1] (n=67)	
Department or Service	*No. of authorities*
Leisure	33
Education	11
Play Service	9
Sport	5
Community Services	4
Children, Young People, Early Years	3
Parks and Open Spaces	2
Regeneration	2
Social Services	2
Community Education	1
Planning	1
Libraries	1
Arts	1
Partnership or independent organisation	*No. of authorities*
Voluntary organisation	6
EYDCP	2

[1] Where nomenclature varies from that used here but functions are likely to be identical, services/departments have been included in this table, under the appropriate heading.

Play Associations and Networks

Between half and two thirds of local authorities have either a play association or network operating within their area:

- Associations or networks supporting play are reported as operating in 117 out of 167 local authorities. In some areas more than one organisation operates, while in others a single organisation covers several authorities (e.g. a county-wide association). In addition, organisations are currently in the process of being set up in four authorities, and in one the local forum is said to be 'dormant'.

- Most of the organisations deliver support, while under half are themselves providers of play. In 98 of the 117 authorities with organisations they promote networking; in 91 they provide information; in 79 they deliver training; while in only 47 do they act as service providers.

- Some of the organisations mentioned have a remit beyond play. For example, some respondents referred to childcare and out-of-school hours groups. But in 85 of the local authorities, there is at least one organisation which has 'play' in its title (35 unitary authorities; 44 district councils; 6 county councils).

1.4.   CONCLUSIONS

The survey suggests that there are a very large number of authorities with no strategic approach to children's play. Around half of authorities, for which information was available, have neither specialist play employees or strategic documents for play. But despite this it is still encouraging that a significant number of local authorities *of all types* and *in all regions* take play provision sufficiently seriously to maintain play officers or play services and to develop play policy documents and play development plans.

The evidence shows that play is more likely to receive significant attention in unitary, urban councils. Notwithstanding this, many rural and semi-rural councils do have employees and planning processes for play, usually based in leisure departments.

We would make two policy-related observations from this evidence:

- There are no local authorities which can sensibly say that 'play isn't for us', because the evidence shows similar councils do take play seriously, whatever their powers or geographic and socio-economic conditions.

- There is a good 'base' of activity in all parts of England from which to build, if policy makers wish to encourage more councils to develop professional structures for the delivery of play. For example, there should be ample scope for sharing good practice and introducing benchmarking.

The number of areas where independent play networks and associations are reported to operate is encouragingly high. A priority for further work should be to investigate the capacity of these organisations to support the development of play, and to assess what resources they need to improve their performance.

The discrepancy between the encouraging number of play services and their low level of involvement in leading preparation plans and policies suggests planning may sometimes take place 'over the heads' of play professionals.

PART 2: THE REGIONAL PICTURE – THE WEST MIDLANDS

2.1. OBJECTIVES

Part 2 of the study collected detailed information about the planning and provision of play from local authorities in the West Midlands region. Information was collected through a questionnaire, which was first piloted on five authorities and then distributed to the remaining 29 unitary and lower tier authorities.

The West Midlands region was chosen because it has both urban and rural areas, and significant pockets of affluence and deprivation. It was felt that it is the region which is most likely to represent conditions across England.

The main objectives of this part of the study were to assemble detailed information about individual local authorities, and to identify patterns and variations across authorities. An additional objective was to provide advice on how to replicate such a data collation exercise in other regions (see Appendix C).

The research aimed to identify patterns in planning and delivering play provision across authorities in the region. In particular, it set out to:

- Report divergences in levels of provision and spending; and identify patterns which might explain differences.

- Identify the main organisational models used by local authorities to plan and deliver play opportunities; assess the extent to which local authorities work in partnership with others; and measure the penetration of government programmes.

- Measure how many authorities have policies and plans for play provision, and assess how these vary; and report the impact of the best value regime for play provision.

Data Sought For Each Local Authority

Provision

- Unsupervised play areas – How many areas are there? How much is spent on them each year?
- Supervised play areas – What types of provision are available? How many of each type are there? How much is spent on them each year?
- Resources projects – Are there any play resources projects? How much is spent on them each year?

Partners and structures

- Which are the key services within the local authority involved in play provision?
- Which partners from outside the local authority are involved in play provision? Is there a local play association or network?
- Do central government programmes support any local play provision?

Planning and Review

- Does the local authority have a play policy, play strategy or any other plans for play? What do these documents cover? Who was involved with writing and implementing them?
- How has the local authority's planning for play fitted into the Best Value process? Which Best Value Reviews cover children's play? Have indicators and targets been adopted for play? Who is being consulted about the development of play provision?

2.2. SURVEY RESPONSE

Thirty-four local authorities were approached and asked to complete the questionnaire. Including five pilot authorities, 16 completed the questionnaire (47%): 12 of the 21 district councils (57%) and 4 of the 10 unitary authorities (40%).

A 50 per cent response rate for a detailed questionnaire was considered to be a satisfactory outcome, and was only achieved through considerable planning and effort. Appropriate officers were telephoned for all authorities. In the conversations, we ensured that we were talking to the right person, explained the purpose and nature of the questionnaire, and gave them an estimate of how long it would take them to complete. Only 2 of the 34 authorities refused to participate at this point. With the remainder, we agreed deadlines for returning the questionnaires, and in the cases when these were not kept, subsequently chased up participants and set alternative deadlines, before the need to draft this report terminated further chasing. The positions held by the people who responded were diverse. Four were play officers, and three community leisure officers. Other respondents worked in parks, leisure, early years or community education services. Full details are listed in Appendix A.

2.3. FINDINGS

The detailed results for each local authority are provided in Appendix A.

Summary Of Findings

Key findings from the survey of 16 West Midlands authorities, with results presented in each case for the typical, mid-range authority (the median):

- The median authority has one play area for every 370 children aged between 5 and 16 and spends about £4 per child on ***unsupervised play***.

- While both levels of spending and number of play areas vary considerably, the two do not always go hand-in-hand. Rather, some higher spending authorities have relatively few, well-funded play areas, and some lower spending authorities have relatively numerous, less well-funded areas.

- Within the median local authority there is one ***supervised play*** project for every 630 children, while the median council spends about £5.20 per child. Not withstanding some discrepancies in reporting, there are large variations in the quantity and characteristics of play provision funded by different local authorities. The highest spending unitary authority spends ten times as much as the lowest, and the highest spending district council also spends more than ten times as much as the lowest.

- Dedicated play officers or services are responsible for supervised play provision in only one third of cases.

- Only five local authorities have policies or plans dedicated to play (some cover play areas only). A further three are currently preparing a play policy or plan for the first time. These results are similar to those for Part 1.

- While play is mentioned in the Best Value Performance Plans of two thirds of the authorities, only four had yet completed any Best Value Reviews covering any dimension of play. Only two planned to conduct cross-cutting reviews of services for children.

- Almost all authorities reported consulting both children and parents in developing play provision.

Play Areas

Local authorities were asked to supply information about all local play areas, both those they funded and independent provision. All 16 authorities provided information about local authority funded areas. In three cases the authorities were unable to give any details of independent provision. In a further five cases the local authority stated that it was the only local provider of play areas.

Table 2.1: Provision of play areas by all organisations, reported by local authorities				
All provision				
	Average	Median	Minimum	Maximum
Number of known play areas	53	39	15	150
Number of children per play area	470	370	170	1,600

Table 2.2: Provision and spending on local authority play areas				
Local authority provision only				
	Average	Median	Minimum	Maximum
Spending by local authority	£73,000	£63,000	£3,000	£200,000
Spending per child by local authority[1]	£4.05	£4.00	£1.70	£7.50
Spending per local authority play area	£2,000	£1,600	£640	£6,500

[1] This row excludes local authorities which are not the main providers of play areas (i.e. Bridgnorth, South Staffordshire, Staffordshire Moorlands, and Wyre Forest).

The council is the only declared provider of play areas in eight of the 16 authorities. In four others, the local authority manages at least twice as many play areas as independent organisations. In four rural district councils, however, the local authority manages under half of the play areas with the other providers usually being parish councils or registered social landlords (often managing former local authority housing).

Among local authorities where most play areas are council-funded there are three important variations in the pattern of provision:

- *Number of children per play area*. There is considerable variation in the ratio of play areas to children aged 5 to 16. When the play areas of all providers are included in the calculations, the authority with the most provision has ten times as many play areas per child as that with the least.

- *Spending per child*. For the 12 local authorities which provide two thirds or more of local play areas, spending per child on local authority play areas is close to five times greater in the highest spending area, compared to the lowest.

- *Spending per local authority play area*. There is also considerable variation in spending on local authority play areas. The highest expenditure per local authority play area is ten times as much as the lowest.

This significant variation in councils' levels of spending per play area is an important finding, which poses two interesting questions. Firstly, what accounts for these variations – levels of staffing, maintenance, capital investment? Secondly, what impact do these variations have for the quality of children's experiences? Both these issues would merit further investigation.

Comparing these variations shows that authorities which spend similar amounts per child may have very different patterns of provision. While both levels of spending and number of play areas vary considerably, the two do not always go hand-in-hand. Rather, some higher spending authorities have relatively few, well-funded play areas, and some lower spending authorities have relatively numerous, under-funded areas. Table 2.3 divides the sample local authorities into four clear 'types':

1. *Few play areas, each with high funding,* resulting in high/medium spending per child.
2. *Few play areas, each with low/medium funding,* resulting in low spending per child.
3. *Many play areas, each with low funding,* resulting in low spending per child.
4. *Many play areas, each with medium funding,* resulting in high spending per child.

Table 2.3: Types of approaches to play area provision, comparing child population, number of play areas and spending – <u>local authority funded provision only</u>[1]					
'Type'	*Type of local authority*	*Child population*	*Play areas relative to number of children*	*Spending per play area*	*Spending per child*
1	Urban met.	50,000	Very few	Very high	Medium
1	Urban district	19,000	Few	High	Medium
1	Rural district	16,000	Few	High	High
1	Rural district	10,000	Few/Medium	High	High
2	Urban unitary	39,000	Few	Medium	Low
2	Urban district	13,000	Few	Low	Low
2	Urban met.	42,000	Few	Medium	Low
3	Urban district	19,000	Many	Low	Low
3	Rural district	6,000	Many	Low	Low
4	Rural district	17,000	Many	Medium	High
4	Urban district	19,000	Many	Medium	Very high
4	Urban district	26,000	Very many	Medium	Very high

[1]This table only includes local authorities which are the main providers of play areas and excludes the four authorities which are not the main providers of play areas.

Play areas relative to number of children – Few: >400 children/area; Many: <300 children/area.

Spending per play area – Low: <£1,000 per area; High: >£1,900 per area.

Spending per child – Low: <£3 per child; High: >£4.50 per child.

Without further information it is inappropriate to speculate too much about the reasons for these variations. It is likely, however, that they result from a combination of differences in geographical characteristics, historical legacies and political priorities. Political decisions are likely to influence the overall level of spending per child. But decisions about concentrating resources among few play areas, as opposed to spreading them more thinly between many, are also likely to be influenced by the distribution of parks, open spaces and other suitable sites, the historical pattern of provision and by the density of the population in the main settlements of each local authority.

It was beyond the scope of this study to assess what impact these varying approaches have on children's experience of play. This is obviously an area where further investigation would be helpful.

Whatever the reasons, this analysis shows that local authorities do have clear alternatives in thinking about how to develop their unsupervised play provision. It would be interesting to explore further the extent to which the alternatives are deliberately chosen and what factors influence councils' decisions.

Supervised Play Provision

Interpretation of data for supervised play provision needs to be approached with some caution, partly because of variation in the quality of responses from local authorities, but more fundamentally because the characteristics of 'supervised play provision' make quantification and comparison difficult (see box for details).

Supervised Play Provision: Data Limitations

There are a series of limitations to the numerical data collected for supervised play, which limit the extent to which the information is comparable. We consider, however, that the results assembled here do highlight important real variations in the extent and characteristics of supervised play provision – even though detailed quantitative comparison is inappropriate.

Limitations with counting supervised play projects: A simple count of the number of play provision settings may not reflect the true availability of provision because it does not allow for:

- Variations in the hours that projects are open (e.g. there is no differentiation between a term time club operating all week, and one that only runs once a week).

- Variations in the number of children that projects cater for. An area with many small play provision settings may appear to have better provision than an area with a few large projects. This gives an indication of the geographic spread of play provision, but it is likely to favour rural areas, compared to urban areas which may provide many more places, but from comparatively fewer locations.

Definitions of 'play': As discussed in the Introduction, we expect that somewhat different definitions of 'play' have been employed by different respondents. This is because out-of-school provision can perform a wide variety of functions and opinions will vary on whether settings have a primary focus on play or other objectives such as childcare, study support, sport or arts. In this respect, the names of services can be misleading.

Age limits: The survey asked about provision for all children over five. We consider it possible, however, that, given most people's association of 'play' with younger children, many respondents have focused on provision for children aged up to 11.

Limitations on local authority knowledge: While local authorities were able to provide us with information about their own provision, many respondents were unable to tell us about provision delivered by independent organisations, schools or county councils. Often the information reported only covers provision funded or delivered by the local authority. Throughout the discussion below, it is made clear whether we are discussing local authority-funded provision or all known provision.

Financial issues: three additional issues have implications for the financial analysis of provision:

- *Charging:* It is not possible to determine whether budgets are net or gross of any charges levied.

- *Part-funding:* When local authorities are not the only funder of services (e.g. when a grant is made to an independent provider) it is not appropriate to compare this spending *per play project* with wholly-funded provision.

- *Accounting practice:* For some local authorities the identified costs of play provision will be delivery expenses, while others will include administration, development and managers' salaries.[1]

---

[1] Our expectation is that this will inflate differences between high and low spending authorities (an authority which makes a few thousand pounds in grants is unlikely to include management and administration in this budget; an authority with a sizeable play service is likely to roll all costs together).

It is, in particular, worth noting that there is no way of systematically collecting comparable financial data for children's play provision. This is an issue policy makers and professional bodies may wish to address in future.

One of the local authorities did not provide any information about supervised play in the area. Seven only provided information about council-funded services, while a further four told us that the information about independent provision was incomplete. Four authorities believed they were supplying complete information.

Thirteen authorities were able to supply information about their spending on supervised play provision. None were able to supply us with information about spending by other providers.

Table 2.4: Delivery of supervised play by all providers, reported by all authorities (n=16)				
All provision				
	Average	Median (mid authority)	Minimum	Maximum
Number of local play projects (known to the local authority)	45	30	0[1]	132
Number of children per local play project (known to the local authority)	1,100	630	90	6,200[1]

[1] A local authority delivering no play provision itself, with no information on independent providers.
[2] A local authority reporting knowledge of only three play schemes in the area, all delivered by the council (the area with no provision is excluded).

The lack of respondents' knowledge of non-council activity is itself a key finding from the survey. It suggests that despite recent developments (e.g. the expansion of childcare and study support, the launch of EYDCPs, NOF consortium bids, cultural strategies and community planning) many local authorities are not well linked into wider out-of-school provision. The pattern was similar where local authorities have play officers or play documents. While two of the authorities which believed they knew of all local providers did have play officers and planning documents, there were four authorities with a play officer or a play document (and in one case both) which had no knowledge of other provision.

There is considerable variation in the reported level of provision available in district council areas, with a setting for every 200 children in three areas, but only a setting for every 1,000 children in four other districts. The four unitary authorities have similar reported levels of provision, with between 300 and 700 children per setting.

Interestingly, out of the four authorities which believed they were supplying complete information about local play facilities, three had very similar total levels of provision. Each reported that one play setting is shared by around 350 children. But there was a marked contrast in the split between local authority and independent provision, with the council funding 80 per cent of settings in one area and 40 per cent in another. The fourth local authority is a remote rural district, with a many more settings, relative to the population (with around 60 per cent council-funded).

As most local authorities report knowing of few independent providers, most of the variations in the level of reported provision result from contrasts in the amount of council-funded provision available. Information about council-funded provision is presented in Table 2.5.

Table 2.5: Delivery of council-funded supervised play				
Local authority funded provision only				
	Average	Median (mid authority)	Minimum	Maximum
Number of play projects (n=15)	35	23	0	110
Number of children per play project (n=15)	1,100	720	140	6,200
Spending by local authority (n=13)	£230,000	£78,000	£10,000	£1.5 million[1]
Local authority spending per child (n=13)	£7.20	£5.20	50p	£30[1]
Spending per local-authority funded project (n=13)	£4,400	£3,500	£800	£15,800

[1] Coventry – see Chapter Four for a full discussion of Coventry's approach to out-of-school provision for children (note, that the average reported is skewed by the authority's very high level of spending).

Spending per child is much greater in the two metropolitan boroughs than elsewhere, including the other two unitary authorities. Most other authorities spend between £3 and £7 per child, while one metropolitan authority spends £15 and the other £30. Factors influencing variations in spending include:

- ***The number of children per council-funded setting*** – in six out of 13 authorities there is a clear relationship between the amount spent and the number of settings available per head (neither of the high-spending metropolitan authorities, however, provide an untypical number of settings).

- ***Spending per setting*** – in seven of the 13 authorities there is a clear relationship between the amount the council spends per child and the amount spent per setting. One of the metropolitan authorities spends the most per setting by far. The considerable variations in spending are, at least in part, explained by the varying hours and numbers accommodated at different settings.

Looking at these various factors in combination shows that local authorities have adopted a wide range of approaches:

Table 2.6: Local authorities' approaches to supervised play, comparing child population, number of play settings and spending – local authority funded provision only – authorities are ranked by spending per child				
Type of local authority	**Child population**	**Play settings relative to number of children**	**Spending per play setting**	**Spending per child**
Urban met.	50,000	Many	High	High
Urban met.	42,000	Many	High	High
Urban district	13,000	Few	High	High
Rural district	7,000	Many	Low	Medium
Urban unitary	39,000	Many	Medium	Medium
Urban district	19,000	Medium	Medium	Medium
Urban district	19,000	Few	High	Medium
Rural district	14,000	Few	Medium	Medium
Rural district	10,000	Many	Low	Low
Urban unitary	26,000	Many	Low	Low
Rural district	16,000	Few	Low	Low
Rural district	17,000	Few	Low	Low
Urban district	19,000	Very few	Medium	Low

Play settings relative to number of children – Few: >800 children/setting; Many: <700 children/setting

Spending per play setting – Low: <£2,000 per area; High: >£7,500 per area

Spending per child – Low: <£4 per child; High: >£9 per child

Findings for different types of supervised play provision are presented below:

Adventure playgrounds

Four of the 16 local authorities reported adventure playgrounds operating locally. In three cases these were local authority-funded, while in the fourth it was independent. A fifth authority had play centres, which they characterised as 'indoor adventure playgrounds'. Interestingly these five authorities are quite different from one other. Four are urban authorities (one metropolitan, one unitary, and two districts) and one is a rural district.

Term time clubs

Six local authorities reported that they were unable to say how many clubs existed. Of the remaining ten, an average of 35 term time clubs were known to each. The maximum number of known clubs was 88 and the minimum one. In seven of the ten authorities there are between 150 and 750 children per setting, while in the other three authorities reported term time provision is extremely scarce, relative to the number of children.

'After-school clubs' were reported in eight of these authorities, 'junior youth clubs' in eight, with both being present in six. Nine councils reported funding some term time provision themselves, with the average number of clubs funded by these local authorities being 23, the maximum 66 and the minimum four.

Holiday play schemes

Authorities had relatively good information on the numbers of holiday play schemes operating, mainly because they were more likely to deliver holiday schemes themselves. Only one authority was unable to provide any information on play schemes (it delivers none itself). Among the remaining 15, the median authority is aware of 19 schemes in the area. The maximum was 49 and the minimum three. There are less than 1,000 children per setting in only five local authorities, and between 1,000 and 1,750 children per setting in a further eight. The median authority funded 18 schemes.

Other provision

Six authorities reported that play buses or other mobile services operate in the area (four rural districts and two metropolitan authorities). One district has six mobile projects. Three authorities reported that a children's farm or urban farm operated (two rural districts and one urban metropolitan authority). Six authorities were aware of projects in the area for disabled children or those with other special needs.

Play Resources Projects

Play resources projects provide facilities to play providers or families to assist them in enriching children's experience of play (examples include toy libraries and scrap stores).

Under half the authorities have any sort of play resources project, with nine of the 16 reporting that no known projects exist in the area. One or more project operates in seven of the local authorities' areas. There are toy libraries in five areas, with other projects mentioned, including scrap stores, equipment loan schemes and bulk buy schemes. Three of the authorities reported providing funding for such projects.

Policies and Plans

All 16 authorities were able to provide some information about their policies and strategic plans relating to children's play.

Table 2.7: Local authorities with policies and plans for play (n=16)		
	Exists	Doesn't exist, but in preparation
Play plan and/or play policy	5	3
Play policy	4	2
Play plan/strategy	3	5
Neither plan or play policy	11	8
No specific play document, but other documents covering play	4	4
No documents covering play	7	1

A minority of authorities have current play policies or plans: five have either a play policy or strategy, while a further three are preparing one or the other (as Table 2.7 indicates, authorities are likely to have both a plan and strategy if they have either). Some of these documents cover only play areas or only supervised play. Other authorities cover play in documents such as Cultural Strategies, Early Years Strategies and Local Plans/Unitary Development Plans, although it was not possible to assess how fully play is dealt with in these cases.

In four authorities documents set out plans or policies for the training of playworkers, while two authorities set out plans for recruitment. Four authorities reported that their documents set out specific policies for targeting particular groups of children (e.g. children in low income families; children with disabilities or special needs; looked-after children; children from ethnic minority backgrounds). Only two authorities reported involving outside organisations in developing their documents.

Best Value and Indicators

Play provision is covered by most, but not all, of the authorities' Best Value processes:

- Children's play is referred to in the 2001 **Best Value Performance Plans**[1] of ten of the 16 local authorities.

- Four of the local authorities reported that they had completed **Best Value Reviews**[2] covering all or part of their play provision and one other was midway through a review. Because most of the completed and planned reviews cover the work of specific departments or services, overall needs and provision of play opportunities are usually not considered (how wide-ranging the reviews are reflects, in general, the remit of existing departments). Two authorities have taken a different approach, with reviews covering all services the council provide for children, so that needs and provision can be considered across the board.

- Only five of the authorities have any targets or local performance indicators for play provision. Another is currently preparing indicators for a new programme. The most commonly collected information relates to play areas' compliance with NPFA standards (three authorities) and attendance information for supervised play provision (three authorities).

Consultation

A very high number of authorities reported consulting both children and parents about play provision. Fourteen of the authorities reported consulting parents, while 13 reported consulting

---

[1] Best Value Performance Plans are annual authority-wide documents which describe progress in improving performance and set out plans for the future.

[2] Best Value Reviews are comprehensive reviews of a set of council services. They are commissioned by local authorities and audited by central government.

children. This is an extremely encouraging finding. The authorities named a range of different reasons for consulting parents and children.

Table 2.8: Reasons given for consulting parents and children (n=14)	No. of local authorities[1]
Planning and development of future provision	10
Customer satisfaction monitoring	4
Design of future facilities	4
To improve activities on offer	2
To spread 'ownership' of provision	2
To inform training	1
To inform funding applications	1
Performance indicator data collection	1

Partners Involved

Play services or a dedicated play officer lead their local authorities' work on supervised play provision in only one third of authorities (a result comparable to the findings from the national survey in Part 1). In other cases work is usually led by an officer in the leisure department who is not a play specialist.

Leisure departments (which may or may not include a play service) are involved in play provision in most areas. Management of play areas is most often led by parks services. Among the lower-tier authorities, only three have play officers, while eight manage supervised play projects as sport or leisure responsibilities. Among the four unitary authorities, two provide activities through play services and the other two through community education. In three of the four unitary authorities, the EYDCP is involved with play, but surprisingly, in the fourth it is not.

Table 2.9 shows the different services that were reported to be involved in play provision, and to lead work on supervised play provision. Fifteen authorities responded to this question, with most stating that more than one service was involved in provision.

Table 2.9: Local authority services reported to have an involvement with play provision[2]		
	Number of local authorities	
Department or Service	Involved in play	Lead supervised play[3]
Parks	7	
Sports	6	4
Play Service	5	5
Recreation/Leisure (with no info. provided about service/sections)	5	3
Early Years/EYDCP (for unitary authorities only)	3	
Community Education	2	2
Arts	1	
Planning	1	
Youth Service	1	

---

[1] Note that several authorities use consultation information for more than one purpose, so the numbers total to more than 14.

[2] Where nomenclature varies from that used here, but functions are likely to be identical, services/departments have been grouped under appropriate categories.

[3] One authority had no supervised play provision.

Schools, parish councils and independent play providers are local authorities' main external partners in planning and delivering play provision. Among the 15 authorities which provided information about other organisations involved with play, an average of four types of independent organisation are involved in each area. The maximum number of types of organisation involved was seven, and the minimum one.

Table 2.10: Other organisations local authorities report working with	
Type of organisation	*No. of authorities*
Schools	11
Town or parish council	8 (plus 1 area committee system)
Other play providers	7
County council (for district councils only)	5
EYDCP (for district councils only)	5
Another authority-wide partnership	5
Neighbourhood zone or partnership	5
Voluntary sector umbrella organisation	4
NHS	4
Neighbouring local authority	3
Regional grouping	2

A play association or network is known to exist in seven of the 16 local authorities (although only four report involving voluntary sector umbrella organisations in planning or delivery). This is a lower figure than for Part 1 of the study, where play associations or networks were known to exist in around two thirds of authorities for which information was available.

Government Spending

Authorities were asked what current central government funding was supporting play provision in the area, and for which funding streams they had plans to apply. Thirteen were able to provide information. Table 2.11 summarises the results.

Table 2.11: Central government funding streams (n=13)[1]		
Funding stream	*Funding (number of authorities)*	*Plans to apply (number of authorities)*
NOF Out-of-school fund	7	1
Sport England	6	
Single Regeneration Budget (SRB)	4	1
Other regeneration funding	2	2
Education Action Zone	1	
NOF Better Play		2
Community Fund		1

[1] Note that authorities may report no government funding, or support from more than one programme, so the figures do not add to 13.

It is surprising that only half of authorities reported NOF Out-of-school funding for play provision. NOF funding is now available in all areas in the country. The low number of councils reporting NOF funding may be a result of the spending going to provision which is not treated as 'play' by the local authority. However, in view of local authorities' limited knowledge of non-council provision, it is also possible that the result could reflect a lack of awareness of the funding that is being accessed by independent providers.

It is encouraging that so many areas are receiving support from targeted regeneration budgets. This suggests that play provision is perceived to have an important contribution to make to alleviating deep social problems. The large number of authorities mentioning Sport England funding is testimony to the blurring of sport and play.

2.4. CONCLUSIONS

For Play Areas

There are some interesting differences in patterns of provision, first between the small minority of councils which are not the main provider and the rest, and second between the four 'types' of local authority provision identified in the findings.

These differences suggest a number of important policy questions, which the survey findings raise rather than resolve.

- Do these variations in approach make a difference for children? In particular what impact do wide variations in the amount spent per play area have on children's play experiences?

- How should local authorities set about resolving the tensions between total spending, quantity and quality, captured by our four-'type' grid?

- Are alternative approaches actively chosen, or accidents of history? To what extent are local authorities 'captives of the past' with little chance of varying radically their spending or pattern of provision?

- Are the plethora of planning processes (new and old) which cover play areas helping local authorities take a fundamental look at existing patterns of need and provision?

For Supervised Play

The findings for play show a great deal of variation in local authorities' activities, both in terms of the level and type of provision. There are two possible reasons for this diversity, apart from obvious variations in responsibilities between authorities with and without education and social services departments. Firstly, there are likely to be longstanding variations in supervised play provision, arising from the discretionary, and sometimes marginal, status of play. Secondly, there is some variation in councils' level of exposure to new government initiatives (for childcare, study support, sport) and the extent to which these have been integrated into (or styled) as play activities.

Another conclusion is drawn, not from the answers that we received, but rather those we did not. Despite our identifying the most appropriate person in each authority, the quality of information we received about non-local authority provision was limited. Finally, the gaps in the answers provided to us show that the quality of information within local authorities about others' provision is often limited. District council leisure departments (even those with dedicated play officers) which have no information about provision, are likely to have little involvement with wider out-of-school initiatives. This suggests that EYDCPs may still have a lot to do to join up the work of providers of out-of-school activities for children.

This finding raises the question of how play provision can become more joined-up – not only within local authorities, but also in multi-agency work with a range of child-focused objectives? One answer may be more dedicated funding for play, but our impression is that the first priority should be to focus on improving the integration of what is happening already.

PART 3: LOCAL AUTHORITY CASE STUDIES

3.1. OBJECTIVES

In parallel with the overall West Midlands data collection, four case study authorities were selected for more in-depth analysis. The purpose of this part of the study was to further map the level and characteristics of play provision, in relation to local needs. It also aimed to understand what approaches and strategies are being followed by local authorities, and suggest why these vary.

The box below lists the principal questions that were asked of each of the four case study authorities.

Issues Explored at Each of the Case Studies

Play provision
What types of provision are available? To what extent does the provision enable non-directed play?
How much of each type of provision is available?
On what basis is provision available? (open access or childcare; free or charged)

Distribution patterns
Where is provision located?
How does the distribution of provision relate to the child population?
How does the distribution of provision relate to social/economic/housing needs?

Inclusion and Targeting
What attempts does the local authority make to ensure the play needs of all children are addressed?

Structures and Processes
Which services within the local authority deliver provision? Which other organisations deliver provision? What relationships exist between different providers?
Who is involved in planning the development of play provision? What written plans and policies are there? What do these documents cover, and how are they implemented?
How does the local authority evaluate and review its provision? Whose views are taken into account? (Best Value regime; quality assurance and self-appraisal; consultation procedures)
Which inspection regimes does provision comply with?
How does play provision fit into other local authority priorities and initiatives? (e.g. childcare; community safety; culture)

Employment
How many paid and unpaid workers are there? How many have playwork qualifications?
What actions do play providers take to recruit, retain and train workers?

Finance
How much is spent on play provision? What is the spending per child resident? How is this spending allocated between different provision?
Where does funding come from? What funding has play provision received in the past? What are the plans for the future? Is provision sustainable?

Background and the future
What factors have influenced the quantity, type and distribution of play provision in the area?
How can play opportunities in the area be enhanced? What plans are there for the future?

An important part of the output of the case study research is a set of maps, one for each authority. These maps are not in electronic form and are, therefore, not physically part of this report. They show the distribution of both supervised and unsupervised play projects, including after-school clubs, distinguishing between:

- Unsupervised *play areas.*
- Supervised *term time* play schemes (usually after-school clubs).

- Supervised *holiday* play schemes.
- Other supervised play schemes.

It should be stressed that our conclusions are not intended to represent judgements on individual authorities or to evaluate their performance. As well as being beyond the remit of a mapping study, there is no agreed yardstick by which to make such judgements. Indeed, since differing patterns of provision ultimately reflect different political choices and priorities in the four authorities, there is no reason why a single yardstick should be expected to exist. This qualification applies both to the overall strategies, to the levels of provision on offer and to the pattern of this provision.

Chapter 5 is devoted to detailed description and analysis of the planning and provision of play in each of the case studies in turn. In this present chapter important points of comparison, and cross-cutting trends and issues, are discussed under the following headings:

- *Characteristics of the four case studies*. The demographic, geographic and socio-economic characteristics of the four areas.

- *The level of provision*. The types and quantities of provision in each area for 5 to 16 year old children, and the basis on which such provision is accessed.

- *The pattern of provision*. How provision relates to the social, housing and economic circumstances of the children in the locality, as well as an assessment of the key factors which influence provision in each area.

- *Inclusion and Targeting*. The local authority's attempts to ensure the play needs of all children are addressed.

- *Playworkers*. The number of people working on provision, whether they are trained, and to what level.

- *Finance*. The amount of money spent on play provision in each local authority area, in relation to the numbers of school-aged children.

- *Planning, review and evaluation*. Local authorities' approaches to planning, Best Value reviews, evaluation and inspection.

3.2. CHARACTERISTICS OF THE FOUR CASE STUDIES

The four case study local authorities are the two rural districts of Bridgnorth and Wyre Forest and the two metropolitan authorities of Coventry and Walsall. They have very different characteristics:

- *Bridgnorth*: a large, sparsely populated district, with only a few pockets of deprivation.

- *Wyre Forest*: a semi-rural district centred on the town of Kidderminster with a greater number of deprived areas.

- *Walsall*: an urban area on the edge of the West Midlands conurbation, with a mix of affluent areas and highly deprived areas.

- *Coventry*: a compact free-standing city, with a mix of affluent areas and highly deprived areas.

Table 3.1 provides some basic geographic and demographic information for each of the four case studies.

Table 3.1: Geographic and demographic characteristics of the case study areas				
	Bridgnorth	Wyre Forest	Walsall	Coventry
Area (sq km)	633	195	106	97
Population density (people/sq. km)	83	494	2,464	3,137
Population	52,000	96,000	261,000	304,000
Children, aged 5 to 16	7,000	14,000	42,000	50,000
Children in low income households[1]	18%	29%	44%	38%

[1] Calculations derived from DTLR Indices of Deprivation 2000. 'Low income' households are defined by the indices as households in receipt of certain means-tested benefits. This is only a proxy for low income. It excludes households which are not claiming their benefit entitlement and households with low paid work who may be ineligible. It is sometimes argued that these households are disproportionately located in rural areas.

3.3. LEVELS OF PROVISION

Table 3.2 shows the total level of provision in each area (note that information about independent provision is incomplete or estimated in some cases). Table 3.3 shows the level of council-funded provision in each area.

Table 3.2: Play Provision Key Statistics – All provision in the case studies				
	Bridgnorth	Wyre Forest	Walsall	Coventry
Number of children aged 5 to 16	7,000	20,000	42,000	50,000
Number of play areas	21	37	89	31
Children per play area	340	340	470	1,600
Number of supervised settings	82	41	132	127
Children per supervised setting	90	350	320	400

Table 3.3: Play Provision Key Statistics – Council-funded provision in the case studies				
	Bridgnorth	Wyre Forest	Walsall	Coventry
Number of children aged 5 to 16	7,000	20,000	42,000	50,000
Number of play areas	3	17	87	31
Children per play area	2,400	840	480	1,600
Number of supervised settings	52	16	110	100
Children per supervised setting	140	900	380	500

The key features of the case studies' levels of provision are:

- ***Children per play area.*** The number of children per play area is similar in three of the four authorities but very much higher (around four times) in the fourth (Coventry).

- ***Children per supervised play setting.*** The number of children per supervised play setting is similar in three of the four authorities but very much lower (around four times) in the fourth (Bridgnorth). All four authorities have significantly more provision than the average authority in the Part 2 survey.

Other notable features of the play provision across the four authorities include:

Conditions of access
The majority of supervised provision is paid for by families. Exceptions include Wyre Forest's council-funded clubs and Coventry's play centres. Almost all provision is run on a childcare basis,

with children being registered for a whole session. Exceptions include Coventry's play centres and some of Bridgnorth's independent summer play schemes.

Responsibility for delivery

1. Play Areas. Neither of the district councils have control of the majority of local play areas (parishes have responsibility in one, while over half are managed by a social landlord in the other).
2. Supervised Play Provision. In Walsall the delivery of council-funded supervised provision is devolved to independent local bodies. In the two districts responsibility lies within the leisure service, while in Coventry different sorts of provision are delivered by different parts of the council. Wyre Forest is the only authority with a dedicated play section, although Walsall and Coventry both have play budgets (in Coventry this only funds a minority of the council's provision).

Non-council provision

All four areas have independent supervised provision receiving NOF and EYDCP support (although in Bridgnorth they are very few in number) plus more traditional youth clubs. Schools or school-based community organisations are key deliverers in all four case study areas. Other partners include community organisations, commercial day-care providers, parish councils, a national charity and a county playing field association.

Term time clubs

All the authorities fund term time clubs, although there is considerable variation in their quantity and style, with some being orientated towards sport, art, study support or childcare. In Wyre Forest clubs have a development remit, running only while the council helps independent provision launch in their place.

Holiday play schemes

There are local authority-funded summer play schemes as well as independent projects in all four case studies. There seems to be little variation in approach, with an unsurprising overlap between play and more organised activities, such as sport and art.

Other provision

Apart from special needs provision, there are several examples of other types of provision from the case studies. For example, Coventry has two council-funded open-access play centres and Bridgnorth has a voluntary sector play bus and children's farm.

Approaches to enhancing levels of provision

The case studies suggested that local authorities have been able to enhance the amount of play provision settings that are available in two ways:

- *Changing the pattern of local authority provision.* Apart from raising overall spending, local authorities have increased the level of their own provision by: making savings through locating provision in multi-use facilities; and shifting away from a higher level of provision for a few children towards more dispersed, shorter-duration provision for many more.

- *Playing a development role.* All four local authorities aim to support the development of independent provision. Examples of this include: facilitating a play forum; joint marketing; co-ordinating opening times; offering free training and staff secondments; advising on start-up and funding. The two unitary authorities lead the work of their EYDCPs, passing on NOF funding to individual clubs, while Walsall also provides development and capacity-building support for the community organisations it funds through devolved budgets. Wyre Forest has completely transformed itself from a traditional play service into a development agency that delivers supervised provision only until it is able to get an independent successor up and running as a replacement.

3.4. PATTERNS OF PROVISION

The four case study areas show considerable contrasts in the pattern of provision. As far as *play areas* are concerned, the following patterns exist:

- *Bridgnorth:* Play areas are, generally, evenly distributed, relative to the geography and distribution of children in the area. In a large rural district many children are still some distance from a play area.

- *Wyre Forest:* Almost entirely located in urban areas, with many in deprived areas with social housing. One quarter of children live in areas without a nearby play area.

- *Walsall:* Generally, play areas are evenly distributed, relative to the geography and distribution of children in the area. One deprived part of the borough, however, has a noticeably below-average level of provision.

- *Coventry:* Play areas are fairly evenly distributed, but the low overall level of provision means that several parts of the city are still some way from an area. The most deprived parts of the city are well served, but other severely disadvantaged areas appear to have little provision.

As far as *supervised play* is concerned, the following patterns exist:

- *Bridgnorth:* Most provision is widely dispersed (i.e. council-funded term time and summer provision; independent summer provision) but much of it available for limited periods of time. More extensive provision is available on a very limited number of sites (i.e. independent term time provision).

- *Wyre Forest:* As with play areas, provision is concentrated almost exclusively in urban areas, ensuring provision is available in deprived areas, but limiting the play opportunities of children in rural communities.

- *Walsall:* Provision is widely dispersed and evenly distributed, with no particular relationship between distribution and levels of deprivation.

- *Coventry:* Provision is widely dispersed and reasonably evenly distributed, although many of both the least and most deprived areas appear to be rather better served than communities 'in the middle'.

The case studies revealed a large number of factors that appear to contribute to variations in the overall quantity, pattern and style of play provision. The overall make up of provision is determined by the pattern of council-funded and independent provision. Some of the factors influencing the two sorts of provision are the same, but others differ, largely because local authorities have the capacity to make area-wide decisions, while independent providers are local in focus and more dependent on the environment they work in.

Factors influencing all provision

- *Geography and population density.* It is obviously desirable for play settings to be as close as possible to children. In an area where children live close together it is possible to guarantee *geographic* access using fewer play settings per child than is the case for rural areas (in urban areas the priority may not be the number of settings but the number of places). Meanwhile, in all communities play areas are traditionally sited in parks and open spaces, so their distribution is dependent on an area's geography and long-term land use strategy. In urban areas, there is more flexibility in the placing of supervised play settings, while in rural areas their location is principally dictated by the pattern of settlements.

- *History*. Historic patterns of provision inevitably have a big influence on the current picture. While other factors will influence change over time, inertia may mean that this does not happen quickly, unless a challenging culture of review and planning develops.

- *Where decision making resides*. In the case studies, parish-level decision making, or decision-making devolved to the community level, tends to result in a more geographically uniform spread of facilities.

- *Decisions about trade-offs between the quality, duration, charges and capacity*. Higher quality, longer duration, lower charges and greater capacity all cost providers money, so if budgets are fixed these may need to be balanced against each other. For organisations delivering provision in more than one setting there may also be a trade-off between these issues and decisions about the number of settings that should be funded.

- *Decisions about styles of provision (for supervised provision)*. Different providers can either chose different priorities – towards sport and arts; towards play and childcare etc – or, if they are large, set different styles for different types of provision (e.g. children clubs, play centres). Often decisions result from institutional or personal preferences. Among local authorities, devolved decision making can result in no obvious style predominating.

- *External influences*. Choices about styles of provision can be influenced by external policy initiatives and funding streams. For example influences include Sport England, Arts Council and NOF funding, the launch of WFTC Childcare credit, and central government's increased emphasis on developing provision which will become self-sustaining.

Factors influencing council-funded provision

- *Whether there is a strategy for 'targeting' areas of high social need*. Targeting may only be possible if decision making or funding allocation is reasonably centralised. Targeting areas of high social need is likely to lead to provision being concentrated in the urban parts of rural districts, and the deprived parts of metropolitan districts. Such a strategy may involve decisions about the location of individual play settings, or in larger areas relate to funding formulae and resource allocation.

- *Whether there is a strategy for maximising 'geographic access'*. A local authority may adopt a deliberate policy of spreading provision as uniformly across an area as possible. In some cases there was evidence that this approach was an alternative to social-need targeting (for example where there are rival options for funding allocations) but this need not be the case. In a rural context the choice may be between 'town' and 'village' based provision, cutting across the issue of targeting social need.

- *Political constraints:* Where provision has historically been spread widely but thinly, moving to a more concentrated but better resourced pattern of provision can lead to political and popular resistance to the loss of local facilities.

Factors influencing independent provision

- *Community capacity.* The success of independent supervised provision often depends on the energy and capacity of local communities or schools. This can lead to patchy distribution of independent clubs, for example some clubs were reported to have struggled in rural and deprived areas.

- *Development support.* The successful launch and sustainability of independent provision is often dependent on the support received from agencies, including EYDCPs and local authorities. These bodies' decisions about the quantity, targeting and form of support on offer could have a big impact on the overall level and distribution of provision that is not funded by the council.

These numerous factors frequently conflict, and it is beyond the remit of this study to assess which should be prioritised in individual circumstances. It is worth commenting, however, that it is not always clear to what extent local authorities or independent providers, when faced with these many influences, have the capacity to alter patterns of provision – although in recent years, two of the authorities have implemented major, plan-led changes. It is quite possible to imagine the interaction of factors resulting in unplanned evolution, with political constraints, corporate inertia or external pressures limiting the extent to which deliberate consideration of alternatives is possible.

3.5. INCLUSION AND TARGETING

The study sought information from the case study authorities on their policies for including specific groups of disadvantaged children. Table 3.4 lists the categories of disadvantage that authorities were invited to discuss, along with the number of authorities indicating that they had specific policies relating to each group. In addition to group-specific policies referred to in the table, three of the authorities commented that their geographic targeting of areas of high deprivation was intended to help many of the groups discussed.

Table 3.4: Number of authorities indicating special provision or policy exists for particular groups of children	
Disabilities; behavioural and learning difficulties	3 (voluntary sector provision in the fourth)
Low income	2
Refugees or asylum seekers	1
Homeless	1
Looked after by local authorities	1
Travellers	1
Different ethnic, cultural and religious backgrounds	0
Excluded from school	0

In commenting on these responses, we would make the following observations, divided between social needs and health-related special needs.

Social needs

All the case study areas have policies in place to improve the inclusion of disadvantaged children. In three cases these policies focus on *where* provision is sited, with funding allocations and the selection of individual sites taking deprivation into account. Two of the authorities operate a discount system for people with low incomes, while another has a referrals programme which offers automatic places to children on the at-risk register, and children in homeless or asylum seeker families.

Special needs

Provision is available for children with disabilities or learning and behavioural difficulties in all four areas. In three of the areas there is local authority-funded provision, and in two, local authority-delivered provision (elsewhere there are voluntary sector services). These two local authorities have programmes which integrate children with special needs into mainstream provision, by allocating them specially trained playworkers.

3.6. PLAYWORKERS

Table 3.5 shows the information local authorities reported about the number of playworkers in the area. For all authorities information was supplied about workers in children's provision rather than about designated playworkers. In the majority of cases workers are part time, but as hours worked vary hugely it is not possible to make comparisons between authorities.

Table 3.5: Information reported on the number of playworkers in each local authority area		
	Local authority	Independent
Bridgnorth	15, year round; 50, holidays-only	Approx. 20 workers, plus 25 volunteers (mainly holidays only)
Coventry	145 year round	No information: assume at least 100 workers
Walsall	None (apart from secondees to local bodies)	Approx 150-200
Wyre Forest	3, year round; 35, holidays-only	Approx 30 (mainly year round)

It should be noted that counting the number of employees caused considerable problems, and did not yield terribly satisfactory results. We asked interviewees how many people were employed, both by local authorities and in independent provision. While it was possible for some officers to give good information about council employees, they were only able to estimate the numbers of staff in provision that is not funded by the council. We also attempted to count employees in each individual setting. This approach, however, proved inappropriate for assessing the total numbers of employees in the area, as so many people worked in more than one setting.

Although the response rate from individual play settings was patchy, from the information we collected it was clear that relatively few settings meet the ideal of having at least one qualified playworker. In the three local authorities which provide services, all workers receive some level of training, although in only one authority are all workers expected to have a playwork NVQ. In two of the authorities there are a handful of people with NVQ3s. Limited information was available about the level of training of workers in independent provision, although there are some qualified playworkers in each area.

All the local authorities identify recruitment, retention and training issues as key challenges for improving play provision. Meanwhile, in all the areas, term-time recruitment is difficult both for local authorities and independent providers, because of short, awkward working hours and low pay. Approaches to resolving problems include: creating packages of work at several sites of provision; introducing flexible rotas; and offering competitive pay. For independent providers the most significant challenge is meeting training needs, with many lacking the capacity to train staff themselves. In the two urban authorities this problem is being addressed through free training from EYDCPs (although levels of take-up are uncertain), while one of the districts has an 'artplay' training programme for potential workers. For local authorities, retention is something of a problem, with trained workers moving onto new careers or into independent provision (although in the latter case staying in the local pool of trained workers).

3.7. FINANCIAL PATTERNS

Overall spending patterns are summarised in Table 3.6 (note that this data is for the local authorities expenditure only). NOF and voluntary sector funding is available in all the local authorities areas but data on this was not available; neither was information available on the amount raised in charges in each area. It should also be noted that the information supplied for the local authorities is on a different basis for the district and metropolitan authorities. The cost bases are:

- *Metropolitan*. Direct delivery costs and also salary and core costs (for Walsall's supervised provision these are the core costs of the independent providers).

- *District*. The costs cover delivery but not officer salaries, administration or development work.

Table 3.6: Overall provision for the four local authorities				
	Bridgnorth	Wyre Forest	Walsall	Coventry
Play areas				
Total local authority spending	£7,000	£40,000	£200,000	£110,000
Local authority spending per child	70p	£2.80	£2.60	£4.00
Spending per local authority play area	£1,700	£2,400	£1,300	£6,500
Supervised play provision				
Total local authority spending	£49,000	£60,000	£660,000	£1.5 million
Local authority spending per child	£6.80	£4.10	£16	£30
Spending per local authority play setting	£940	£3,700	£6,000	£15,000

Our observations on these spending patterns include:

Play Areas

There is a clear disparity in the amount local authorities spend on each play area. In the urban areas variations in spending in part mirror the significant variations in the number of play areas in the two authorities, but Coventry also spends far more per area than Walsall. In the two districts the local authority is not the main funder of play areas.

Supervised Play

There is some relationship between authorities' spending and the number of play provision settings each operates. But other factors which influence variations in spending are the duration, capacity and style of different authorities' provision.

3.8. PLANNING, REVIEW AND EVALUATION

The case studies reported different approaches to planning, review and evaluation:

Planning

Within the local authorities the main focus is on service-level planning, with little ongoing co-ordination between departments. Joint planning takes place in response to external pressures (e.g. NOF funding bids), while organisations outside the local authorities have little involvement in planning possesses. In recent years the two districts have both implemented plan-based changes in the pattern of their provision, while there have been few major shifts in the urban areas. All the authorities were in a new phase of strategy development. Only in Walsall was this specifically focused on play (elsewhere the focus was on cultural strategy development or Children's Fund bid preparation).

It was pleasing to note that Walsall's decision to embark on play-focused planning was taken as a result of the launch of Better Play and our invitation for them to participate in the research.

Best Value Reviews

In the rural districts, Best Value Reviews are not scheduled to cover play provision for some time. In both urban areas, reviews have been undertaken: in one, a cross-cutting review of all services for children; in the other, supervised provision delivered by Community Education was reviewed alone.

Evaluation and performance

Two of the councils have internal quality assurance programmes. The other two councils measure performance using indicators, although these only measure level of use.

Inspection

In all areas a surprisingly low level of provision is registered as childcare under the Ofsted inspection regime. In Wyre Forest the council had recently registered its provision, in part to set a positive example, while some of Coventry's clubs have registered in order that parents can claim WFTC. In Walsall the council is encouraging all funded bodies to register.

3.9.   CONCLUSIONS

The case study phase of the study highlights the diversity of practice in both the delivery of play provision and in professional structures and processes.

In terms of provision, while there are play areas and childcare-based play settings in all the areas, in most respects there is considerable variation between the authorities. They have different approaches to the quantity, geographic distribution and style of provision. To some extent these variations are linked to the characteristics of the authorities, but the clear contrasts between Coventry and Walsall, and between Wyre Forest and Bridgnorth, indicate that factors such as history and local priorities are also important.

In terms of professional structures each of the four local authorities has a different approach, with only Wyre Forest having a dedicated play service. Both metropolitan authorities present interesting – although possibly unusual – models, Coventry because of its diverse styles of provision and fragmented management, and Walsall because of the devolution of responsibility for delivery. While all have planning and review processes covering play delivery, only Walsall has taken a cross-cutting approach (with both a Best Value Review of all services for children, and plans to develop a play strategy). A key finding from the study was that both districts had implemented major, plan-led changes to their provision in recent years.

There are several important questions arising from the case studies which could merit further work:

- What relationship should there be between play and other out-of-school-hours priorities and forms of provision? In all the authorities, designated 'play provision', and non-directed play within all types of provision, had to co-exist with alternatives. Policy makers need to resolve what status play should have within out-of-school provision in general.

- How can play provision and other out-of-school services resolve their human resources issues? The case studies revealed significant challenges relating to the status, pay, recruitment, and training of playworkers.

- Should local authorities transform themselves, at least in part, from delivers of play provision into development agencies? If so, how should they go about this, and what support might they need from external bodies, including the government?

RESULTS FOR THE FOUR CASE STUDIES

CASE STUDY 1: BRIDGNORTH

Bridgnorth is a rural district in Shropshire, with a population of about 50,000. Its play areas are mostly managed by town and parish councils. Voluntary organisations, parish councils and schools run some term time clubs and holiday play schemes, but most play provision is delivered by the district council. The council has a strong emphasis on sport and arts, and provision focuses on children's development in these areas. Provision is well dispersed around the smaller communities of the district

ABOUT THE AREA

Bridgnorth has a population of around 50,000, including around 7,000 children aged 5 to 16. The district covers a very large rural area and outside the market town of Bridgnorth the population is dispersed around four larger settlements, as well as smaller villages. Although the area is prosperous there are some areas with noticeable deprivation, with 30 per cent of children in the former pit village of Highley living in low income families.

BACKGROUND

Play provision in Bridgnorth was traditionally the preserve of town and parish councils. Parish councils still run most play areas and deliver a number of holiday activities, either themselves or through the county Playing Fields Association. The district council has a more recent interest in play arising from its cultural development objectives. Schools and the county EYDCP have little involvement with play provision and as a result term time provision is relatively sparse.

District Council Management: All district council play provision is funded and managed by the council's Leisure Development service. Responsibility for play is split between Art and Youth Sport Development officers, while the manager of the service is directly responsible for council-funded play areas, and for the leisure facilities where some play provision is located. Other services in the council have minimal involvement with children's play.

In 1994/95, the council produced a leisure strategy which paved the way for a big increase in Leisure Development, with the service expanding from one to five people. Play did not have a specific place within the plan but was covered under sport and art. The plan led to the creation of the youth sports and arts positions. Both had initial funding for three years. This influenced the approach of the local authority, as it was a high priority to prove the value of both roles, to ensure they were 'mainstreamed'. This led officers to quickly set up a high volume of council-delivered services, to produce tangible results (as a result councillors decided to make both positions permanent).

More recently officers have turned their attention to activities with less obvious outputs, such as encouraging the development of non-council provision. Another key priority of the last few years has been to increase the dispersal of play provision. In the past most activities were provided from the area's three leisure centres. Now there is provision in smaller, rural communities.

PROVISION IN THE AREA

Description of provision; Quantity of provision; Scope for non-directed play

Play Areas

There are ***21 play areas*** in the district. Most are managed by parish councils and there is considerable variation in their age and quality.

School Holiday Provision

The district council provides holiday programmes in every school holiday period, through two programmes. Both are focused on cultural development rather than non-directed play, and despite their names it is not possible to assess how much scope for play they offer. ***Kidsplay*** provides activity and sport sessions across 19 settings, either for a single day or as part of a three to five day course. Over the summer 2001 there were 240 sessions, lasting for an average two-and-a-half hours. ***Art Play*** offers a series of one-off two hour sessions at seven settings. They combine imagination-based games with arts and crafts.

There are ***nine other holiday play schemes***, run either by parish councils or voluntary organisations. Some of these schemes operate one-day a week, while others run Monday to Friday, although in some cases for only a handful of weeks.

Term Time Provision

There are ***four school-based after-school clubs*** in the district. In addition the district council provides after-school clubs once a week in 25 primary schools. These are **TOP Play** and **TOP Sport** activity sessions funded by Sport England. They allow limited scope for non-directed play although Top Play (for 4 to 7 year olds) aims to integrate play with acquiring sport skills. There are *16 children's or youth clubs* operating in the district (5 are county council run, 11 voluntary sector). They cater for children aged over eleven and the activities on offer vary from club to club. One club operates from its own premises, the rest use community centres and schools.

Other Provision

There is one voluntary sector play bus, one farm with activities, and one special needs project. There are two private nurseries delivering year-round, all-day childcare for children aged up to 11. The district has three leisure centres, which are used to host play provision, in addition to providing other leisure activities. These are all based on secondary school sites. Elsewhere activities take place in community centres and open spaces, of variable quality.

Access restrictions

There is a charge for almost all supervised provision in the area (two town councils provide free holiday play schemes). Most provision is run on a childcare basis, although at some parish council and voluntary sector holiday schemes older children are free to come and go.

DISTRIBUTION PATTERNS

Bridgnorth's 21 play areas are reasonably well distributed through the borough despite the absence of co-ordination of parish council provision. This is because so many parish councils take it upon themselves to provide an area in their own village (only a handful of larger communities appear to lack a play area). Inevitably in such a rural area, there are still many children without a play area in their ward or parish.

The district's limited number of term time play settings are well distributed, as a result of the district council offering an after-school club to every primary school one day a week. With only three other term time clubs independent provision is inevitably inaccessible for the majority of the area's children. Holiday provision is also well distributed, with many larger settlements being served by two or more settings. This pattern is a result both of district council's out-reach policy, and the efforts of parish councils, sometimes in conjunction with the county PFA. It should, however, be noted that many settings in smaller villages only offer provision for a week or so in the summer holidays. As there are only small

areas of deprivation, matching provision to social need is not a massive issue in Bridgnorth.

INCLUSION

Addressing the play needs of all children

Social Need: Families with low income are eligible for a Leisure Express card, which halves the price of all council holiday activities, but officers report that take-up of the scheme has been disappointing. The scheme is to be reviewed in 2002 in the development of a district Sport Strategy.

Disabilities: There is one voluntary sector special needs project which serves children with learning difficulties and disabilities (the district council acknowledges that there is little public provision for children with special needs, in part because there are no special schools in the district).

STRUCTURES AND PROCESSES

Local authority services involved with delivery of provision; Other organisations involved; Relationships between providers

Organisations involved in delivering play provision in Bridgnorth include the district council, numerous parish councils, schools and voluntary organisations.

Play Areas: Eighteen play areas in the district are managed by town and parish councils. These councils act in isolation, with minimal contact with the district council. The district council is responsible for three play areas (one is managed in-house, another is based on a school site, and a third is run by a voluntary committee). These are district rather than parish-delivered through historical accident and the district does not view their management as a core function on which it can justify significant expenditure.

Supervised Play: In addition to two private year-round providers and school-based clubs, Bridgnorth, Broseley and Shifnal town councils each deliver summer play schemes. The largest voluntary sector provider is the Shropshire Playing Fields Association. It provides six schemes for parish councils (in one case using a play bus). The uptake for its provision tends to be low, partly because of the small size of the communities, but also because not enough is done to investigate demand before services are set up.

The district council has recently begun to improve co-ordination between supervised play providers across sectors. In 2001, for the first time, the council's summer activities brochure attempted to list all provision in the district. The council hopes in the future to improve co-ordination and planning by providers, in particular by co-ordinating the weeks that summer schemes are open, to ensure there are not too many places available in any one week.

The district council participates in two Shropshire-wide partnerships related to play provision. The Shropshire Sports Partnership is a formal relationship which exists to pool resources to access Lottery match funding. There is also a county Creative Arts Team bringing together arts development staff across the county.

Organisations involved in planning or developing provision; Written plans and policies for developing play; Coverage of plans; Implementation of plans

The district and county councils are the main organisations involved in planning for the development of play, while parish councils, schools and voluntary organisations have little role. The district council aims to review and develop its own provision as part of the development of a new Sports Strategy. Increasingly it also aims to assist other organisations with their provision.

The county-wide EYDCP and Early Years Unit has a development officer focusing on out-of-school and holiday activities. Her role is to advise potential new providers and to develop county-wide NOF consortium bids. The EYDCP has a three-year and one-year plan, with DfES targets for the creation of number of new places.

Bridgnorth district council does not have plans or policies exclusively focused on play. This reflects the council's division of 'play' into art-based and sport-based activities. Instead play is covered by sport and art strategies.

An *art strategy and art audit* were completed in 2001. They were prepared by external consultants in liaison with Leisure Development officers and councillors. The strategy set out plans for three years, committing £25,000 each year. The plan is funded in partnership with West Midlands Arts.

A district *sports strategy* is in preparation and will be completed in 2002. The strategy covers leisure and recreation facilities (including play schemes), green spaces, play areas and playing fields. Key issues for the review include addressing geographic funding iniquities, and pairing down the number of overlapping standards services are required to meet.

In addition a county-wide *cultural strategy* and *community plan* are both in preparation (with perceived overlap between the two processes). Bridgnorth is feeding into them, and for the community strategy, there will be a more detailed plan for the district. The cultural strategy will replace a 1994/95 district leisure strategy.

Review and evaluation of provision (Best Value, quality assurance and self-appraisal); Views taken into account during reviews

Play provision will not be subject to any Best Value Reviews for some time. A review of leisure facilities is scheduled for 2003/04, while the review of the council's sport development, art development and countryside activities will not take place until 2004/05.

The district council has a system of internal quality checks for all its own provision. There is little monitoring or evaluation of grant-funded clubs, as the grants tend to be small-scale.

The council asks both parents and children for their views on individual play programmes. This information is used to develop future training and projects, and to ensure activities on offer are wanted. There has been no consultation on the area's play provision in general.

Compliance with inspection regimes

Five programmes in the area currently register their provision under the Children Act. Three are parish council-delivered holiday schemes, and two are private day care holiday programmes.

The district council does not register its play provision. This is because most of it lasts for less than two hours.

Play provision's relationship with other local authority priorities and initiatives

The district council's play provision is largely motivated by its ambitions for cultural development in the area, with play being targeted at developing children's potential for either art or sport. There is no real integration with other areas of district council activity.

Provision shows little sign of being integrated with other educational objectives, through study support initiatives. The development of voluntary and private provision is linked to the National Childcare Strategy, with providers receiving support from the county EYDCP. The district and parish council provision is not linked to the development of childcare

EMPLOYMENT

Numbers of paid and unpaid workers; Numbers of workers with playwork qualifications

Forty-five employees and seven volunteers work in district council provision at some point in the year, usually for short periods each week. There are 15 year-round, freelance workers, who are topped up during the holiday periods, largely with students.

The Art Play programme is delivered by a private contractor and paid trainees.

The county council youth service has three permanent employees.

Around 20 employees and 25 volunteers work in parish council, voluntary and private provision, at some point in the year. Most only work during school holidays.

Across the district there are two playworkers with NVQ3 and four with a lower qualification or in training. The district council's workers all have sport coaching qualifications. The area suffers from a massive skills shortage. The council's officers were aware of only a handful of playworkers with NVQ3 qualifications in the whole of Shropshire.

Recruitment, Retention and Training Issues

There are significant local recruitment problems. The district council reports difficulty recruiting people for after-school provision, as the hours are inconvenient. Summer programmes are less of a problem as the council is able to employ students returning from university.

The Art Play programme has a specific training remit, with training adults seen as high a priority as provision for children. 8 to 10 trainees receive three days of (paid) training before participating in sessions with children, under supervision from their trainers. The programme is targeted at parents, playgroup volunteers and some professional play and youth workers. The council believes that the programme is having results. It boosts participants' confidence and in at least one case a trainee has gone on to set up her own after-school club. There is a problem with continuing development as participants have to travel to Telford or Shrewsbury to pursue more advanced courses.

TOP Play and TOP Sport leaders and assistants receive a day of training before working with children, while head coaches require national qualifications to lead sessions.

FINANCE

Spending on play provision; Spending per child resident; Budget allocation issues

The district council spends £7,000 per year on maintaining play areas (70p for every 5 to 16 year old) and £49,000 per year on delivering supervised provision (£6.80 for every 5 to 16 year old). These costs do not include officers' salaries, administration or development. The council also generates resetting of over £40,000 from charges.

Information was unavailable on parish or voluntary sector spending (although the district council makes several £500 grants to voluntary clubs for children).

The geographic allocation of spending is currently under review, as part of the preparation of the district's sport strategy.

Present funding sources; Funding in the past and plans for the future; Sustainability of provision

The district council's TOPs clubs receive support from Sport England. Some individual after-school clubs have received NOF funding through the EYDCP. Shropshire Playing Fields Association's programme is funded by a Communities Fund grant.

PLANS FOR THE FUTURE

Plans for the future; How to enhance play opportunities in the future

After five years of expansion the expectation is that levels of leisure provision will remain stable over the next few years. There is no prospect of budget cuts.

The district council is now aiming to take on a much greater co-ordination and development role. The hope is that the council can enable other organisations plan and develop their provision, so that its provision only fills the gaps left by others. Officers commented that this shift will require careful consideration to ensure existing services are maintained. They also perceive time and resources conflicts between short- and medium-term objectives, as maintaining high quality council-delivered provision distracts from taking on a wider development function.

The council also wants to support the development of improved recreation facilities apart from at the three leisure centres. In particular they want to see community centres and open spaces improved.

CASE STUDY 2: COVENTRY

Coventry is a compact city, with a population of around 300,000. It has 30 play areas, close to 50 holiday play schemes, and almost 100 term time clubs providing opportunities for play. There are also two open access play centres. In terms of funding and organisation there is a clear demarcation between provision that mainly focuses on childcare, and provision that focuses on children's development, with study support or sport activities.

ABOUT THE AREA

Coventry has a population of around 300,000, which includes 50,000 children aged 5 to 16. The city is compact, and on the whole densely populated. There are high levels of deprivation and child poverty (one third of wards are in the government's list of most deprived areas, while around 40 per cent of children live in low income households).

BACKGROUND

Responsibility for play provision lies with three parts of the council, Cultural Development, Children and Family Education and Early Years. Provision begun many years ago with the development of Play Centres, with a play budget. Subsequently the Youth Service established Children's Clubs. These were later demerged and now form part of the Children and Family Education Service within Community Education. They were called Children's Clubs to differentiate them from the city's existing play provision, and to highlight their educational emphasis. More recently the Early Years Unit has been established to manage the EYDCP and existing school-based 'Wraparound' provision which predated the explosion of school-based clubs. The pattern of provision of local authority play areas has remained reasonably static in recent years.

PROVISION IN THE AREA

Description of provision; Quantity of provision; Scope for non-directed play

Play Areas

The city council manages *30 play areas*, all situated in parks and open spaces. One third are designated 'neighbourhood' areas, and two thirds 'local' areas. There is one skate park.

Year Round Provision

There are *two play centres* in the city open all year (with variations in hours). There are also *around 20 voluntary sector groups and clubs* for young people (most are targeted at children aged 11 and over). In addition there are *two Arts Clubs* run by the local authority. Many other sites deliver both out-of-school clubs and holiday schemes at different times of the year. These are discussed below.

School Holiday Provision

The city council's provision consists of *41* Children and Family Education *children's clubs* (24 are asked at the setting of a term time club) and a *summer school for asylum seeker children*. In addition there are Cultural Development *Activity Zone sessions* (park-based drop-in activity sessions) and *seven Holiday Sports Programmes* delivering sport activities in deprived neighbourhoods. Finally *four term time 'Wraparounds'* also provide day-care over the summer.

There are also *24 Independent Holiday Play Schemes* (seven of which share a setting with a term time club).

Term-time Provision

Clubs in the city are perceived to focus on sport, children's learning and development, or childcare. Local authority officers suggested, however, that there is not always great variation in children's experiences of the different types of provision. The city council's provision consists of: Children and Family Education's *41 children's clubs* (most of these are 'after-school', but others begin later, for example running between 6pm and 8pm); Cultural Development's sport-focused *Tops clubs* running in *29 schools* (sports activities and skills for 9 to 11 year olds); and five Early Years funded *'Wraparounds'* (school-based clubs operating before and after school, typically starting at 8am and finishing at 6pm)

There are also *24 independent after-school clubs* and *15 independent breakfast clubs* run at 25 settings by voluntary or private organisations, or voluntary committees linked to schools. Sixteen of the settings are schools.

Access restrictions

The two play centres are free, drop-in facilities, where children are free to come and go. The Tops programme is free at most schools, with children required to register. The holiday sport programme is a drop-in scheme, and children are asked to pay.

The Children and Family Education children's clubs have a range of access policies. Some (for example the ICT Clubs) are free, drop-in schemes; at many other clubs there are charges and children register for a place, sometimes after a referral from another agency.

The independent clubs and wraparounds tend to charge, and tend to expect children to be registered for sessions.

DISTRIBUTION PATTERNS

Coventry has very few play areas, relative to its child population (about a quarter Walsall's number). Two of the city's wards have no play areas, and a further nine have only one (shared on average by more than 4,000 children). Some wards do better than this, including the city's two most deprived, but beyond this there is no obvious sign of targeting, as three of the least deprived wards also have good provision.

Supervised provision is more numerous and evenly distributed. There is holiday scheme for every 1,200 children and a term time club for every 1,100. The distribution of term time clubs, in particular, is extremely uniform, with a noticeably low level of provision in only three wards (six wards have noticeably below average level of summer provision). Interesting many of the wards with poor supervised provision have middling levels of deprivation, while the most and least deprived wards tend to have rather better levels of provision (this pattern tallies with the commonplace observation that communities either need to be deprived or vocal to secure services).

INCLUSION AND TARGETING

Social Needs: The play centres and summer sport programmes, and a large number of the Children and Family Education children's clubs are sited in locations with high levels of deprivation, and aim to target children who would otherwise be unable to take part in the activities on offer. Children and Family Education funding is split between three districts of the city, using needs-weighted allocation formulae. Within each district, officers also aim to locate provision according to need. In addition, clubs in more affluent areas are expected to raise a higher proportion of their costs through charging families, so that more resources can be targeted towards disadvantaged areas.

Social Services refers to Children and Family Education children's clubs, and to the play centres, children on the at-risk register, asylum seeker children and children living in hostels. These children are allocated places at clubs without having to join a waiting list. Similarly, traveller children automatically receive places, when a referral is made by an officer working with the traveller community.

Children with Disabilities and Asylum Seeker Children: The Play Partners programme is a scheme for integrating children with particular needs into mainstream provision, by pairing children with partner workers. Targeted groups include children with disabilities or behavioural problems, looked-after children (funded by the LEA Education Access service), and refugee and asylum seeker children (with NOF-funded language support). In the summer of 2001 the council delivered a three-week NOF-funded summer school for 47 asylum seeker children, from several different cultural groups.

STRUCTURES AND PROCESSES

Local authority services involved with delivery of provision; Other organisations involved; Relationships between providers

There are two city council services involved in delivering play services while another is a key funder. In addition services are delivered by a large number of voluntary and community organisations, including voluntary committees linked to schools.

The *Children and Family Education Service*, part of the Community Education department, delivers children's clubs, holiday play schemes and special needs provision. Its provision has a strong emphasis on children's development and study support, and it is often linked to support for parents, such as family literacy and parenting programmes.

The *Cultural and Economic Development* department manages sports development, parks and the two play centres.

The *Early Years Unit* carries out the work of the EYDCP and is responsible for the development of childcare provision. But in addition the unit is a direct funder for the five 'Wraparounds'.

Other sections of the LEA with a role to play include: Education Access, which places looked-after children in clubs; Minority Groups Support Services, which supports ethnic minorities, including asylum seekers; the Study Support officer who works with schools to improve the quality of their own after-school activities. There is also an LEA-run Parental Partnership, which supports and represents the parents of children with special needs.

Relationships between local authority services, and between different providers, are primarily practical and delivery-orientated, rather than strategic.

There are no permanent city-wide arrangements for co-ordinating council provision. In the past groups have come together to carry out practical short-term projects such as developing NOF consortium bids.

Children and Family Action Teams, however, exist in each of the six districts of the city. These groups include council officers, voluntary sector leaders and community representatives. They are co-sponsored by Children and Family Education, social services and Early Years.

There is little co-ordination between officers delivering play areas and the different services delivering supervised play. The exception is when new services are being planned, when parks officers do consult children in Children and Family Education clubs in 'Planning for Real' exercises.

For independent providers there is both a city ***Play Forum***, which brings together out-of-school clubs and the ***Coventry Voluntary Youth Service Council***, an affiliate of the CVS, which serves youth clubs and groups. The relationship between the council and the voluntary sector is not particularly strong. Local, delivery-focused networks, such as the Children and Family Action Teams, are better established than strategic, city-wide arrangements. The expectation is that this will change when all work together to develop and implement the city's Children's Fund programme.

Organisations involved in planning or developing provision; Written plans and policies for developing play; Coverage of plans; Implementation of plans

Different parts of the local authority co-operate on individual projects (such as a recent combined NOF bid). But there is minimal strategic co-ordination.

In most cases individual services have their own plans or policies. For example Children and Family Education clubs are covered by documents for three successive tiers of operation – a Children and Family Education Policy, a Community Education Policy, and a Student and Community Services Plan. Play centres, play areas and sport-based provision is covered by the Cultural Development Strategy and childcare development by the Early Years and Childcare Development Plan.

All the documents were prepared in consultation with councillors, but without the involvement of independent organisations. The documents specifically discuss how the needs of target groups will be met. These groups include: low income families, ethnic minority children, children on the at-risk register, asylum seeker children and children at risk of offending.

Review and evaluation of provision (Best Value, quality assurance and self-appraisal); Views taken into account during reviews

A Best Value Review of the Children and Family Education Service was conducted in 2001 by external consultants. The service is currently waiting for external scrutiny from Ofsted. Officers felt that the process had been protracted and difficult, but ultimately valuable. The review was largely positive, but focused on shortcomings as well as successes. The review led to members and other officers becoming more aware of the value of the service's work. As a result of the review there was cross-party agreement that the service should receive extra money for marketing its provision. Meanwhile a Cultural Services Best Value Review is planned.

The Children and Family Education service has its own internal Quality Inspection Process (QUIP). This is a peer inspection regime with a framework based on youth service and social services childcare criteria. There is then a participative moderation process, where the aim is to discuss problems. The result is feedback to individual provision, and the developing of an action plan.

The Cultural Development and Children and Family Education provision is accredited with Investors in People.

The EYDCP has established a Quality Assurance Group, which is aiming to develop a 'Coventry Kitemark' for all out-of-school hours provision including under-5s' playgroups, nurseries, childcare-orientated clubs, and study support-orientated. They are developing a framework, which covers health and safety, but also curriculum quality. Clubs will be able to bypass requirements, if they have already had to fulfil these for another regulation scheme.

Compliance with inspection regimes

Wraparound clubs have all recently registered under the Children Act, specifically so parents can claim the WFTC childcare allowance. Independent clubs are also mainly registered.

Children and Family Education clubs are not registered. Officers feel that it will be appropriate to register in the future, as this will demonstrate quality to stakeholders. There are, however, concerns that Ofsted childcare standards are not appropriate for activity-based clubs lasting for one to two hours.

Play Provision's relationship with other local authority priorities and initiatives

Different elements of Coventry's play provision are well linked to other objectives, perhaps to the detriment of good co-ordination between play providers. The Children and Family Education clubs are linked to family literacy and skills programmes. Sport-based clubs are tied to the public health agenda. Independent clubs fall under the framework of the National Childcare Strategy. All the council's provision appears to address inclusion priorities, partly through targeting within provision, and also through referrals from other council services.

Coventry is a second wave Children's Fund authority, which is currently engaged in mapping needs and existing provision in order to develop a programme, commencing in April 2002. The programme will focus on preventative services for children with 'moderate' levels of need. Officers hope that the process of drawing up and delivering the Children's Fund package will improve the strategic relationships between providers of play provision.

EMPLOYMENT

Numbers of paid and unpaid workers; Numbers of workers with playwork qualifications

There are 106 workers in Children and Family Education Children's Clubs. Almost all are part time. The play centres are run by around 15 paid workers, with support from four volunteers. Only one of these workers has a playwork NVQ3. There are 25 paid workers involved in delivering the Tops programme and Holiday Sport Programme. In addition, each school is encouraged to recruit a volunteer to assist with sessions. All the workers have training in sports skills and child protection.

Recruitment, Retention and Training Issues

There are considerable problems with recruitment. The Children and Family Education service has 20 per cent rolling vacancies. As it operates an integrated service it is able to spread staff shortages between clubs. Within the service there are many long-serving staff, but turnover is reasonably high, as staff frequently move on to higher education or better paid work. There are plans to advertise all vacancies in a single advert, and encourage applicants to apply for a portfolio of work, to overcome the problem of unattractively short hours.

Staff working in Children and Family Education Service provision are paid to participate in off-site training for 30 hours each year. Although voluntary sector clubs are encouraged to provide training for their staff, levels of training remain low.

FINANCE

Spending on play provision; Spending per child resident; Budget allocation issues

The council spends £200,000 per year on play areas (£4 for every child aged 5 to 16) and £1.5 million on

supervised play (£30 for every child aged 5 to 16). £140,000 is allocated to the two play centres.

Present funding sources; Funding in the past and plans for the future; Sustainability of provision

There has been a massive increase in funding over the last two years, with most of the new money coming from central government. Over the next year this will rise again, through Coventry's Children's Fund allocation. Funding has come from Education Action Zones, NDC, Neighbourhood Renewal Fund, and NOF. The NOF bid was made by a council-wide consortium, with funding across all services. The city received £400,000 for out-of-school activities and £126,000 for summer schools.

Children's Clubs are funded by the council, and through charges from families. The proportion of funding raised through charges varies depending on the level of deprivation in individual clubs; some clubs are expected to be self-sufficient.

Independent clubs are supported by NOF funding. The aim is for this provision to become self-sustaining from fee income, provided WFTC take-up is high.

Summer schools were funded by the Standards Fund, while summer play schemes were funded by NOF.

The Wraparounds are intended to be self-sustaining, with profitable clubs subsidising clubs in more deprived areas. At present, however, they receive £300,000 subsidy per year.

PLANS FOR THE FUTURE

Plans for the future; How to enhance play opportunities in the future

Managers are positive about the future of provision, with major government initiatives such as the Children's Fund and Neighbourhood Renewal Fund expected to have a big impact. The expectation is that activity-based provision will become more targeted and preventative, with additional funding linked to the pursuit of measurable targets, with a focus on improved outcomes. The importance of demonstrating quality will increase. While all this will involve time-consuming bureaucracy, it is recognised that this is a price worth paying.

CASE STUDY 3: WALSALL

Walsall is an urban and suburban borough with a population of 260,000. It is committed to devolving power to neighbourhoods within the area, both through the use of area committees and through service delivery by local community associations. All supervised play provision is delivered by these play associations or by local schools. There are a large number of play areas, although many are in need of renovation.

ABOUT THE AREA

Walsall is an urban borough at the northern edge of the West Midlands conurbation, with a population of 260,000 (including 42,000 aged between 5 and 16). The borough is severely deprived and has very high levels of child poverty (over half Walsall's wards are in the government's list of most deprived areas, while 44 per cent of children live in low income families). The west of the borough is both more built up and more deprived than the east.

BACKGROUND

Much of Walsall's supervised provision is delivered by around 40 community associations. These associations were formed as part of a radical initiative to devolve and out-source provision of community services (other devolved services include adult education, youth services, sport and community development). Community associations were initially established around schools, to open up facilities to wider community use. They tend to be charitable companies with boards made up of local residents, service users and councillors. Traditionally community associations have tended to have slightly parochial attitudes. The council is trying to change this by encouraging neighbouring associations to come together under 14 Youth and Community Partnership Areas. These will then be merged into seven district partnerships, with funding decisions taken by the council's seven district committees.

PROVISION IN THE AREA

Description of provision; Quantity of provision; Scope for non-directed play

There are **86 play areas** located in the council's parks and open spaces. In addition two areas are located in housing estates. All 'neighbourhood' play areas have been refurbished in the last five to ten years. Officers acknowledge, however, that many smaller 'local' play areas are of poor quality. A decision has been taken to keep them all in place to preserve their status as play areas, so they have a chance of being refurbished should funding become available.

School Holiday Provision

There are **40 holiday play schemes** running in the borough. Among these, 32 are provided by

community associations, with support from the borough council. The remainder are run by schools, voluntary organisations and a commercial day-care provider.

Term Time Provision

There are **43 term time clubs**. Twenty-seven of these clubs are delivered by schools, sometimes through a voluntary committee. Nine are provided by community associations, in two cases from a school site. Among the 43 clubs, there are 21 clubs running both before and after school, and a further 18 clubs running after school only. One club runs in the evening, and a special needs club provides weekend day-care.

Access restrictions

All providers who provided information reported that families needed to pay to use their service. Almost all provision in the borough requires children to be registered by parents and remain for the entire session. There are six term time clubs and two holiday schemes where children are free to drop in as they choose.

DISTRIBUTION PATTERNS

Walsall's 80 play areas are distributed reasonably evenly. Across the borough there is a play area for every 700 children, and in most wards there is not much deviation from this figure, regardless of levels of deprivation (this constant level of provision per capita does mean that walking distances to play areas tend to be greater in the less populated east of the borough). Standing out from the pattern of uniformity, three adjacent wards, with high levels of deprivation (Birchills Leamore, Bloxwich East and Bloxwich West) have considerably fewer play areas, with one for every 2,000 children.

A uniform pattern of provision is also found with supervised play provision. Across Walsall there is one term time club and one holiday scheme for every 1,400 children, and in most wards the variation from this level is not that great (particularly for holiday provision). Again there is no evidence of particular concentrations of provision in deprived areas; only three deprived wards have an above average number of term time clubs, while four have less than half the average.

INCLUSION AND TARGETING

Addressing the play needs of all children

Social Need: The council targets funding at areas with social need by using formulae to allocate resources to districts of the city and community associations which are weighted to take account of relative deprivation. This favours poorer parts of the borough, although is unable to cope with pockets of deprivation in affluent areas. The extent of weighting has, however, just been significantly cut following the Conservative group gaining control of the council. No mainstream clubs, however, go further and target specific groups of children.

Disabilities: Provision for children with special needs is funded. separately from the delegated youth and community services budgets. There are four schemes. Funding is limited to £14,000 including transport. In addition NCH Action for Children provides an out-of-school club and summer scheme with NOF funding.

STRUCTURES AND PROCESSES

Local authority services involved with delivery of provision; Other organisations involved; Relationships between providers

Play areas are managed by the Parks section of the Leisure and Community services department.

Community association and some voluntary organisation-delivered provision is funded by the council's Community Education service. Most other provision is delivered by schools, often through voluntary committees.

Organisations involved in planning or developing provision; Written plans and policies for developing play; Coverage of plans; Implementation of plans

The council's Early Years unit has a strategic role covering all services for children. It services the EYDCP and operates the Children's Information Service (it is currently drawing together a directory of provision for parents).

There are several Children and Family Partnerships in the borough. These are local forums which bring together parents and service providers to identify needs and priority areas. Recent meetings have, for example, highlighted the lack of opportunities for outdoor play.

The council has recently decided to bid to NOF Better Play for funding for a play strategy. The hope is that a review of play provision will focus on play overall, and offer the scope to think again about contentious issues such as the trade-off between the quality and quantity of play areas, and the interaction between play areas and the planning system.

Community associations providing play services aim to plan their own provision according to their assessment of local needs (they also have to reflect the council's strategic agenda, as far as this is reflected in their funding allocations). They produce their own development plans, which need to link into EYDC planning, for example to access NOF funding. Officers commented that in reality Community Association planning did not take much account of identified local needs, as it was so driven by the demands of funders.

Review and evaluation of provision (Best Value, quality assurance and self-appraisal); Views taken into account during reviews

Devolved services underwent a Best Value Review in the first year of the regime. The process was in its infancy and the review has not been viewed as a great success. It was felt that it had not dug very deeply. The review concluded that responsibility for funding devolved play delivery should be transferred to the Early Years Unit. This was opposed by officers because the unit currently has no delivery functions and is intended to be an entirely strategic body. Councillors and management decided to hold a feasibility inquiry rather than proceeding immediately. The inquiry recommended enhanced partnership working rather than a transfer of play from Community Education to Early Years.

The council itself is accredited with Investors in People. The council is now encouraging and supporting community associations in meeting IiP standards.

Compliance with inspection regimes

Community associations and other providers receiving council funding are closely monitored to ensure that services are delivered. Every three months each provider is required to pass on information on the level of use of their services. This information is used to allocate resources, with higher-volume providers receiving greater funding.

In the past individual play provision has not needed to register with social services because most was school-based. In recent years, however, most providers have been encouraged to register. Officers suggested, however, that some providers may not be fulfilling their registration obligations, because managers are inexperienced and under-trained.

Prior to the handover to Ofsted, there were only two Youth and Community Officers in the borough to enforce registration. They reported spending their time 'fire-fighting' when problems emerge, rather than supporting and advising providers.

Play provision's relationship with other local authority priorities and initiatives

Play provision's devolution to community associations is part of an ambitious agenda to devolve service delivery and empower local communities.

Some of the recent school-based play opportunities have emerged as a result of the childcare development work of the EYDCP. Most of the community association provision however comes from existing play and community development spending.

EMPLOYMENT

Numbers of paid and unpaid workers; Numbers of workers with playwork qualifications

At least 150 to 200 people are involved, at some point of the year, in delivering play services.

Community association staff are a mix of council officers on secondment and direct employees.

Recruitment, Retention and Training Issues

There is a general shortage of playworkers in the area. There are particular difficulties recruiting holiday workers. Community associations report struggling to recruit, police-check and train seasonal staff within tight deadlines. There have been examples of fully funded provision being unable to open because of a lack of staff. The EYDCP is hoping to improve matters by creating a pool of workers, who they would police-check, as well as train on behalf of the community associations. Community associations themselves have limited budgets or capacity to provide training for workers. The Early Years Unit wants to provide training free-of-charge to community associations. Community associations are also being encouraged to sign up to Investors in People.

FINANCE

Spending on play provision; Spending per child resident; Budget allocation issues

Annual spending on the maintenance of play areas is £110,000 (£2.60 for every child aged 5 to 16). For the last two to three years there has been no capital funding available for refurbishing play areas. In 2000/01 community associations and other providers reported spending £687,000 on play provision (around 21 per cent of their total spending). This is around £16 per child aged 5 to 16 in Walsall.

It is worth noting that this spending is well above the council's 'target' for spending on play, which is 10 per cent of total community association expenditure (the council does not have direct means of influencing the mix of provision community associations decide to provide as most funding follows the hours delivered). In addition Community associations are free to raise additional funds, from charges or other grants, and allocate them as they chose between their services.

The council has been criticised for under-resourcing community associations' core-costs (in particular the salary costs of senior managers), which has led either to funding designated for provision being transferred to administration, or to management weaknesses within community associations.

Present funding sources; Funding in the past and plans for the future; Sustainability of provision

Many of the school-based clubs have received NOF funding through the Early Years Unit. The borough is due to receive a Children's Fund allocation. In addition, it is planning to bid for a Better Play grant to develop a Play Strategy.

PLANS FOR THE FUTURE

Plans for the future; How to enhance play opportunities in the future

The council hopes that developing a play strategy will lead to a more joined-up approach to play. There is considerable pressure for the EYDCP to deliver, but so far the results have been mixed and there has been insufficient participation from the community associations.

Co-ordination between community associations should improve as they form into area partnerships. The 14 area partnerships should come to be funded through seven council 'district committees' which would lead to further geographic co-ordination.

A key issue is the sustainability of the community associations which deliver play and so many other key services. They have an increasing workload, while their budgets are falling. The council will face a choice between increasing investment in the associations or letting them erode away and then having to find alternative ways of delivering services.

CASE STUDY 4: WYRE FOREST

Wyre Forest is a semi-rural district in the North of Worcestershire with a population of 100,000. The main town in the district is Kidderminster. Supervised play provision is delivered by both the district council and schools, although the council aims to develop new provision and then withdraw and move on, rather than indefinitely running clubs from the same settings. Play areas in the district are managed by the council or a registered social landlord.

ABOUT THE AREA

Wyre Forest has a population of 100,000, with around 20,000 children aged 5 to 16. Around three quarters of the population live in the district's three towns, with the rest in rural areas. There are some pockets of deprivation, including one ward in the government's list of most deprived areas. Around 30 per cent of children live in low income households.

BACKGROUND

The district has a long history of play provision. The council's chief executive has a play background and play has historically been better funded than sport, art or the like.

Between 1972 and 1997 the district's play provision consisted of one Play Centre in a deprived area of Kidderminster. The building was unsuitable and poorly used, while a large amount of the play section's budget was spent on its maintenance. A decision was taken to close the centre and use the resources to fund development work and the delivery of after-school clubs from hired premises. This led to protests, but now the changes are complete no one seriously doubts that it was the right decision to make.

The council's play development role has changed as the central government childcare agenda has developed. External funding means it is now possible to set up clubs and then pull out. In addition there is a much greater level of professionalism, and the council is able to concentrate on training and capacity-building. All this would have been unrecognisable five years ago.

PROVISION IN THE AREA

Description of provision; Quantity of provision; Scope for non-directed play

Play Areas

There are 37 play areas in the district. Seventeen are managed by the council's parks service, while 20 are the responsibility of a social housing company, following the recent transfer of the council's housing stock.

School Holiday Provision

The district council delivers **holiday play schemes at 11 sites** around the area. **Eight independent holiday**

schemes are largely delivered by school-based after-school clubs.

Term Time Provision

The district council provides **five after-school 'Kids Klubs'**, in local first schools (5 to 8 year olds). These are used almost exclusively by children attending these schools. They run one night a week, for two and a half hours. Clubs are sited at each school for between 6 and 18 months before switching to a new location (hopefully once an independent club has got going in its place). There are **15 independent after-school clubs** in the area. These are located at schools and are usually run by an independent committee. The most well used club in the area is located at Franch First School, where the provision has evolved into a complete 'wrap-around' package from 7am till 6pm running throughout the year and also operating two buses to ensure transport links.

Access restrictions

The district council's after-school clubs are available free of charge. Independent clubs charge parents and usually run for five nights a week. Families are expected to pay for the council's holiday play activities. Charges vary from £2 to £7 per session, depending on the facilities available. Independent schemes are more expensive, typically costing £15 per day. All provision in the area is on a childcare basis, with children required to register.

DISTRIBUTION PATTERNS

Wyre Forest has a high number of play areas, with one area for every 500 children. The distribution of play areas is, however, extremely uneven, with urban wards being favoured at the expense of rural areas (although more than half the areas are now managed by a social landlord their location is a legacy of former council control). While there is an extremely high number of play areas in more than half of the wards (including one where four play areas are shared by just 900 children), in five wards there are no play areas and in a further two there is just one. This leaves around a quarter of the district's children with poor access to a play area.

Although there was insufficient information to carry out a full mapping exercise the general pattern is similar for supervised provision. The council's own provision is targeted at deprived urban areas, while independent clubs have flourished whether at locations where council provision once operated or in urban communities with the capacity to support them. In contrast, officers reported that clubs in smaller settlements had struggled to take off. This leaves children outside the three towns with extremely limited provision.

TARGETING AND INCLUSION

Addressing the play needs of all children

Social Need: The district council has a deliberate policy of rotating the location of its five after-school clubs. Its aim is to set up clubs in communities where there is no provision, and then assist others in taking ownership, for example by supporting schools with NOF or EYDCP funding bids. Ideally the council hopes to pull out after six months, although it is prepared to stay for longer if necessary. This approach is perceived to be particularly important in deprived areas, which lack the initiative to start their own provision. The council's commitment to supporting areas with limited community capacity is reinforced by its policy of identifying areas in need and offering a service, rather than waiting for approaches. So far there have been three examples of clubs becoming self-sustaining. This policy has some problems. Councillors are reluctant to see services withdraw from their communities and parents resent being asked to pay for services that were initially free. Officers commented that sustainability is particularly difficult to achieve in more remote rural areas. The council, however, views this development work as an efficient and equitable way to spend its limited resources.

Special Needs: In 2001 the district council started working with the EYDCP to provide places for children with special needs. The county council part-funds special needs workers to operate in three district council services. Currently three or four children with special needs attend each setting. Most of the children have behavioural problems, although one is physically disabled. The places are publicised through the EYDCP Children's Information Service. In the future the district council intends to expand provision and employ its own special needs worker.

Access to summer play schemes is free for children from families claiming benefits.

STRUCTURES AND PROCESSES

Local authority services involved with delivery of provision; Other organisations involved; Relationships between providers

Organisations involved in delivering provision include the district council's Parks and Play Development services, and independent school-based clubs.

Provision of council play services and the play development function is the responsibility of a play development officer working in the Cultural, Leisure and Commercial Services department. A district Play Forum operates to bring all providers together. It plays a role in co-ordinating provision, especially during holidays (through the forum the council ensures that each week there is a choice of provision without excessive competition that could lead to schemes becoming unsustainable). The forum also provides training for playworkers, registers all members to Kids Club Network and produces a newsletter (with contact details for all the areas' play providers) and it provides some specialist provision to children.

The county council, through the EYDCP, provides funding and training. There are NOF-funded development officers throughout the county. But the county and district council have tried hard to avoid replicating each other's work, leading to the county only employing a worker in Wyre Forest part time, to concentrate on pre-school provision, where the district has less of a role.

Organisations involved in planning or developing provision; Written plans and policies for developing play; Coverage of plans; Implementation of plans

The main organisations involved in the development of play provision are the district and county council.

The district council is in the process of finalising a Play Facilities strategy. It already has a detailed play policy presented in two documents, a Prospectus setting out what parents can expect from the service and a Code of Conduct and Ethics for staff, which also acts as a resource pack for independent play providers.

A county cultural strategy is in preparation. It will be county-wide and fairly broad brush, although there will be district input. District council officers see fitting play development into the vision set out in the strategy as a major challenge for the years ahead.

Review and evaluation of provision (Best Value, quality assurance and self-appraisal); Views taken into account during reviews

A Community Development Best Value Review is planned to take place, but is not on the immediate agenda.

The district council monitors the take-up of its services through the use of two Performance Indicators. Firstly it measures attendance at after-school clubs and holiday schemes as a proportion of the children in the area; secondly it measures the percentage take-up on after-school clubs.

Parents and children have both been asked for their views on council-run play provision. This information is being used for Performance Indicators and Best Value.

Compliance with inspection regimes

Until 2000 the district council chose not to register with social services. As there was already a good working relationship with the county council and the district council had its own standards this suited both parties. In 2000 the district council decided to register, in part to set an example to independent providers. The district has found registration valuable, because it has led to recognition of excellence (e.g. in training) and useful advice on how to improve.

Play provision's relationship with other local authority priorities and initiatives

The district council's play provision is tightly integrated with its other community development functions (art, sport, environmental work). This makes joint working possible and gives all four sections more clout. It also fits into the EYDCP's childcare development work. In addition, the district council makes an effort to join up its provision of clubs with other initiatives in deprived areas (for example, one club is operating in a Sure Start area).

EMPLOYMENT

Numbers of paid and unpaid workers; Numbers of workers with playwork qualifications

At the independent clubs, there are at least 30 paid workers. The council employs three part time playworkers. It aims to recruit playworkers with NVQ2 or equivalent. It also employs around 35 workers during summer holidays (these are often students or teachers).

Recruitment, Retention and Training Issues

The council reports that it has significant problems recruiting qualified staff who want to work for 12½ hours a week, during mid-afternoons. This is despite the council paying good hourly rates compared to what is typical locally. Almost all staff are women, which is perceived as a problem, because it means boys have few role models.

Retention is a significant issue for the council. The council often trains staff only for them to quickly move on to work for other play providers. While this creates recruitment problems, officers are reasonably relaxed because their former employees tend to remain working locally, adding to the local pool of experienced playworkers. This is one way the council can contribute to the wider development of

play in the area. There is good retention of seasonal workers, with approximately half of workers returning each year.

Many independent clubs employ workers who also act as classroom assistants or nursery workers at the same schools. This allows employees to build up a more attractive portfolio of work, rather than simply working in the mid-afternoon. Independent clubs however also face problems with recruitment and retention. There is some co-operation through the Play Forum, with clubs sharing workers in emergencies. The EYDCP hopes to improve matters by establishing a database of registered childcare workers. There are concerns, however, that sharing information may not be possible because of data protection legislation.

The council aims to support its full-time staff through to NVQ3 qualification. It provides one week of full-time paid training for seasonal workers, before they are able to work with children. The EYDCP offers training to independent play providers.

FINANCE

Spending on play provision; Spending per child resident; Budget allocation issues

The direct costs of council provision are around £60,000 (around £4 for every child aged 5 to 16). The council's play development budget, however, is £180,000, including salaries and other costs. The expectation is that funding will remain stable, rising with inflation over the next few years.

The district council spends £40,000 on play areas.

Present funding sources; Funding in the past and plans for the future; Sustainability of provision

District council provision is funded from mainstream community services' budgets. Independent provision is funded from fees and NOF grants. The council reports that play providers in the more rural areas of the district face problems with sustainability.

The high price of most independent summer schemes has meant they have had limited success in attracting children. The council reports that most families in the area chose to use council provision or the well-established club at Franch First School.

PLANS FOR THE FUTURE

Plans for the future; How to enhance play opportunities in the future

The district council hopes to extend its development and facilitation role by providing more advice, supporting new providers and developing networks.

In the near future the council hopes to expand summer holiday provision through a NOF funding bid. In time, officers would also like to introduce Easter and half-term activities.

In the medium term, the aim is to link play development into the cultural strategy, which is in preparation, and to improve provision in more remote rural communities, where current policy is working less well. The possibility of mobile play provision and a viable toy library will be explored.

APPENDIX A: PART 2 RESULTS BY LOCAL AUTHORITY

1A   RURAL DISTRICT COUNCIL

Number of children aged 5 to 16:	7,000	Deprivation ranking (1 = most deprived, 354 = least deprived)	259

Local authority officer supplying information: Arts officer

Unsupervised Play

Number of play areas:	21	Children per play area:	300
Number with local authority funding:	3	Children per play area:	2,400

Local authority spending on play areas:	£5,000	*Per Child Resident:* £0.69	*Per Play Area:* £1,700

Notes: 18 play areas are funded by parish councils.

Supervised Play Projects

Number of play projects:	82	Children per play project:	100
Number with local authority funding:	52	Children per play project:	100

Local authority spending on play schemes:	£49,000	*Per Child Resident:* £6.80

Term time clubs

Number with local authority funding:	29	Other *known* clubs:	20

Holiday Play Schemes

Number with local authority funding:	21	Other *known* schemes:	9

Notes: Most after-school and holiday provision is provided by the district council; there are also independent after-school and youth clubs, holiday schemes, a play bus, special needs project and children's farm.

Policies and Plans

Art Plan 2001 (a training provider, parents, parish councils and councillors were involved in planning; it covers recruitment, retention and training of playworkers); Youth Sports Strategy being updated.

Best Value and Consultation

Best Value Performance Plan	Play not mentioned in the Best Value Performance Plan
Best Value Reviews	Leisure Best Value Review planned for 2004/05
Indicators and targets	No PIs or targets
Consultation – Parents	Parents consulted to help develop training and projects
Consultation – Children	Children consulted to ensure training and programme is popular with children

Partners involved in play

Within the local authority	Arts and Sports Development (Leisure Development)
Outside the local authority	Neighbouring councils, county council, parish councils, schools, play providers, voluntary sector respresentative body

Play Associations and Networks

County Playing Fields Association

Central Government Funding

Sport England funding

1B   RURAL DISTRICT COUNCIL

Number of children aged 5 to 16:	17,000	Deprivation ranking (1 = most deprived, 354 = least deprived)	157

Local authority officer supplying information: Community Development officer

Unsupervised Play

Number of play areas:	68	Children per play area:	200
Number with local authority funding:	58	Children per play area:	300
Local authority spending on play areas:	£80,000	*Per Child Resident: £4.81*	*Per Play Area: £1,400*

Notes: 10 areas are managed independently.

Supervised Play Projects

Number of play projects:	13*	Children per play project:	1,300
Number with local authority funding:	13	Children per play project	1,300
Local authority spending on play schemes:	£10,000	*Per Child Resident: £0.60*	

Term time clubs

Number with local authority funding:	0	Other _known_ clubs:	0

Holiday Play Schemes

Number with local authority funding:	13	Other _known_ schemes:	0

Notes: 13 play schemes are grant-funded by council and delivered by other organisations; an unknown number of youth clubs, mobile services and special needs schemes are delivered by county council.

Policies and Plans

Play Policy exists; new policy in preparation (covers training of playworkers) Play Strategy in preparation

Best Value and Consultation

Best Value Performance Plan	Play not mentioned in the Best Value Performance Plan
Best Value Reviews	Best Value Review planned
Indicators and targets	PIs for grant-funded schemes including numbers attending and ethnic breakdown
Consultation – Parents	Parents consulted to assess popularity of provision
Consultation – Children	Children not consulted

Partners involved in play

Within the local authority	Sport Development and Parks and Countryside (Community Services department)
Outside the local authority	Parish councils, schools, EYDCP, neighbourhood partnerships

Play Associations and Networks

No known play association

Central Government Funding

No information provided

The Planning and Location of Play Provision in England   167   *Appendix A: Part 2 Results By Local Authority*

1C   RURAL DISTRICT COUNCIL

Number of children aged 5 to 16:	10,000	Deprivation ranking (1 = most deprived, 354 = least deprived)	192
Local authority officer supplying information: Community Leisure officer			

Unsupervised Play

Number of play areas:	39	Children per play area:	200
Number with local authority funding:	26	Children per play area:	400
Local authority spending on play areas:	£50,000	*Per Child Resident:* £5.17	*Per Play Area:* £1,900
Notes: 13 play areas are managed by parish councils.			

Supervised Play Projects

Number of play projects:	68*	Children per play project:	300
Number with local authority funding:	38	Children per play project	100
Local authority spending on play schemes:	£33,000	*Per Child Resident:* £3.40	

Term time clubs

Number with local authority funding:	12	Other *known* clubs:	15

Holiday Play Schemes

Number with local authority funding:	24	Other *known* schemes:	10

Notes: There are 12 council funded after-school clubs, but others are delivered by schools; 20 summer schemes are delivered by the council; there is 1 play bus, 3 children's farms and 1 special needs service.

Policies and Plans

Leisure and Cultural Strategy in preparation (coverage will include supervised and unsupervised play; the plan will ensure that looked-after children and children with disabilities receive free places)

The Community Plan and Crime and Disorder Strategy both identified need for additional play provision

Best Value and Consultation

Best Value Performance Plan	Play mentioned in Best Value Performance Plan
Best Value Reviews	Leisure and Development Best Value Review planned (coverage will include play areas, summer schemes, play buses)
Indicators and targets	No PIs or targets
Consultation – Parents	Parents are consulted about future plans
Consultation – Children	Children are consulted on improving provision and to inform funding bids

Partners involved in play

Within the local authority	Recreation and Leisure
Outside the local authority	County council, parish councils, schools, other play providers, authority-wide and neighbourhood partnerships

Play Associations and Networks

No play association operates

Central Government Funding

NOF, Sport England and Coalfield Regeneration funding; plans to apply to Communities Fund

* Incomplete information available for non-local authority provision.

1D RURAL DISTRICT COUNCIL

Number of children aged 5 to 16:	16,000	Deprivation ranking (1 = most deprived, 354 = least deprived)	222

Local authority officer supplying information: Community Services manager

Unsupervised Play

Number of play areas:	36	Children per play area:	400
Number with local authority funding:	36	Children per play area:	400

Local authority spending on play areas:	£86,540	*Per Child Resident: £5.48*	*Per Play Area: £2,400*

Notes:

Supervised Play Projects

Number of play projects:	25*	Children per play project:	800
Number with local authority funding:	19	Children per play project	600

Local authority spending on play schemes:	£25,000	*Per Child Resident: £1.60*

Term time clubs

Number with local authority funding:	4	Other _known_ clubs:	0

Holiday Play Schemes

Number with local authority funding:	9	Other _known_ schemes:	0

Notes: Most provision is delivered by the council; 5 holiday schemes council funded and independently delivered.

Policies and Plans

Cultural Strategy in preparation (covers all play; councillors and RCC involved in process; it targets children with low income and working parents, children with disabilities and children from ethnic minorities; includes policy for training playworkers)

Best Value and Consultation

Best Value Performance Plan	Play mentioned in Best Value Performance Plan
Best Value Reviews	Parks and Open Spaces Best Value Review complete (covered play areas)
	Lesiure Services Best Value Review planned (covering holiday schemes)
Indicators and targets	No PIs or targets
Consultation – Parents	Parents consulted to identify priorities, allocate resources and spread ownership
Consultation – Children	Children consulted to identify priorities, allocate resources and spread ownership

Partners involved in play

Within the local authority	Operations manager and 4 leisure centre managers in Lesiure and Community Services
Outside the local authority	Play Association

Play Associations and Networks

A play association operates, promoting networking and delivering information and play provision

Central Government Funding

Sport England funding

* Incomplete information available for non-local authority provision.

1E   RURAL DISTRICT COUNCIL

Number of children aged 5 to 16:	6,000	Deprivation ranking (1 = most deprived, 354 = least deprived)	176
Local authority officer supplying information: Sports and Leisure Development officer			

Unsupervised Play

Number of play areas:	22	Children per play area:	300
Number with local authority funding:	22	Children per play area:	300
Local authority spending on play areas:	£15,000	*Per Child Resident:* £2.49	*Per Play Area:* £700
Notes:			

Supervised Play Projects

Number of play projects:	34*	Children per play project:	200
Number with local authority funding:	34	Children per play project	200
Local authority spending on play schemes:	–	*Per Child Resident:* –	

Term time clubs

Number with local authority funding:	30	Other _known_ clubs:	0

Holiday Play Schemes

Number with local authority funding:	4	Other _known_ schemes:	0

Notes: The district council only has information on sports-related clubs; the county PFA delivers some holiday schemes; some schools deliver NOF-funded after-school clubs.

Policies and Plans

Cultual Strategy in preparation

Best Value and Consultation

Best Value Performance Plan	Play not mentioned in the Best Value Performance Plan
Best Value Reviews	Leisure Service Best Value Review completed in May 2001
Indicators and targets	PIs for Active Sport programme are in preparation
Consultation – Parents	Parents not consulted
Consultation – Children	Children not consulted

Partners involved in play

Within the local authority	Sports and Leisure Development Officer
Outside the local authority	County council, parish councils, schools, a local authority-level partnership

Play Associations and Networks

No known play association

Central Government Funding

NOF Out-of-school Learning and Sport England funding

1F   RURAL DISTRICT COUNCIL

Number of children aged 5 to 16:	15,000	Deprivation ranking (1 = most deprived, 354 = least deprived)	256

Local authority officer supplying information: Leisure Services oficer

Unsupervised Play

Number of play areas:	15	Children per play area:	1,000
Number with local authority funding:	1	Children per play area:	15,200

Local authority spending on play areas:	£3,000	*Per Child Resident:* £0.20	*Per Play Area:* £3,000

Notes: 14 areas managed by other organisations.

Supervised Play Projects

Number of play projects:	6*	Children per play project:	2,500
Number with local authority funding:	6	Children per play project	2,500

Local authority spending on play schemes:	–	*Per Child Resident:* –

Term time clubs

Number with local authority funding:	0	Other _known_ clubs:	0

Holiday Play Schemes

Number with local authority funding:	5	Other _known_ schemes:	0

Notes: Information was only available about holiday programmes; term time clubs also exist.

Policies and Plans

No plans or policies

Best Value and Consultation

Best Value Performance Plan	Play not mentioned in the Best Value Performance Plan
Best Value Reviews	No information supplied
Indicators and targets	No PIs or targets
Consultation – Parents	No information supplied
Consultation – Children	Children consulted in planning the design of play areas

Partners involved in play

Within the local authority	Leisure Centre managers and Lesiure Development officers
Outside the local authority	Neighbouring councils, county council, parish councils, schools

Play Associations and Networks

No play association operates

Central Government Funding

No information provided

* Incomplete information available for non-local authority provision.

1G   RURAL DISTRICT COUNCIL

Number of children aged 5 to 16:	14,000	Deprivation ranking (1 = most deprived, 354 = least deprived)	190
Local authority officer supplying information: Head of Leisure Services			

Unsupervised Play

Number of play areas:	39	Children per play area:	300
Number with local authority funding:	12	Children per play area:	1,100
Local authority spending on play areas:	£34,000	*Per Child Resident:* £2.51	*Per Play Area:* £2,800
Notes: 27 areas are managed by other organisations.			

Supervised Play Projects

Number of play projects:	0*	Children per play project:	–
Number with local authority funding:	0	Children per play project	–
Local authority spending on play schemes:	–	*Per Child Resident:* –	
Term time clubs			
Number with local authority funding:	0	Other *known* clubs:	0
Holiday Play Schemes			
Number with local authority funding:	–	Other *known* schemes:	–
Notes: No information about supervised play provision was supplied.			

Policies and Plans

Parks and Countryside Strategy in production (will cover unsupervised play)

Best Value and Consultation

Best Value Performance Plan	Play mentioned in Best Value Performance Plan
Best Value Reviews	Leisure Best Value Review planned (covering unsupervised play areas)
Indicators and targets	PIs for play areas (NPFA standards)
Consultation – Parents	Parents consulted to decide on location of new play areas
Consultation – Children	Children consulted to decide on location of new play areas

Partners involved in play

Within the local authority	No information
Outside the local authority	No information

Play Associations and Networks

No known play association

Central Government Funding

No information provided

* Incomplete information available for non-local authority provision.

1H   RURAL DISTRICT COUNCIL

Number of children aged 5 to 16:	14,000	Deprivation ranking (1 = most deprived, 354 = least deprived)	161
Local authority officer supplying information: Play officer			

Unsupervised Play

Number of play areas:	37	Children per play area:	400
Number with local authority funding:	17	Children per play area:	800
Local authority spending on play areas:	£40,000	*Per Child Resident:* £2.79	*Per Play Area:* £2,400
Notes: 20 by social housing company.			

Supervised Play Projects

Number of play projects:	41	Children per play project:	900
Number with local authority funding:	16	Children per play project	300
Local authority spending on play schemes:	£59,000	*Per Child Resident:* £4.10	

Term time clubs

Number with local authority funding:	5	Other *known* clubs:	17

Holiday Play Schemes

Number with local authority funding:	11	Other *known* schemes:	8

Notes: 5 after-school clubs and 11 play schemes are delivered by the council; all other provision is independent.

Policies and Plans

Play Policy exists. Play Development Plan exists (targets children from low income, working and lone parent families; policies for recruiting, retaining and training playworkers)

Play mentioned in parks and open spaces, community safety, LA21 and EYDCP plan

Best Value and Consultation

Best Value Performance Plan	Play mentioned in Best Value Performance Plan
Best Value Reviews	Community Development Best Value Review planned
Indicators and targets	PIs for number of attendances at after-school clubs and holiday schemes
Consultation – Parents	Parents consulted for PIs and Best Value
Consultation – Children	Children consulted for PIs and Best Value

Partners involved in play

Within the local authority	Play Development, Parks and Countryside officers (Culture and Leisure and Commercial services)
Outside the local authority	Play forum, county council, schools, play providers, EYDCP, regional grouping

Play Associations and Networks

A play forum operates, promoting networking and provides training, information and provision for children

Central Government Funding

NOF funding

2A   URBAN DISTRICT COUNCIL

Number of children aged 5 to 16:	19,000	Deprivation ranking (1 = most deprived, 354 = least deprived)	138
Local authority officer supplying information: Parks and Open Spaces manager			

Unsupervised Play

Number of play areas:	38	Children per play area:	500
Number with local authority funding:	32	Children per play area:	600
Local authority spending on play areas:	£75,000	*Per Child Resident:* £4.01	*Per Play Area:* £2,300
Notes: 6 areas managed independently.			

Supervised Play Projects

Number of play projects:	3*	Children per play project:	6,200
Number with local authority funding:	3	Children per play project	6,200
Local authority spending on play schemes:	£10,000	*Per Child Resident:* £0.50	

Term time clubs

Number with local authority funding:	0	Other _known_ clubs:	0

Holiday Play Schemes

Number with local authority funding:	3	Other _known_ schemes:	0

Notes: After-school clubs and youth clubs operate but the district council has no details; apart from 3 holiday schemes, the county council has responsibility for all supervised play.

Policies and Plans

Play policy and stratgey exists as a single document, covering play areas only. The document targets children in low income families and children with disabilities and special needs

Local Plan exists (covers play areas)

Best Value and Consultation

Best Value Performance Plan	Play mentioned in Best Value Performance Plan
Best Value Reviews	No details available
Indicators and targets	No PIs or targets
Consultation – Parents	Parents consulted during development of new sites
Consultation – Children	Children consulted about design of play areas and wider play strategy

Partners involved in play

Within the local authority	Sports Development (Community Services), Parks, Planning
Outside the local authority	Neighbouring council, county council, parish council, NHS, schools, play providers

Play Associations and Networks

A play association operates, promoting networking and providing informaiton

Central Government Funding

SRB funding, plans to tap into NDC funding

* Incomplete information available for non-local authority provision.

2B   URBAN DISTRICT COUNCIL

Number of children aged 5 to 16:	19,000	Deprivation ranking (1 = most deprived, 354 = least deprived)	111
Local authority officer supplying information: Community Leisure officer			

Unsupervised Play

Number of play areas:	67	Children per play area:	300
Number with local authority funding:	67	Children per play area:	300
Local authority spending on play areas:	£43,000	*Per Child Resident:* £2.25	*Per Play Area:* £600
Notes:			

Supervised Play Projects

Number of play projects:	19*	Children per play project:	1,000
Number with local authority funding:	19	Children per play project	1,000
Local authority spending on play schemes:	£100,000	*Per Child Resident:* £5.20	

Term time clubs

Number with local authority funding:	0	Other _known_ clubs:	0

Holiday Play Schemes

Number with local authority funding:	18	Other _known_ schemes:	0

Notes: The district council runs 18 holiday schemes, two of which are able to cater for children with special needs; there is one other special needs service; no information was available on independent provision.

Policies and Plans

A Play Strategy is in preparation (covering play areas only)

Best Value and Consultation

Best Value Performance Plan	Play not mentioned in the Best Value Performance Plan
Best Value Reviews	No details available
Indicators and targets	No PIs or targets
Consultation – Parents	Parents consulted to monitor customer satisfaction
Consultation – Children	Children not consulted

Partners involved in play

Within the local authority	Community Recreation (Leisure) and Landscape Development (Parks and Amenities)
Outside the local authority	Schools

Play Associations and Networks

No play association operates

Central Government Funding

Intend to apply for NOF childcare funding

* Incomplete information available for non-local authority provision.

2C URBAN DISTRICT COUNCIL

Number of children aged 5 to 16:	19,000	Deprivation ranking (1 = most deprived, 354 = least deprived)	258
Local authority officer supplying information: Play officer			

Unsupervised Play

Number of play areas:	80	Children per play area:	200
Number with local authority funding:	80	Children per play area:	200
Local authority spending on play areas:	£115,000	*Per Child Resident:* £6.15	*Per Play Area:* £1,400
Notes: All known play areas are council managed.			

Supervised Play Projects

Number of play projects:	26*	Children per play project:	700
Number with local authority funding:	26	Children per play project	700
Local authority spending on play schemes:	£115,000	*Per Child Resident:* £6.10	

Term time clubs

Number with local authority funding:	0	Other *known* clubs:	0

Holiday Play Schemes

Number with local authority funding:	24	Other *known* schemes:	0

Notes: The district council runs 2 adventure playgrounds and 24 holiday schemes; information about other providers was not available.

Policies and Plans

Cultural Strategy exists (covers supervised play)
Parks and Open Spaces Strategy exists (covers play areas)

Best Value and Consultation

Best Value Performance Plan	Play mentioned in Best Value Performance Plan
Best Value Reviews	Sport and Recreation Best Value Review planned (covering parks and play areas)
Indicators and targets	No PIs or targets
Consultation – Parents	Parents consulted on new play areas and priorities for cultural stragegy
Consultation – Children	Children consulted to deliver youth facilites

Partners involved in play

Within the local authority	Play Development (Leisure)
Outside the local authority	Parish councils, play providers, neighbourhood partnerships

Play Associations and Networks

No known play association

Central Government Funding

Sport England and SRB funding; intend to apply for NOF Better Play

* Incomplete information available for non-local authority provision.

2D   URBAN DISTRICT COUNCIL

Number of children aged 5 to 16:	13,000	Deprivation ranking (1 = most deprived, 354 = least deprived)	132
Local authority officer supplying information: Community Leisure officer			

Unsupervised Play

Number of play areas:	29	Children per play area:	400
Number with local authority funding:	29	Children per play area:	400
Local authority spending on play areas:	£21,581	*Per Child Resident: £1.70*	*Per Play Area: £700*
Notes: No information on any non-council play areas			

Supervised Play Projects

Number of play projects:	13*	Children per play project:	1,100
Number with local authority funding:	12	Children per play project	1,000
Local authority spending on play schemes:	£118,000	*Per Child Resident:*	£9.30

Term time clubs			
Number with local authority funding:	0	Other *known* clubs:	1

Holiday Play Schemes			
Number with local authority funding:	9	Other *known* schemes:	0

Notes: An adventure playground, holiday programmes, and a special needs scheme are delivered by the council.			

Policies and Plans

Play Policy in preparation
Play Strategy in preparation

Best Value and Consultation

Best Value Performance Plan	Play mentioned in Best Value Performance Plan
Best Value Reviews	Leisure and Amenities Best Value Review under way (covering play areas and holiday schemes)
Indicators and targets	No PIs or targets
Consultation – Parents	Parents consulted to assist with planning
Consultation – Children	Children consulted to assist with planning

Partners involved in play

Within the local authority	Community recreation, sport and play development officers, leisure cente manager (all Lesiure and Amenities department); Parks and Open Spaces department
Outside the local authority	Play association, schools, other local partnerships

Play Associations and Networks

A Play association operates, promoting networking and delivering information and training

Central Government Funding

SRB funding

* Incomplete information available for non-local authority provision.

4A   URBAN METROPOLITAN BOROUGH

Number of children aged 5 to 16:	50,000	Deprivation ranking (1 = most deprived, 354 = least deprived)	67
Local authority officer supplying information: Children and Family Education manager			

Unsupervised Play

Number of play areas:	31	Children per play area:	1,600
Number with local authority funding:	31	Children per play area:	1,600
Local authority spending on play areas:	£201,000	*Per Child Resident:* £4.00	*Per Play Area:* £6,500
Notes:			

Supervised Play Projects

Number of play projects:	127*	Children per play project:	500
Number with local authority funding:	100	Children per play project	400
Local authority spending on play schemes:	£1,525,000	*Per Child Resident:* £30.30	

Term time clubs

Number with local authority funding:	43	Other *known* clubs:	24

Holiday Play Schemes

Number with local authority funding	49	Other *known* schemes:	0

Notes: All provision is delivered by council except for 24 after-school clubs, an urban farm, and 2 special needs schemes. The council also runs 2 Play Centres and offers 350 places for those with special needs and asylum seeker and looked-after children

Policies and Plans

Children and Family Education Policy and Community Education Policy; Cultural Development Strategy; Early Years and Childcare Development Plan

Best Value and Consultation

Best Value Performance Plan	Play mentioned in Best Value Performance Plan
Best Value Reviews	Children and Family Education Best Value Review completed (covered children's clubs; holiday schemes; play centres)
	Cultural Services Best Value Review planned (covering other play centres and holiday schemes)
Indicators and targets	No PIs or targets
Consultation – Parents	Parents consulted to influence planning and design
Consultation – Children	Children consulted to influence activities, planning and design

Partners involved in play

Within the local authority	Children and Family Education (delivered by three area offices); Cultural Development; Early Years
Outside the local authority	NHS, schools, play providers, EYDCP, other local partnerships

Play Associations and Networks

Play Forum and Council for Voluntary Youth Service both operate

Central Government Funding

NOF, EAZ, NDC and Neighbourhood Renewal funding currently; Children's Fund programme about to begin

* Incomplete information available for non-local authority provision.

APPENDIX B: THE PART 3 SPATIAL MAPPING EXERCISE

An important element of the Part 3 case study research was a spatial mapping exercise. It has not been possible to include the results of this part of the study in this report, although key findings are highlighted in Chapters 4 and 5. This appendix describes the approach we adopted in carrying out the spatial mapping exercise.

Using post code data we indicated on Ordinance Survey maps where play provision is located within the four local authorities. Play provision was divided into four types, and each was given a colour coding (play areas – green; summer play projects – red; term time play projects – yellow; special projects – blue). Incomplete post code/address information meant that we were not able to map all provision for all the case study areas, but we consider that the data available was sufficient to give a good impression of the spatial distribution of play provision.

In addition, to simply indicate the location of provision, the mapping exercise was used to compare levels of play provision to child population, at the level of local authority wards. Ward boundaries were marked on the maps, and the number of sites of play provision in each ward were counted. Estimates for the number of children (aged 0 to 16 years old) living in each ward were obtained from National Statistics. This enabled us to calculate how much provision was available per capita in different wards, and indicate which parts of each case study area had low and high levels of provision.

In addition we obtained data on the level of deprivation of each local authority ward, using the DTLR Indices of Deprivation 2000. We ranked wards in terms of what proportion of children were estimated to live in families with low incomes.[1] We were then able to consider how levels of provision per capita compared to levels of deprivation, allowing us to assess whether deprived areas had particularly high concentrations of provision.

---

1 The definition of low income used by the Indices of Deprivation 2000 counts children living in the households where certain major benefits are being claimed (e.g. Income Support, Job Seekers Allowance (income based), Family Credit, Disability Working Allowance). Although the indicator is an adequate proxy for the level of low income in a community it does not capture all dimensions of income poverty (e.g. non claiming of benefits and low paid work above benefit thresholds), or social disadvantage and exclusion that is unrelated to low income.

APPENDIX C: REPLICATING THE WORK

PART 2: THE REGIONAL PICTURE

Part 2 of the project was designed so it could be replicated in other regions of the country, drawing on the lessons of our piloting of the survey in the West Midlands.

To assist such replication, this appendix provides some information about the approach we adopted. We would be very pleased to discuss our methodology in greater detail with anyone interested in a conducting a similar survey.

1. The questions were designed in liaison with the Children's Play Council (CPC) and the project steering group. Topics were set by CPC, with questions tested on the play professionals on our steering group.

2. The questionnaire was piloted on four local authorities. A short summary of responses was compiled and discussed with CPC and the steering group. Respondents were asked to comment on the questionnaire's style and content. New questions and amendments were made at this stage.

3. All local authorities were contacted by telephone, with the aim of identifying the most appropriate officer to answer the questionnaire. This is a time-consuming process, although speeded somewhat by having steering group members with good contacts in the regions. In the telephone conversations, we ensured that we were talking to the most appropriate person, explained the purpose and nature of the questionnaire, and gave them an estimate of how long it would take them to complete (30–45 minutes). We also warned they might need to consult with colleagues to answer some questions. Finally a deadline was agreed by when the questionnaire would be returned.

4. Some local authorities failed to return their questionnaires in time. These were phoned on several occasions with reminders. Eventually a final deadline was set to time limit the exercise.

5. Data on each local authorities' child population (5–16) was obtained from the Office of National Statistics Populations Estimated Unit (www.statistics.gov.uk).

6. All data was inputted into an Excel spreadsheet. This was used both to analyse numerical data (e.g. ratios of play areas to child populations) and as a source for presenting tables of data in word documents.

Problems along the way

The length of the questionnaire: We wanted to collect a large amount of information, so the questionnaire was inevitably long. This is off-putting to many respondents, particularly if they are unable to answer some sections. A shorter questionnaire might well have produced a higher response rate.

Definitions: Different local authorities use words differently, so there is always likely to be ambiguity in how questions are read (and how you read answers). Particular issues are how terms such as 'children', 'play' and 'after-school clubs' are used. Another issue is how different authorities account for their costs. While it is possible to provide explanation of your terms, the more words you use the more you may put off respondents. A degree of misunderstanding is almost inevitable.

Identifying knowledgeable respondents: In many cases, respondents did not have information on all aspects of a council's work. In particular, different people were often needed to provide answers on supervised and unsupervised play. Although officers were sometimes happy to pass the questionnaire among themselves, it might be better to split the questionnaire into halves targeted at play area and play activities staff respectively. Finally, our experience suggests it would be well worth contacting the EYDCP as well as local authorities for information about non-council provision.

PART 3: THE LOCAL AUTHORITY PICTURE

Replicating the methodology

We recruited the four case study local authorities with advice from playwork specialists in the West Midlands. In the first instance, each authority was invited to take part in Part 2 of the study. This helped the authorities decide if they wanted to go on to become case studies and gave us useful basic information about each authority.

The evidence for the case studies was gathered using the following approaches:

1. *Visit and structured interview:* In all cases we interviewed several representatives of the local authority. In each interview we first invited participants to briefly 'introduce' their work to us, and then worked through a standard list of questions. In all instances we made subsequent telephone calls to the interviewees, or others suggested by them, to clarify details or gain another perspective.

2. *Reviewing written material:* Before and during our visits we collected any written documents of interest. These included play policies, best value reviews, brochures and newsletters.

3. *Data collection: unsupervised play areas:* The participants were asked to fill in a form for each of the play areas in the area. Where these were delivered by others they were asked to arrange for them to be filled in.

4. *Data collection: supervised play provision:* The participants were asked to fill in a form for each play provision site or programme in the area. For non-council providers, we asked either for the local authority to fill in the forms using its existing information, or for the forms to be distributed to providers.

5. *Assembly of statistical data:* For the mapping exercise, we obtained two sources of ward-level data. The first were estimates for child populations, available from the Neighbourhood Statistics Unit, Office for National Statistics (www.ons.gov.uk). The second was the Indices of Deprivation 2000, available from the Department of Local Government, Transport and the Regions (www.dtlr.gov.uk).

There were three stages to understanding and interpreting the data we collected:

- In the first instance we simply set out to 'tell the story' of the local authority by presenting facts in a digestible manner.

- Our analysis first consisted of the mapping exercise which involved charting provision, using the information from the data collection forms, and cross-referencing the information against the official statistics, to produce the ward-level tables.

- Finally, we undertook a comparative analysis of the four local authorities to expose and understand differences in patterns and approaches.

Section 4

The State of Play

A Survey of Play Professionals in England

March 2001

The State of Play
A Survey of Play Professionals in England

Contents

Summary   **187**

1   **The survey**   **189**
1.1   The questionnaire   189
1.2   Respondents   189
1.3   Play services and provision   189
1.4   The children who used the provision   190
1.5   Access to play services and provision   190

2   **The value of play**   **193**
2.1   The benefits of play provision to children   193
2.2   Benefits of play provision to the children's families   194
2.3   Benefits of play provision to local communities   195

3   **The development of play services and provision**   **196**
3.1   Background to provision   196
3.2   The changing face of play provision   197

4   **Play and public policy**   **198**
4.1   Play and the Government's policy agenda   198
4.2   Formal links with the national and local initiatives   199
4.3   Play provision in local planning   200
4.4   Involvement of play staff in the planning process   201
4.5   Involvement of children in planning and evaluation   201

5   **The Government's quality agenda**   **202**
5.1   Best Value Reviews   202
5.2   Meeting legal requirements for inspection and regulation   202
5.3   Quality Assurance schemes   202

6   **Conclusions**   **204**

Appendix 1: Questionnaire   **205**

Tables and figures

Table 1: Types of play provision in urban and rural areas   **187**
Table 2: Age range of children using services and provision   **187**
Table 3: Access to play provision in urban and rural areas   **189**
Table 4: Benefits of play provision to children   **190**
Table 5: Benefits of play provision to families   **191**
Table 6: Benefits to the community   **192**
Table 7: Main reasons respondents felt play services in their area were   **193**
provided in the way they were
Table 8: Single most important reason respondents felt play services in   **193**
their area were provided in the way they were
Table 9: Policy objectives addressed by play services and provision   **195**
Table 10: Numbers of play services and provision linked to national   **196**
and local policy initiatives
Table 11: Play services referred to in different local authority plans   **198**
Table 12: Ways in which children are involved in the planning process   **198**

Figure 1: Proportion of services linked to combinations of initiatives   **196**
Figure 2: Number of services or provision mentioned in combinations   **197**
of plans

Acknowledgements
CPC would like to thank all members of the CPC Executive Committee, DCMS and the play professionals who piloted and completed the survey.

Available from:
Children's Play Council
8 Wakley Street
London
EC1V 7QE
020 7843 6016
cpc@ncb.org.uk

Issy Cole-Hamilton
Policy and Research Officer
Children's Play Council
March 2001

Summary

i.   In September 2000 the Children's Play Council surveyed the views of play professionals on the ways in which their services benefited children and their families and how those services were linked to the Government's policy and planning agendas. (Section 1)

ii.   Exactly 200 play professionals responded, representing many types of play provision, including both staffed and unsupervised, and coming from all over England. In most areas a wide range of children used the services, which could be accessed via a variety of means including open access, referrals and 'paid for' places. In some areas provision was targeted for specific groups of children, in particular, those who were disabled or had special educational needs and those who had been identified as 'in need' or at risk of social exclusion. (Section 1)

iii.   The primary benefit of play services to children was seen to be the opportunity for them to socialise with other children, make new friends and have a good time. Also important were the health benefits, the safety aspects and the opportunity to gain new experiences. Families were benefiting from children's play services, in particular through enabling parents to work or train and in ensuring parents felt their children were happy, safe and enjoying themselves. Play provision was also seen as important in promoting community well-being and security. This was achieved by providing economic benefits, primarily through allowing parents to work and train and ensuring children were occupied. These benefits all linked closely with the Government's policy agenda for children and families. (Section 2)

iv.   To plan for the future of play services it is important to understand the reasons why services exist as they do now. When asked to prioritise the factors behind the rationale for existing provision, the most frequently cited reason was the availability of resources. Children's needs, local government agendas, history and parents' needs were also seen as high on the list. The factor cited by the smallest number of respondents was children's wishes. (Section 3)

v.   Looking to the future there was a cautious optimism. Over half the respondents thought their service or provision would change in the future. Of these, the largest group thought their service would improve. Many saw the Best Value review process as having an impact but were not clear, as yet, what changes it would bring. A small number of people felt their service would suffer, from lack of funding and as a result in the change of emphasis from play to childcare. (Section 3)

vi.   Amongst the play professionals responding there was a high level of liaison with other local services and planning although there were a significant number of areas where these links were not being made. Almost half the services were referred to in the Early Years Development and Childcare Plan and one in four in the Children's Services Plan, but a significant number of services were not linked in at all with local policies and initiatives. Eight services said they had or were developing a Play Policy or Strategy. (Section 4)

vii.   Involvement of children in planning was also prominent. In some areas there was extensive and rigorous consultation with children whilst in others it was much less formal. (Section 4)

viii.   Awareness of Best Value Reviews was high amongst play professionals with almost all of those in local authorities aware of an impending review even if it was not planned for the near future. Many had or were completing reviews at the time of the survey. (Section 5)

1   The survey

1.1   The questionnaire

In September 2000 the Children's Play Council distributed a questionnaire to the 6,000 recipients of *Play Today*, a free, bi-monthly newspaper for professionals with an interest in play and play provision for school-aged children. The questionnaire was aimed specifically at those managing, providing and supporting local play services and provision in England. (See Appendix 1)

1.2   Respondents

A total of 200 completed questionnaires were received from people in rural and urban areas, representing a range play provision, including service managers and people who worked with children on a daily basis and those involved in training, support and planning.

Of the 200 play professionals in England, who completed questioannaires:
- 68 (34%) were service managers
- 39 (20%) managed some type of play provision
- 25 (13%) were involved in development work
- 18 (9%) worked directly with children
- 13 (7%) were involved in supporting play services and provision
- 10 (5%) were involved in planning.

The remainder were involved in training, campaigning and other support activities.

Over half the respondents worked for local authorities, of whom three in five worked for district or borough councils. One in four were in the voluntary sector, most of whom worked for local organisations. The remainder worked in education, the health service and the private sector.

Responses came from all over England with:
- 42% from people working in urban areas
- 37% from people working in mixed urban and rural areas and
- 21% from people working in rural areas.

1.3   Play services and provision

Of those replying, almost 40 per cent were involved with only one type of provision. Of these almost one in three worked with unsupervised play spaces and one in five in year-round provision. However, most respondents were involved with a range of play provision. The most likely combination, for one in five respondents, was of holiday play schemes, after-school clubs and year-round provision.

Amongst all the respondents
- 53% were involved with holiday play schemes
- 35% were involved with after-school clubs
- 25% were involved with unsupervised play provision
- 24% were involved with specialist provision, of whom nearly two thirds provided for disabled children and those with special educational needs
- 20% were involved with adventure playgrounds
- 16% were involved with mobile play projects

There were also two hospital play projects.

The respondents working in urban areas were more likely to be involved in providing adventure playgrounds, after-school clubs, year-round out-of-school play provision and provision for disabled children than those in rural areas. Those in rural areas were more likely to be involved with mobile play projects than those in urban areas. Similar proportions of respondents in rural and urban areas were involved in providing holiday play schemes and unsupervised play provision. (See Table 1)

Table 1: Types of play provision in urban and rural areas

Type of play provision	Urban n=80*		Rural n=38*	
	n	%**	n	%**
Adventure playground	19	24	4	11
Holiday play scheme	46	57	21	55
Unsupervised play space	15	19	7	18
After-school club	34	42	13	34
Year-round out-of-school provision	33	41	10	26
Mobile play project	10	13	9	34
Provision for disabled children	15	19	2	5
Other	25	31	9	24

* Total numbers are less than 100 so percentages are for comparison only
** Proportion of respondents in urban and rural areas involved with each type of play provision
n= number of respondents

1.4 The children who used the provision
The play services and provision described in the survey were almost all used by children of under eight years old as well as older children. (See Table 2) Four services were used only by children up to eight years old and three services were used only by children over eight years old.

Table 2: Age range of children using services and provision

Minimum age of children using service or provision	Number of services/provision with children of a maximum age of:			
	8 to 11 years	12 to 14 years	15 years and over	Total
Under 3 years	6	25	37	68
3 and 4 years	14	26	15	55
5 to 8 years	14	26	20	60
Total	34	77	72	183

1.5 Access to play services and provision
In most areas there were a variety of ways in which children were able to use the services or provision. For example:
- 66% of services offered open access
- in 42%, children were referred by other agencies
- in 50%, parents bought places for their children

- in 24%, places were targeted to a specific group of children
- in 12%, there were other means of accessing provision, including first come first served, children from the local school and workplace provision.

Of the 124 services offering some open access provision, 44 said all their provision was open access. Of these 44, there were:
- 25 providing unsupervised play spaces
- 13 providing adventure playgrounds
- 12 providing holiday play schemes
- 6 providing year-round provision
- 4 providing after-school clubs.

Nineteen respondents were involved with provision only available to children if their parents bought places. This included:
- 8 providing holiday schemes
- 8 providing after-school clubs
- 7 providing year-round provision
- 2 specialist schemes for disabled children.

The children specifically targeted for places or referred by agencies were predominantly those who were disabled or had special educational needs and those who had been identified as 'in need' or at risk of social exclusion. Of the 44 services targeted for specific groups of children:
- 16 were aimed at children who were disabled or had other special educational needs
- 7 were for children from the locality
- 7 for children identified as 'socially excluded'
- 5 were for children defined by their social services as 'in need' under Section 17 of the Children Act 1989
- 3 schemes were specifically for children in the school and two were workplace provision.

Other types of access included emergency care for children in distressed families, children in hospital and children visiting prisoner parents.

The main referring agencies were social services departments. Of the 77 services accepting referrals 37 (48%) took referrals from social service departments. The rest accepted children referred by schools, health services and other local projects.

Provision in rural areas was more likely to be paid for by parents than in urban areas where there was more open access provision, referrals from other agencies and provision targeted at specific groups of children. (See Table 3)

Table 3: Access to play provision in urban and rural areas

Access to play provision	Urban n=80*		Rural n=38*	
	n	%**	n	%**
Open access	54	68	20	53
Referred by other agencies	34	43	13	34
Parents pay for places	38	48	23	60
Targeted to specific groups of children	27	34	6	16
Other	7	9	4	11

* Total numbers are less than 100 so percentages are for comparison only
** Proportion of respondents in urban and rural areas involved with each type of access to play provision
n= number of respondents

2 The value of play

2.1 The benefits of play provision to children

Providing children with the opportunity to socialise and develop friendships was seen as the most important benefit of the play service or provision to the children themselves. Of the 501 perceived benefits, reported by 179 respondents, over one in four involved children's opportunities for social interactions (see Table 4). The following are comments about the benefits of play services to children, and are representative of many:

- Increase individual's self-awareness, self-esteem, self-confidence and self-respect.
- Mix with children from other backgrounds.
- Increase in confidence through developing new skills.
- Socially excluded children able to interact with others.
- Offer good opportunities for social learning and interaction.
- Meeting new friends from other areas.

Between them, the 179 play professionals describing the benefits of their play provision to children cited children's opportunities to meet other children and socialise, 130 times. This was by far the most frequently mentioned benefit.

Table 4: Benefits of play provision to children (179 respondents)

Benefit to children	% of responses n= 501	Number of responses
Social interaction	26	130
Can play and have fun	19	96
General child development	9	42
Keeps children safe	8	40
Childcare	5	27
Gives children new experiences	5	25
Physical activity	5	23
Developing learning skills	4	20
Children feel respected and listened	3	17
Supervised, quality provision	3	17
Emotional development	3	16
Keeps children occupied	3	14
Developing creativity	2	12
Other	2	10
Access to indoor and outdoor space and local provision	1	6
Special provision for special needs	<1	4

Opportunities for children to play and have fun were mentioned 96 times, over twice as frequently as the third most mentioned benefit, child development. Play provision was also seen by many as being important in keeping children safe, offering them childcare, giving them physical activity and helping their developing learning skills.

Typical comments included:
- Stretching imaginations, curiosity, creativity.
- Caring, safe environment with fun, music, craft, etc.
- Physical challenge and enjoyment, e.g. climbing/swinging/sliding.
- Play can then be developed into sport.
- Assist with intellectual and educational development.
- Children do things they normally would not be able to.
- Keeps them occupied when not at school.
- Good quality play with trained workers.

2.2 Benefits of play provision to the children's families
Play professionals clearly felt that their provision was valuable to families as well as to the children who used it: 174 respondents cited 470 benefits to families of children using the play provision or service. The most commonly mentioned benefits, cited 86 and 76 times respectively, were that parents were able to work or train and that they could be sure their children were enjoying themselves and being well cared for. (See Table 5) Typical comments included:
- Low cost, high quality childcare enables parents to take up work or study.
- Children as young as six weeks can attend so young single parents can continue education and gain qualifications.
- Able to work, knowing child is happy and safe after school.
- Pleasure from watching children play.
- Knowledge/peace of mind that equipment/sites are as safe as possible.

Allowing parents the opportunity to have time away from their children was also seen as an important benefit of play provision. In addition, families were thought to benefit from having healthier, happier children (see Table 5). For many play professionals the fact that their provision gave parents an opportunity to meet and socialise with other adults was also important.

Table 5: Benefits of play provision to families (174 respondents)

Benefits to families	Per cent of all responses n= 470 %	Number of responses
Able to work or train	18	86
Peace of mind	16	76
Break from children	14	67
Healthier children	13	61
Childcare	10	49
Social contact with other adults	10	45
Benefits to family and community life	9	40
Parenting support and advice	6	28
Other	2	8
Access to other services	1	6
Feelings of involvement	1	4

2.3   Benefits of play provision to local communities
Play provision was also seen as important in promoting community well-being and security and in providing economic benefits, primarily through allowing parents to work and train.

Buildings and facilities used by play services were frequently seen as a focal point for communities. Play services were thought to offer opportunities for social interaction for the wider community and to support the development of a greater sense of community spirit.

Local communities were also seen to benefit from the fact that parents were able to work or train and that children were occupied, had somewhere safe to go, and, in many cases, were not involved in criminal or anti-social behaviour. (See Table 6)

Table 6: Benefits to the community (number of respondents = 169)

Benefits to the community	Per cent of responses n=405 %	Number of responses
Places where children are occupied	32	129
• Less anti-social or criminal behaviour in public places		(55)
• Giving children something to do		(42)
• Places where children are safe		(32)
Community well-being, i.e.	30	121
• Resource or focal point		(51)
• More integrated community		(30)
• Greater sense of community		(29)
• Local provision for children		(11)
Economic benefits to families and community	14	57
Development of children's social skills	12	47
Play and creativity for children	5	21
Support for families	4	15
Positive images of children	1	5
Providing affordable childcare	1	4
Other, including healthier children, opportunities for consultations, promoting good practice	1	6

3   The development of play services and provision

3.1   Background to provision

Two recent, major changes in the Government's approach to planning for children have been the expansion of out-of-school childcare and greater emphasis on the importance of consulting with children and parents. We wondered what impact this had had on the way provision exists and asked respondents to identify, from a list, the three main reasons why services in their area were provided in the way they were. They were then asked to identify the single most important reason.

The availability of resources was the most frequently cited reason for the way services were currently provided. Nearly 60 per cent of the respondents put this as one of the three main reasons. Children's needs, local government agendas, history and parents' needs were also seen as high on the list. The factor cited by the smallest number of respondents was children's wishes. (See Table 7)

Table 7: Main reasons respondents felt play services in their area were provided in the way they were

Reason	Number of responses*	Proportion of respondents n=179 %	Proportion of responses n=497 %
Availability of resources	106	59	21
Children's needs	76	43	15
Local government agendas	75	42	15
Historical reasons	73	41	15
Parents' needs	70	40	14
National government agendas	39	22	8
Parents' wishes	28	16	6
Children's wishes	19	11	2
Other	11	7	2

*   Respondents gave up to three answers each

When asked for the single most important reason, availability of resources was still the most likely to be cited. However, historical reasons and local government agendas displaced children's needs and moved higher up the list. (See Table 8)

Table 8: Single most important reason respondents felt play services in their area were provided in the way they were

Reason	Proportion of respondents n=134 %
Availability of resources	24
Historical reasons	18
Local government agendas	17
Children's needs	14
Parents' needs	10
Children's wishes	5
National government agendas	5
Parents' wishes	4
Other	3

3.2   The changing face of play provision

'With additional government funding now available there will be a great increase in the amount and type of provision.'

In order to identify potential changes in play services and provision we asked whether the professionals expected any significant changes to the way play services are provided in their locality in the next few years. Fifty-five per cent of the respondents anticipated changes. Twenty-three per cent were not sure and 22 per cent felt little would alter.

'There seems to be money available and a group of enthusiastic people who are working very hard to get things set up in this area.'

Of the 106 people describing likely changes, 43 felt that play provision would improve. This included:
- 22 who anticipated an increase in play provision
- 19 who thought play would have a higher profile in local planning and development.

Two respondents thought there would be better co-ordination of the play service.

'We are currently producing a comprehensive play strategy to include summer play schemes, etc. We are also working with County and District partners to raise the profile of play.'

However, 12 respondents thought that local play services would suffer from lack of funding; and nine, that the emphasis on childcare and education was taking resources from play provision. Three respondents felt that difficulties with insurance and perceived risks to children would have a negative impact on their provision.

'I see provision decreasing substantially for two reasons. Authorities are under pressure to cut costs and play is an easy target.'

One in three of those anticipating change did not specify if the changes would be good or bad but were clear that Best Value Reviews, the Government's childcare and education policies and the 'Social Inclusion' agenda would have a marked impact on local play services and provision.

4   Play and public policy

4.1   Play and the Government's policy agenda

The Government's children's policy agenda relates to children's health and well-being, education, family income and community well-being. Play professionals see play provision and services as very closely linked to these overall policy goals.

Play provision and services are seen as having an impact on children's social, physical and mental health, their safety and their general inclusion in society. Over 90 per cent of the respondents perceived the play provision or service they were involved with played a role in addressing these policy goals (see Table 9). Crime prevention and community safety were also seen as important spin-offs of play provision. However, play provision was less likely to be seen as a means of supporting children's formal education, or of reducing child poverty. Unless specifically designed as a resource to enable parents to work and train it was also less likely to be seen as achieving this. (See Table 9)

Table 9: Policy objectives addressed by play services and provision

Policy objective addressed n=180	Not addressed %	Incidentally addressed %	Intentionally addressed %	Specifically designed to address %
Improving children's social skills	2	13	39	46
Improving children's physical health	5	22	44	29
Improving children's mental health	7	30	38	25
Reducing social exclusion	8	19	39	33
Protecting children from danger	8	28	34	30
Promoting children's cultural lives	13	24	44	19
Promoting caring communities	16	30	34	21
Crime prevention	16	48	27	9
Improving safety in the local community	17	40	32	11
Education children about lifestyle choices	19	38	31	12
Educating children about safety	20	37	33	10
Allowing parents to work or train	30	15	18	37
Increasing children's learning at school	32	44	18	6
Reducing child poverty	44	29	19	8
Increasing children's attendance at school	54	33	9	3

4.2 Formal links with the national and local initiatives

Amongst the play professionals responding there was a high level of liaison with other local services and planning. For example, over three quarters of the respondents said their service or provision was linked to at least one national or local government policy initiative. (See Table 10)

Table 10: Numbers of play services and provision linked to national and local policy initiatives (n=179)

Policy initiative	Number of services	Proportion of services %
Early Years Development and Childcare Partnerships	108	60
Single Regeneration Budget	57	32
Health Action Zones and Healthy Living Centres	27	15
Community Safety Strategy	27	15
New Deal for Communities	24	13
Education Action Zones	23	13
On Track	8	4
National Lottery funding	4	2
Regional Development funds	4	2
Other, including Youth Justice Board, Sure Start, Sport England	4	2
Communities that Care	3	2

Just over one third of services or provision were linked with one other policy initiative, the majority (42 of 61) being linked with the Early Years Development and Childcare Partnership (EYDCP). One in eight services, however, were linked with four or more initiatives. (See Figure 1). Forty-two services (23%) of those answering were involved with both the EYDCP and the Single Regeneration Budget, the most common combination. Thirty-two of these were also linked in to other policy initiatives.

Figure 1: Proportion of services linked to combinations of initiatives (n=179)

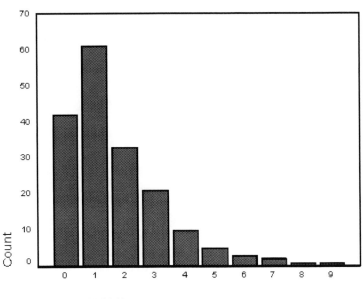

Number of initiatives

Of the 42 respondents whose services or provision were not linked in with other policy initiatives 21 were local authority services which might have had opportunities to be linked more closely to local planning. This included 13 providing unsupervised play provision and eight involved in supervised play services. The other 21 respondents whose service or provision was not liked to other initiatives included those run by local voluntary organisations and dedicated arts and sports projects.

Of the 24 respondents involved solely with unsupervised play provision, 13 were not aware of links with other initiatives but the remainder were linked to Community Safety Strategies, EYDCPs, Education and Health Actions Zones, Single Regeneration Budgets and On Track.

4.3 Play provision in local planning

In the majority of areas there was some recognition of play services and provision in local authority plans. Respondents were asked to identify the local plans in which there services were explicitly mentioned; 70 per cent of respondents named at least one plan. (See Figure 2)

Figure 2: Number of services or provision mentioned in combinations of plans

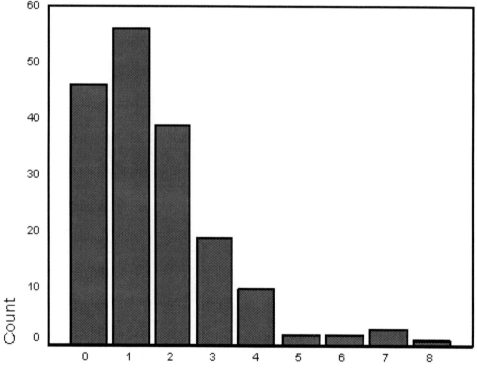

Number of plans referring to service or provision

Almost half the play services were referred to in the Early Years Development and Childcare Plan and one in four in the Children's Services Plan. Eight services said they had or were developing a Play Policy or Strategy. (See Table 11)

Table 11: Play services referred to in different local authority plans
n=178

Local Plan	Number of services	Proportion of services %
Early Years Development and Childcare Plan	87	48
Children's Services Plan	42	24
Best Value Performance Plan	34	19
Local Cultural Strategy	23	13
Community Safety Strategy	22	12
Local Plan/Unitary Development Plan	20	11
Quality Protects MAP	10	6
Assessment Framework for Children in Need	9	5
Neighbourhood Renewal Plan	8	4
Community Strategy	8	4
Play Policy/Strategy	8	4
Working Together to Protect Children	5	3
Local Transport Plan	5	3
Other	9	5

Of 187 respondents answering the question, 22 (11%) were not linked in with any local policy initiative nor referred to in local plans. Most of these were involved with a single provision, for example a holiday play scheme, specialist services or unsupervised play provision.

4.4 Involvement of play staff in the planning process
Almost two thirds of the 157 people answering the question said that they, or their colleagues, had been consulted over the development of local authority plans. The extent and nature of this consultation varied widely. In some areas play professionals were taking a leading role in the development of policies and initiatives and in others they were consulted in an ad hoc manner.

4.5 Involvement of children in planning and evaluation
One in three respondents said the children using their service had been consulted in the planning process. The level of involvement varied widely. Some examples of comments are given below. (See Table 12)

Table 12: Ways in which children are involved in the planning process.

- Workshops, seminars and fora
- Questionnaire surveys and needs assessment
- Children's Taster Days
- Large-scale, randomised surveys
- Dedicated children's participation projects
- Village appraisals and involving children and young people
- At Children/family events, e.g. National Play Day
- Regular children's meetings and daily surveys

5 Play and the Government's quality agenda

5.1 Best Value Reviews

Awareness of Best Value Reviews was high amongst play professionals. Only four of the respondents who had never heard of Best Value worked in local authorities and these all worked in local play projects. The other 30 respondents who had not heard of Best Value were almost all in voluntary organisations providing local play services.

Of the 97 respondents involved in local authority play provision:
- 9 had completed a Best Value Review
- 30 were in the process of the Review
- 44 knew that a Review was planned.

The remaining 12 were not aware of any impending Review.

Amongst the voluntary organisations represented in the responses 11 play associations and local voluntary providers were aware of Best Value Reviews in their areas, including one in which the Review was complete, three where the Review was in progress and seven where the Review was planned.

5.2 Meeting legal requirements for inspection and regulation

Of the 176 respondents answering a question about the regulation and inspection of their services, over 90 per cent (161) said their service or provision was subject to regular inspection. Of these, 114 (71%) were inspected under the Children Act 1989 and 12 (7%) under Health and Safety legislation. In addition:
- 28 services (17%) described regular, internal, physical inspection of equipment; these almost all involved unsupervised play provision
- 19 services (12%) had their own local standards and guidelines
- 14 (9%) were subject to Ofsted inspections.

A small number of services were subject to inspections by their grant-giving body and one scheme was inspected by the EYDCP.

Sixteen respondents were involved in provision or services which were not subject to inspection. Whilst some of these were support services others did have direct contact with children. Reasons for not being subject to inspection included:
- the local authority having a policy of not inspecting open access provision
- short-term provision outside the legal scope of the Children Act inspections.

5.3 Quality Assurance schemes

When asked whether there were formal quality assurance (QA) schemes for monitoring the provision or service, of the 182 people answering the question:
- 32% used formal QA schemes
- 32% were in the process of developing schemes
- 36% did not use QA schemes.

Of those using or developing QA schemes 42 per cent had their own local schemes, frequently based on the PQASSO scheme and 25 per cent used 'Aiming High', published by Kids' Club Network. Other schemes included 'Quality in Play', developed by Hackney Play Association and the then draft 'Play Wales' scheme, now published as 'The First Claim'.

Two in three respondents said that the children who used the service or provision were formally involved in evaluation or monitoring. This involvement varied from informal discussions with children about the day to day activities of the play provision to active involvement in the design and purchase of equipment. Children were involved through informal discussions, regular meetings, questionnaires, children's panels and organised consultation events. In one area children were actively involved in the development of a skate park. They were involved in designing the equipment specification, drawing up the tender requirements and evaluating the bids.

6   Conclusions

A survey of 200 play professionals working in England, carried out in September 2000, indicates that:

- Play professionals see play provision as important for the social lives of children, the social and economic lives of families and the well-being of communities.
- Play professionals are aware of play provision as an important element in the implementation of the Government's policy agenda for children an families, in particular in relation to social exclusion and children's health and development.
- Most play services are creating good links with other local services and initiatives, especially those connected to childcare and regeneration, although a significant minority are not well linked.
- Play is integral to local planning, in particular in relation to the expansion of childcare and overall services for children.
- Play services are currently widely inspected under the provisions of the Children Act 1998 and Health and Safety legislation.
- Children are frequently involved in the planning and evaluation of play services.
- There is a cautious optimism about the future of play services.

Appendix 1

Questionnaire

Play provision for children of school age

This questionnaire has been sent to all readers of *Play Today* and we hope that most of you will be able to complete all or part of it. Although many of the questions, in particular those in Section 2, are aimed at people who either work in or manage local play services and provision for school aged children, replies from everyone who is interested in contributing are welcome.

From the replies we hope to start formulating a picture of ways in which local play provision for school aged children in England is currently linked with the Government's policy agenda and how it is monitored and regulated.

In order to see if there are any particular patterns in the way these things happen we need to know something about you and your work, the children who use services* and provision*, the services and provision themselves and how Local Authorities and other providers plan their play provision.

The result of this survey will be used as part of the work the Children's Play Council (CPC) is undertaking for the Department of Culture, Media and Sport (DCMS). The work will look in detail at many aspects of children's play provision in England and aims to promote greater interest in children's play throughout both national and local government.

The questionnaire is divided into three sections.
Section 1 asks for information about you, the respondent, and your views on the importance of play for children, families and communities.
Section 2 asks about local provision* and services* and is aimed mainly at those working in or involved in planning and developing local provision.
Section 3 asks for your experience of the links between local policy and practice and the current Government's policy agenda.

* In this questionnaire the term 'provision' means a setting or project in which children play and the term 'service' means a collection of play provision under one management structure.

Please answer all parts of all the questions you feel able to. After each question there is an indication about how we would like you to approach the answer.

Section 1: Please tell us about yourself

1.1   Which of the following best describes your main role in children's play? (tick one box only)

☐ Direct work with children
☐ Supervising/managing provision
☐ Managing/co-ordinating/planning a service
☐ Development work
☐ Training and education
☐ Supporting play services and provision

☐ Strategic development or planning
☐ Student
☐ Campaigning
☐ Other (please specify)
....
....

1.2   What is your full job title, if any? (please state)

1.3   What is the name of the organisation you work for, if any? (please state)

1.4   What type of agency is this? (tick one box only and give the descriptive information below)

☐ County Council (*specify department)
☐ District/Borough Council (*specify department)
☐ Metropolitan Borough (*specify department)
☐ Unitary Authority (*specify department)
☐ Parish/Town Council
☐ Play Association
☐ National Voluntary Organisation
☐ Local Voluntary Organisation
☐ National Government Agency

☐ Government Department (*state section name)
☐ Education/Training (*state type of institution/agency)
☐ National Health Service (*state NHS sector)
☐ Private sector (*state nature of business)
☐ Joint Agencies (*state which agencies)
☐ Other (please specify)
....
....

*Description

Section 2: Please tell us about the service or provision you are most involved with

The way in which you answer the questions below will depend on whether you are referring to a service or a provision (see page 1 for the definitions used here).

2.1   Are you answering the questions below in relation to a service or a provision? (tick one box only)
☐ Service
☐ Provision

2.2   How old are the children who use the provision or service? (give age range)

2.3   Approximately how many individual children use the provision or service in an 'average' week? (state number)
        a) in school term time ………………….
        b) during school holidays ……………..

2.4   How do children get to use the provision or service? (tick as many boxes as necessary)
        ❏ There is open access
        ❏ They are referred by other agencies (please specify)
        ❏ Their parents buy places for them
        ❏ Priority access for children from specifically targeted groups (please specify)
        ❏ Other (please specify)

2.5   What are the main ways in which children benefit from using the provision or service? (please give up to three examples)
i.
ii.
iii.

2.6   What are the main ways in which families benefit from their children using the provision or service? (please give up to three examples)
i.
ii.
iii.

2.7   What are the main ways in which the local community benefits through children using the provision or service? (please give up to three examples)
i.
ii.
iii.

2.9   In what sort of area is the provision or service located? (tick one box only)
            ❏ Rural
            ❏ Urban
            ❏ Mixed urban and rural
            ❏ Other (please specify)

2.10   How would you describe the play provision or service? (if describing a provision tick one box only. If describing a service tick as many boxes as necessary)
❏ Adventure playground
❏ Holiday play scheme
❏ Unsupervised play space
❏ After-school club
❏ Year-round out-of-school provision
❏ Mobile play project
❏ Hospital play project

❏ Specialist provision for specific groups of children (please specify which)
❏ Other (please specify)
…………………………………………
…………………………………………

2.11 Do you think the provision or service supports Government attempts to address any of the following objectives? (Please mark each box with a number from 0 to 3 where: 0 = No, 1 = Incidently, 2 = Intentionally and 3 = Specifically designed to meet this objective)

.... Reducing youth crime
.... Protecting children from danger
.... Educating children about safety
.... Educating children about 'lifestyle' choices
.... Improving safety in the local community
.... Reducing social exclusion
.... Improving children's physical health
.... Improving children's mental health
.... Improving children's social skills

.... Increasing children's attendance at school
.... Increasing children's learning at school
.... Promoting caring communities
.... Increasing opportunities for parents to work
.... Reducing child poverty
.... Promoting children's cultural life
.... Other (please state)

2.12 Why do you think play services in your area are provided in the way they are? (tick up to three boxes and mark the single most important with an *)

❑ Historical reasons
❑ Availability of resources
❑ Children's needs
❑ Children's wishes
❑ National Government agendas

❑ Local Government agendas
❑ Parents' needs
❑ Parents' wishes
❑ Other (please state)

2.13 Do you expect any significant changes in the way play services are provided in your locality in the next few years? (circle appropriate answer)
        Yes* / No / Don't know
*If 'Yes' please describe and give reasons

2.14 What inspection or regulatory framework/s does the service or provision operate under? (please describe)
        If 'none' please state the reason for this

2.15 Do you have a formal Quality Assurance (QA) system for monitoring the provision or service? (circle the appropriate answer)
        Yes* / No / It is being developed* / Don't know
* If you are developing or using a scheme, what scheme is it? (please state)

2.16 Are the children who use the service or provision formally involved in evaluation or monitoring?
        Yes* / No
*If 'Yes' please describe the process briefly

2.17 Has the Local Authority undertaken a Best Value Review of the service or provision? (tick one box only)

❑ Yes, the first review is complete*
❑ Yes, the first review is in progress*
❑ No but the first review is planned for .... *(give date)
❑ No there is nothing planned
❑ I have not heard of a Best Value Review

*Please describe briefly the way in which the Best Value Review has or will be undertaken

Section 3: Questions about the extent to which local play services and provision are linked to Government and other national initiatives. (If you are not directly involved in a service or provision please tell us about examples you know of)

3.1 Is the service or provision linked to any of the following initiatives? (if 'yes' tick box)

❑ Education Action Zone
❑ Health Action Zone
❑ On Track
❑ Communities that Care
❑ Community Safety Strategy
❑ New Deal for Communities
❑ Single Regeneration Budgets

❑ Early Years Development and Childcare Partnerships
❑ Other (please state)

....
....

If 'Yes' please give brief details

3.2 Do any of following plans and procedures, developed by the Local Authority in which the service or provision is located, refer *explicitly* to play provision? (if 'yes' tick box)

❑ Children's Services Plan
❑ Early Years Development and Childcare Plan
❑ Quality Protects MAP
❑ Assessment framework for Children in Need
❑ Working Together to Protect Children
❑ Local Cultural Strategy
❑ Neighbourhood Renewal Plan
❑ Local Transport Plan

❑ Community Safety Strategy
❑ Local Plan/Unitary Development Plan
❑ Best Value Performance Plan
❑ Community Strategy
❑ Other (please state)

....
....

3.3   Were you, or relevant colleagues, consulted about the development of any of these plans? (circle appropriate answer)
Yes* / No / Don't know
*If 'Yes', please state briefly which and to what extent you were consulted.

3.4   Were any of the children who use the provision or service consulted about the development of any of these plans? (circle appropriate answer)
Yes* / No / Don't know
*If 'Yes', please state briefly which and to what extent they were consulted.

3.5   If you have any other views about how an understanding of the importance of play can influence Government policy, please comment.

... and finally

3.6   If you know of any studies relating to play provision in your or other localities please tell us about them here.

Thank you for your help